ANXIETY IN RELATIONSHIP

Understand and Overcome Anxiety, Remove
Negative Thinking and Win over Jealousy.
Feel Secure in Love, Eliminate Couple Conflicts
and Live Healthier Relationships

By Morgan Coyle

Published in the United States of America

ISBN 9798697118252

TABLE OF CONTENTS

INTRODUCTION _____ 1

Chapter 1: UNDERSTANDING ANXIETY _____ 3

Chapter 2: UNDERSTANDING ANXIETY IN RELATIONSHIP _____ 12

Chapter 3: ANXIETY AND DEPRESSION _____ 24

Chapter 4: THE INSECURE FEELING _____ 42

Chapter 5: DOUBT CAUSED BY ANXIETY IN RELATIONSHIP _____ 49

Chapter 6: NEGATIVE THINKING IN YOUR RELATIONSHIP _____ 64

Chapter 7: THE NEGATIVE EFFECTS OF ANXIETY ON INTIMATE RELATIONSHIPS _____ 89

Chapter 8: OVERCOMING ATTACHMENT ISSUES _____ 93

Chapter 9: HOW TO HANDLE JEALOUSY IN YOUR RELATIONSHIP _____ 108

Chapter 10: EXERCISES TO HELP YOU RELAX ANXIETY _____ 126

Chapter 11: OVERCOMING ANXIETY IN RELATIONSHIP _____ 140

Chapter 12: 7 MOST COMMON DISAGREEMENTS IN RELATIONSHIPS AND HOW TO RESOLVE THEM _____ 163

Chapter 13: HOW TO RECOVER FROM A TOXIC RELATIONSHIP _____ 190

Chapter 14: ESTABLISHING AND SUSTAINING RELATIONSHIPS QUALITY _____ 196

Chapter 15: UNDERSTANDING THE IMPORTANCE OF SELF-CARE _____ 209

Chapter 16: THE BENEFITS OF MEDITATION _____ 222

Chapter 17: THE PURPOSE OF RELATIONSHIPS _____ 236

Chapter 18: THE BEST RELATIONSHIP GOALS TO NURTURE INTIMACY _____ 242

Chapter 19: THOUGHTS AND STYLE OF THOUGHT: THE ART OF PRACTICAL THINKING _ 259

Chapter 20: UNDERSTANDING BODY LANGUAGE AND FACIAL EXPRESSIONS _____ 276

Chapter 21: EMOTIONAL INTELLIGENCE _____ 283

Chapter 22: THE SECRETS TO RELATIONSHIP CONTENTMENT _____ 294

Chapter 23: HOW TO BUILD HEALTHY TIES AND AVOID UNHEALTHY RELATIONSHIPS _ 297

Chapter 24: LOVE FINDING TOOLS: HELP YOU FIND THE PARTNERSHIP YOU WANT ____ 308

Chapter 25: 10 POSITIVE SUCCESS AFFIRMATIONS THAT WILL CHANGE YOUR LIFE ____ 321

CONCLUSION _____ 325

INTRODUCTION

Love is probably the most powerful emotion possible. It's not unusual for it to have a profound impact on your relationship and your quality of life when you begin to experience anxiety over that love. Anxiety about relationships is confusing, meaning different things to different people, but there's no denying that once you've got it, you'll do anything you can to stop it.

Many individuals experience a kind of long, drawn-out, chronic anxiety with which they live each day. This type of anxiety reduces the quality of life. Still, it is manageable because it rarely gets too intense and instead provides this persistent unease feeling, which takes away from your daily activities.

So many factors in relationships may cause anxiety, and often that anxiety differs depending on what it has brought about. Because of the problems raising children, abusive relationships cause anxiety for reasons that are entirely different from those which develop anxiety. First, some people have anxiety that, in other ways, spills into their relationship. It's such an overwhelming subject that whole books were written about how and why certain people develop anxiety about relationships and the struggles they are going through. These are all potentially complicated problems that need to be resolved for it to succeed in a relationship, and all potential causes of anxiety.

The anxiety may, in some cases, be for other, unrelated reasons. Some people worry about their partner's going to leave them. Some people experience anxiety because something is "too" to their partner: too rich, too good-looking, too busy, too talkative, etc. The partner (boyfriend, husband, girlfriend, wife) has anxiety-inducing qualities. Evaluating the quality of the relationship effectively is critical in determining how the discomfort can be reduced.

We discuss this even more in this book, and if you are looking for tips to help someone with anxiety, we encourage you to read it. But obviously, anxiety not only stresses the person who is suffering. It may also cause tension within the relationship as a whole. It can be frustrating to date someone with anxiety or to marry someone with anxiety, and it is not unusual to have to find ways to overcome it.

There is nothing that keeps a relationship healthy and safe better than understanding. Many become more acquainted with communication, and the various ways we can connect once proven communication is formed.

When contact includes talking to our families, friends, individuals in general, when things are not going so well in their relationship, individuals tend to turn to their others first (partner, spouse, friends, etc.). With that in mind, it has more to do with you managing your relationship anxiety than it does with them, and you can't expect them to contribute. The following are fundamental techniques to ensure that your relationship will recover.

Chapter 1: UNDERSTANDING ANXIETY

What is Anxiety? What's the distinction between fear and anxiety? What about worries and anxiety? How does stress or a "stressed-out" feeling fit in? What about Nervousness? Anger? Panic? Terror? Dread?

One of the greatest challenges to working through anxiety is knowing what we mean when we use the word. If we are not sure about what it is, it is hard to determine where it comes from and what to do about it. So let's begin by defining our terminology and describing other similar definitions exactly what we mean by anxiety.

Defining anxiety using the three experience levels

When it comes to talking about something psychological in nature, like anxiety, it is important to differentiate between three basic levels of our experience: physical, cognitive, and emotional.

Body sensations are physical experiences: warm, cold, tingly, numb, achy, painful, dry, moist, tense, relaxed, etc.

Any mental or intellectual phenomena or anything else about thoughts is cognitive experiences. Often in nature, they're verbal. For example, the voice in your mind that interprets and narrates your daily life and says things such as "I just know that I'm going to blow this answer," "How could she do that to me! Or "You have this, champ." But thoughts can also be visual or imaginary. The memory of the face of your father when you told him that you were dropping out of school to go to clown college, or maybe imagining that after eight more weeks of kale smoothies and spin class, you're going to have a six-pack.

The most difficult of the bunch to pin down are emotional experiences because they are essentially a mixture of physical and cognitive. For example, when we're amid anger, there are usually plenty of cognitive thoughts and inner monologues, but we also feel things like warmth, tension, or restlessness. Likewise, despair is often a mixture of negative tinged thoughts or images, plus a sense of low energy, tiredness, sluggishness, etc. After we perceive something cognitively, the subjective feelings we encounter are emotions.

Actions vs. Events

Note that both cognitive and physical experiences can happen to us. Our tummy grumbles and churns, and the thought of picking up bananas from work on the way home pops into our mind. These are events. However, we can also initiate both cognitive and physical experiences: waving to a friend, working through a problem 24-7 in your head. Those are actions.

On the other hand, emotional feelings are purely occurrences that occur to us; after realizing that a loved one has passed away or remorse after a transgression, we feel sorrow. They don't act, we can't personally initiate them. We can't just turn our happiness dials up or shut our anger off. This distinction between events and behavior is crucial because when we wrongly believe that feelings are something we can do or have direct control over, we mentally get into all kinds of trouble. A core tenant in most mental health (and basic neuroscience) theories is that we can only indirectly alter our emotions by how we want to think and what we do or the situations we expose ourselves.

Now that we have our three basic levels of physical, cognitive, and emotional experience and their status as either events or acts, let's see if we can put anxiety and some associated words within this structure.

ANXIETY AND THE PRINCIPLES ASSOCIATED

What follows is a list of the most popular words linked to anxiety and my perspective on how different they are. No official party line defines these words, so they are open to interpretation. But I want to describe them upfront for this book purposes, so I can be consistent.

Stressor

A stressor is considered dangerous or difficult in our world (for example, a tiger chasing you or an upcoming exam).

Stress

Stress is the physiologic response of the body to a stressor. It is mainly characterized by the release of adrenaline and fight or flight response activation. The most common symptoms associated with a fight or flight response are rapid breathing, elevated heart rate, muscle tension, blood pressure (especially chest tightness). Other symptoms are butterflies/stomach tightness/nausea, dizzy feeling, transpiration, lightheadedness, and extremities such as toes or hands often face numbness or tingling. These feelings are all manifestations of your brain attempting to train you (more on this later) to effectively handle a threat by either running away or fighting.

Stressed or Stressed-out

Stressed or stressed-out is the informal terms that we use when we are in a chronic or long-term state of high stress to explain how we feel physically. Notice that all of these arise at the physical level, while we use the terms stress or stressed-out often (mistakenly) to explain how we feel emotionally.

Fear

Fear is an emotion that typically occurs in response to a threat or danger that is perceived. On the hiking trail in front of us, we see a dark, curvy shape, and we feel fear as we consider the possibility that it may be a poisonous snake. But as we get closer, we know that it's just a fallen branch of a tree, our anxiety subsides, and we keep hiking. Fear appears to be present-oriented, transient in length, and based on a rational danger assessment.

Anxiety

Anxiety, similar to fear, is an emotion that occurs in reaction to the perception of a threat or risk. But while fear is typically a reaction to a plausible threat in the present that subsides rapidly, anxiety is generally a reaction to an abstract danger, often imagined or hypothetically probable to occur in the future, no matter how impossible, and tends to persist in frequency and intensity. For instance, we are beginning to decline invitations to go hiking after watching a National Geographic documentary about the most venomous snakes on the planet, imagining that we might encounter and get attacked by a deadly snake. Soon, we can avoid remote areas, golf courses, lakes, and zoos in the park. We spend a lot of time planning our days to avoid even the risk of running into a snake.

Panic

Panic is a sudden burst of extreme fear that, after 10-20 minutes, peaks in a few minutes and then subsides. Usually, panic is caused by a catastrophic perception of symptoms associated with the reaction to fight or flight (e.g., "I'm going to have a heart attack and die because my heart beats too quickly."). Panic is also caused by anxiety about experiencing a panic attack in individuals with frequent periods of sustained panic (i.e., panic attacks). Panic is fear over uncertainty, in a way.

Worry

Although we use the word worried casually to describe how we feel emotionally, on the cognitive level, worry is the best thought of and is a problem-solving method that tends to be repetitive, quick, negative, and self-evaluative but is typically unproductive or unhelpful. The key thing that sustains anxiety and stress or causes it to recur regularly is almost always a concern. It is equivalent to, but different from, problem-solving or planning.

Horror, terror, dread, nervousness, etc.

All these are emotional variants of anxiety or fear. For example, dread is similar to fear, but in nature, it is always more abstract and omnipresent, more severe, maybe not as acute, and slightly more existential.

Set your phone timer for 60 seconds to see how many of the anxiety variants you can mention (e.g., fear, terror, nervousness, etc.). I once had a customer come up with 18, which I thought was very amazing.

Hopefully, this brief discussion has helped explain how anxiety is connected to several related terms but different from them. From this discussion, two major takeaways are:

1. Being as precise as possible about how we feel is crucial. For any given experience, I think a reasonable structure for doing this is to ask: A) Is it predominantly physical, cognitive, or emotional? And B) Is it something (action) that I'm doing or something (event) that's happening to me?

2. I said before that, since they are mixtures of physical and cognitive stages, emotions are harder to describe. Feelings are the product of a particular perception of something that happens to us or is interpreted by us. Interpretation is the key word here. Without taking some form of cognitive action first, you simply can't have an emotion. This is good news because even though we can't change our feelings, even though

these cognitive behaviors are long-standing patterns, we can change how we choose to perceive and view ourselves and the world. By the way, this concept is the foundation of both cognitive therapy and stoicism, its philosophical precursor.

But before we get into techniques to improve how we think and work through our anxiety, when it reaches a therapeutic stage and becomes a disease, let's quickly run through what anxiety looks like.

POPULAR DISORDERS OF ANXIETY

Anxiety reaches a therapeutic stage and becomes a condition when it lasts for a long period, and our functioning is greatly affected. In other words, when it becomes a habit and affects your life in a significant way, anxiety is a disease. However, remember that anxiety should not be diagnosed if another mental or physical health condition or the effects of any form of drug, treatment, or other substance are best accounted for. In other words, you have to rule out hyperthyroidism, cocaine misuse, ADHD, etc., before you can diagnose an anxiety disorder. Some of the most common diagnoses/disorders linked to anxiety are below, along with a brief overview.

Anxiety Generalized

Persistent anxiety is characterized by extreme worry (e.g., failing a test, not being able to sleep, what happens when you die, etc.) over various topics. "Individuals with generalized anxiety are often described colloquially as "the well concerned." While at first blush, it is counterintuitive, people with generalized anxiety simply use the mental act of worrying as a way to momentarily relieve themselves from the feelings associated with whatever it is they are worried about. Sadly, this habit of fear contributes to persistently high anxiety and stress levels in the long run (more on this later).

Panic attack

Technically, a panic attack is described as a sudden surge of extreme fear or anxiety that peaks in minutes and are usually characterized by symptoms of a fight or flight reaction, such as sweating, rapid heart rate, chest tightness, lightheadedness, etc. When someone experiences frequent panic attacks with constant fear about having potential panic attacks or their effects (e.g., going insane, dying), they have panic disorder. In Chapter 3, we will closely look at how to recognize a panic attack and deal with it.

Specific Phobia

Anxiety is associated with a particular circumstance or item, such as flight, snakes, confined spaces, etc. These are comparatively rare true real phobias. A panic condition that looks like a particular phobia is much more common. In other words, individuals are irrationally fearful that fear could arise from a particular event or circumstance, not that the specific thing or circumstance itself is harmful.

Social Anxiety

Social anxiety is anxiety in social circumstances, generally when a person is subjected to others' real or imagined attention or judgment. Social anxiety also presents as unnecessary worry and concern for how others view or judge you.

Obsessive-Compulsive Disorder (OCD)

The continued existence of obsessions, compulsions, or both is known as OCD. Obsessions are repetitive and persistent thoughts, images, or impulses that cause severe anxiety or depression that the person tries to suppress or neglect (e.g., imagining your house burning because you forgot to turn off the stove). Compulsions are repetitive activities or rituals performed by a person to relieve the discomfort associated with addiction (e.g., washing your hands seven times before drying them, counting the number of steps you enter in each house, etc.). With OCD, the main theory is that individuals treat intrusive mental behavior (an event) as harmful or bad because they feel that they are either responsible for it or that it means something (i.e., they interpret it as though it were an action).

Post-traumatic stress (PTSD) disorder
PTSD happens when an individual is subjected to a real or threatened trauma (e.g., rape, murder, etc.) and results in the continuing experience of:

- Intrusive and distressing chronic memories of trauma
- Avoidance of trauma-related artifacts or circumstances
- Changes in mood and thought due to trauma
- Increased arousal after trauma (e.g., hypervigilance, increased startle response).

One way of thinking about PTSD is that it is like a memory phobia. People are afraid of something triggering a recollection of a traumatic experience in their world and the negative thoughts, emotions, and sensations that might go along with it. As a result, they become concerned with preventing their trauma from some sort of signal or cause. This avoidance, not to mention higher anxiety levels, can quickly lead to loneliness, depression, and drug abuse.

Separation Anxiety
Age-inappropriate distress over separation from an attachment figure, usually a parent, is separation anxiety. In adolescence, it is commonly seen (e.g., school denial behaviors), but may also arise in adults (e.g., anxiety when a partner leaves the city for business).

We've addressed what anxiety is (and isn't), how clinically it's conceptualized, and what are the most common therapies for it, so why do we have anxiety at all? Why do we get frightened of something irrationally and keep afraid? In other words, how, exactly, does anxiety work? And how do we make use of the information for our benefit?

I'm going to let the cat out of the bag right off the bat and propose that avoidance is the single most powerful notion when it comes to anxiety. More precisely, the reason why psychiatric anxiety levels continue is that, in the first place, we strive to prevent our anxiety. I realize that this assertion sounds best counter-intuitive and maybe just incomprehensible (we can stop it, of course, it feels awful!) so let me break it down a little bit.

Most anxiety disorders are essentially the same at their heart. Although they can look and, to some degree, feel very different, the same dynamics are present from a mechanical perspective. People with anxiety disorders have conditioned themselves to be fearful of anxiety-related thoughts, feelings, and emotions. And they did so quite by mistake. In reality, the very thing they are doing to try to boost their anxiety, resisting it, is the thing that makes it worse counterintuitively.

Chapter 2: UNDERSTANDING ANXIETY IN RELATIONSHIP

What is the "anxiety around relationships," and why do certain people have it? When either or both individuals in the relationship spend more time worrying anxiously about the relationship than turning toward the relationship itself.

Expectations may differ, but awkward thoughts are the same. A fear of rejection, feeling as though they care more, a constant fear of infidelity or an overall apprehension of the relationship's stability contributes to a lack of confidence.

There are several reasons why you might have anxiety about a relationship. Manipulative spouses may have set the tone for potential anxieties: parent attachments, abusive exes, poor communication, and ineffective therapy as causes.

An individual with anxiety about relationships doesn't always have a partner that isn't trustworthy, but if you don't voice your worries and desires, your significant other may very well be just living their lives, utterly unaware of your concerns. "Any conduct that causes one partner to doubt the other at the same time creates conflict. Secretive conversations, text messages, micro-cheating, and failure to communicate with your partner can spike fear."

Similarly, when you don't feel your best and most comfortable, your anxiety could skyrocket. "The game of comparison and contrast fosters anxiety that your relationship isn't as good as others, and causes nervous thoughts to grow as you ruminate why your relationship isn't as 'successful' as others." That's all imagination, of course.

ANXIETY IN RELATIONSHIP IS NATURAL

If you're in a long-term, committed relationship or fresh off a Tinder swiping session, anxiety about relationships can – and will definitely – pop up anywhere.

Whether it is due to lack of confidence, fear of rejection, questioning the compatibility, or worrying about non-reciprocal feelings, most people are experiencing some sort of discomfort about their partner's future. The real issue occurs when everyday worries turn into deteriorating tension or result in self-sabotage that hurts your relationship.

Anxiety about relationships can cause people to indulge in habits that end up driving away their partner. The first step to maintaining it at a manageable level is to recognize that some anxiety is entirely natural. When you start seeing things spiraling out of control — and have ripple effects that start affecting your relationship and your mental health — here's what you need to know about finding the cause and keeping it under control.

HOW DOES ANXIETY AFFECT US IN RELATIONSHIP

When we shed light on our history, we quickly recognize many early factors influenced our pattern of attachment, our psychological defenses, and our vital voice inside. All these factors contribute to our uncertainty about relationships and can lead us in many ways to sabotage our love lives.

Having to hear our inner critic and giving in to that fear can lead to the following actions.

Cling - Our propensity to behave aggressively towards our partner could be when we feel nervous. When we entered the relationship, we may stop feeling like the independent, influential people we were. As a consequence, we can easily fall apart, behave jealously or dangerously, or no longer participate in separate activities.

Control - We can try to dominate or influence our partner when we feel threatened. We should lay down rules about what they can and can't do just to relieve our feelings of fear or anxiety. This action can alienate our partner and make us feel resentful.

Reject - If we are uncertain about our relationship, it is aloofness that is one of the defenses we can turn to. To defend ourselves or to beat our partner to the punch, we may become cold or refuse. These acts can be subtle or explicit, but in our partner, it is almost always a sure way to cause distance or build vulnerability.

Withhold - Often, we prefer to withhold from our partner when we feel nervous or scared, as opposed to outright rejection. Maybe things got close, and we feel stirred, so we withdraw. We hold back little affections or give up entirely on any part of our relationship. It may seem like a passive act to withhold, but it is one of the quietest desire and attraction killers in a relationship.

Punish - Our reaction to our distress is often more violent, and we are merely punishing, taking our feelings out on our partner. We-shout and scream or give the cold shoulder to our partner. It's essential to be mindful of how much our acts are a response to our partner and how much they are a response to our vital voice inside.

Withdraw - We can give up real acts of love and intimacy when we feel scared in a relationship and withdraw into a "fantasy bond." A fantasy bond is an illusion of attachment that replaces real acts of love. In this fantasy state, we concentrate on shape over substance. We will stay in the relationship to feel safe but give up on the essential parts of the relationship. In a bond of illusion, we frequently indulge in many of the above described detrimental behaviors as a way of creating distance and protecting ourselves against the discomfort that inevitably comes with feeling free and in love.

WHAT CAUSES ANXIETY IN RELATIONSHIPS

Everybody is different, and every couple has their quirks. Relationship anxiety can grow in both parties over time; one partner can come in furious from the start; one individual does something to instigate anxiety; there are countless possibilities. Either way, it is important to recognize the root cause to snap it in the bud or whittle it down to a manageable size. Let's look at some possible reasons.

A preceding diagnosis

Some diagnosable disorders, such as social anxiety disorder, may contribute to anxiety in relationships or feed them. Because social anxiety is rooted in fearing others' judgment or constantly worrying about what others think about you, it is not difficult to see how those thoughts could cause a fire of relationship anxiety.

Breach of confidence

If your partner in the past has been unfaithful to you (and you have evidence or they have coped with it), this may lead to mistrust and uncertainty about the relationship going forward. You might also find yourself wondering whether they have improved, recognizing that previous partners may have been unfaithful to them.

Abusive actions or vocabulary

Physical, verbal, mental, any form of violence can contribute directly to anxiety. Physical mistreatment is never OK. If your partner is abusing you physically, please contact the National Domestic Violence Hotline. Physical and emotional violence breaks down people or, by words, instills fear. If your partner regularly "jokes" about your flaws or pretends to be cruel more often than they are truly kind, this form of emotional and verbal abuse might cause you to experience relationship anxiety.

Fights that are unproductive
A.K.A Wars that end in hollow apologies. Effective wars result in learning about yourself or your partner and developing as a couple together.

Worrying for the future
Would the two of you marry? Do they want to get the same stuff out of life? When are these questions a good time to ask?

Anxious connection
Many with anxious attachment are continually unsure of the commitment of their mate, in contrast to individuals who demonstrate stable attachment. In exchange, this leads to negative habits that can potentially drive the partner away.

The myth of the perfect partner
It is extremely counterproductive to continually wonder if there's anyone else out there better for you than the person you met. News flash: There isn't your dream match. Relationship therapist (and cultural icon) Esther Perel repeats this reality adamantly to her clients. This implies that neither you nor your partner will ever hope to ideally or rationally treat every situation. It also means not thinking about greener grass in any other yard when you've found a wonderful thing.

So, is that fear, or is that plain old stress? Here's the thing: Everyone probably feels some anxiety about a relationship at some point. We could be sociopathic if we didn't. We hope they like us too when we like

16

someone! We work hard at it when we're married to somebody, and it's not always easy. What needs some significant rewiring is persistent, crippling anxiety about relationship-specific problems.

Fortunately, in recent years, the stigma surrounding mental health has been challenged, and individuals are becoming more open to addressing anxiety issues and learning how to handle them, one step at a time.

THE SYMPTOMS OF ANXIETY THAT YOUR RELATIONSHIP GIVES YOU

When it comes to relationships, the most important piece of data you need to pocket and never forget is that relationships require effort. Every one of them. Even those who look so good from the outside have their kind of confusion and tension behind closed doors, especially if you want to make them last.

But relationships are about trying to make them work and putting in the effort and how they make us feel about the whole relationship and how they make us feel about ourselves. Some relationships can take such a mental toll that anxiety may also be induced by individuals who do not generally suffer from anxiety.

Behavioral Scientist & Relationship Coach Clarissa Silva informs Bustle that the most prevalent cause of this type of anxiety is uncertainty about the relationship's future. "Sometimes, over time, with small incidents, anxiety increases steadily," Silva says. "Sometimes, we are not even aware that it is the person who is the root cause of the distress that happens."

Does your relationship trigger anxiety? Perhaps it is, and you might not even be conscious of it. Here are seven signs that the source of your anxiety may just be your relationship.

1. With your partner, you are preoccupied with

"If you're constantly wondering what they're doing, checking their social feeds, or feeling insecure in the relationship. That diverts attention on what you need to be happy without you in it and focuses only on their happiness," Silva says, "if you're constantly wondering what they're doing."

While there's nothing wrong with checking your partner's social media, because, hey, it's there, if you're checking in on it to look for something that's not even there, it can be a concern.

2. You're overthinking what you wish you could tell

Communication is important in a healthy relationship. But it's only normal that if you can't express what you want and let it build up inside you, it's going to give you anxiety. In certain cases, there is nothing quite like thinking over and over in your head what you wish you could think or say to push your anxiety levels up.

"Without getting a complete script written or predicting their responses to you if you feel like you can't convey what you feel," says Silva, "this will gradually turn into more regular episodes of anxiety over time."

3. You struggle with yourself and your partner

It doesn't only stem from the arguments you have with your partner when anxiety strikes, but the arguments you have with yourself. For those of us who suffer from anxiety, there is an inner struggle as we compete with ourselves to make sense of circumstances, circumstances that concern us, and concern our relationships.

Silva says, "When small arguments produce physiological symptoms of anxiety, you're battling with yourself." If someone: a) needs to have it their way all the time, or b) is not able to compromise and becomes deceptive (i.e., dishonest, tries to demean you, purposely attempts to build self-doubt inside you, violent, or aggressive) when they do not get their way, it can only get worse over time.

4. You struggle to resolve arguments

The need to settle conflicts, in addition to the internal and external battles, is something that can be troublesome when your relationship causes you anxiety and dominates you. As Silva points out, "Before they continue to be in the relationship, your partner needs to overcome what causes their control and uncompromising conduct," particularly because you are nervous about their actions.

5. Safely, you are unable to compromise

In a partnership, it is one thing not to compromise because you are headstrong and will not shift, but it is another thing to compromise in a way that still helps your partner get what they want. In reality, that's not even a compromise on your end; that's just giving up, and you lose some of yourself in doing so, which leads to more anxiety.

"Relationships need a lot of compromises, and it is often difficult to find a balance where both parties are satisfied," Silva says. "Yet, if you acquiesce to the needs of your spouse much of the time ... it may intensify anxiety."

6. You replace your desires for their desires

"You could be replacing the needs of your life in the long run, increasing symptoms of anxiety, by deciding what you want to be based on someone else to satisfy them," says Silva.

Since your ability to over compromise is not enough to deplete your self-esteem and crank your anxiety into much higher gear, it's like you begin to vanish as you let your partner's needs replace yours. More anxiety will follow when more of you are lost to your partnership.

7. You're moving to unsafe coping ways

Eventually, if you don't realize the detrimental impact your relationship has on anxiety, a major indication that it's hard to overlook is that you're turning to unhealthy ways to deal with the relationship-induced anxiety. In certain instances, they can resort to alcohol and narcotics because they want to numb the anxiety or erase it.

"You can turn to something to help you cope when you deal with problems you don't want to deal with," says Silva. "Drinking or recreational drugs are ways of dealing with the issue or self-medicating it. You may not be aware that you are binging because your subconscious is constructing for you a different reality and your level of tolerance rises with time-based intake."

Suppose all of these symptoms are true to your life and relationship. In that case, it is time to seek help and reassess the relationship, particularly if the toxic behavior of a partner is what triggers your anxiety. While it is common to experience small amounts of anxiety inside your relationship from time to time, it is a problem when it becomes persistent. Try to connect with your partner.

SIGNS THAT YOUR RELATIONSHIP ANXIETY HAS REACHED AN ALARMING DEGREE

"It's important to remember that everybody has some anxiety about relationships, and that's to be expected," said Dr. Amanda Zayde, a clinical psychologist. "However, if you find yourself hyper-vigilant for signs that something is wrong, or if you encounter recurrent anxiety that affects your everyday life, please take some time to fix it. All in their relationships needs to feel safe and connected."

Not only is this constant state of mind psychologically draining and harmful to your health, but it can also eventually lead to the disintegration of the relationship.

"The uncertainty about relationships can cause people to participate in activities that end up driving their partner away," Dr. Zayde says. "To call 20 times in a row, leap to conclusions, or become emotionally detached, for example. It can also cause immense anxiety and frustration because people spend hours trying to decipher the actions of their partner." Dr. Forshee, Doctor of Psychology, continues, "They may bother with social media accounts of their lover, google them incessantly or have their friends assist in doing some research. They may wrongly accuse their new lover of things they have no proof for, or become excessively clingy, just to fulfill the desire for euphoria and attachment."

Although these behaviors can cause fear or anxiety to decline for the moment through mini-neurochemical bursts, Forshee says, they're just a short-term diversion. You have to do some intense, inner searching for the long-term easement, and then work proactively to reduce the anxiety. And this step begins by discovering the actual reason behind the primary cause of the anxiety.

Childhood: Root Cause of Anxiety in Relationship

"Relationship anxiety also arises from patterns of attachment, which form in early childhood," Zayde says. "A child builds a blueprint of what to expect from others based on their experiences in early care."

She says that a child can learn to either communicate or inhibit his or her emotional and physical needs, depending on the exactness and quality of the caregiver's response. This coping mechanism may work at the time, but when extended to adult, intimate relationships, it may turn into maladaptive behaviors. Sometimes, anxiety about relationships stems from patterns of attachment that grow in early childhood.

A typical example of maladaptive behavior is what psychologists term an enmeshed relationship, or a situation in which a parent is excessively involved in the life of a child, as described in the book of Greenberg,

Cicchetti, and Cummings, Attachment in the Years of the Preschool. This can result in "reciprocally invasive, controlling conduct," and "a great deal of uncertainty and anxiety on both sides over the actual or threatened separation."

For those who feel easily suffocated in a relationship, on the flip side, they may have had childhood experiences, which caused them to avoid relationships and bonding. For example, a child with an inattentive parent may learn to suppress their inherent tenderness towards bonding to escape heartache and rejection feelings. As an adult, the child can have a difficult time committing to a relationship or being insecure in it.

If this is true to your experience, it may be worth looking further into attachment theory, which has profoundly influenced the way relationship experts and contemporary psychologists think of relationships. You can also use a questionnaire to decide what kind of relationship style you and your partner have. In Chapter 8, we will talk more about attachment theory and the various attachment styles.

Your Ex Might be the Blame for Your Anxiety

Besides your upbringing, past relationships can also play a role in the relationships you act in. "When you experience the kind of relationship anxiety that you fear being cheated on or lack of faith in your new admirer, this might result from past relationship interactions embedded within your brain. Our brain will never forget", Forshee said. "The brain circuitry has become conditioned to connect those characteristics, smells, sounds, and emotions with previous memories of a lover and relationship. Your brain has developed a powerful pattern from previously acquired experiences, and your brain maintains remnants of that circuitry, even after you have fallen for someone new."

Finally, the body releases massive quantities of strong chemicals like oxytocin, dopamine, cortisol, and vasopressin when you start a new relationship. When combined, these "heart chemicals" make bonding and engagement more accessible. While they make us feel very passionate, they can also make us feel emotionally unstable, insecure, and obsessed with new partners. When we're around our partners — especially when we embrace, kiss, or have sex — this development of hormones goes into overdrive.

"When we're away from our new love, are afraid of rejection, or are rejected, it can make us feel like we're going through the withdrawal of addiction," Forshee explained, which can lead to unhealthy obsession and fear.

Chapter 3: ANXIETY AND DEPRESSION

Disorders of anxiety are also related to depression. Both conditions must be dealt with at the same time. People with anxiety disorders — a disease of social anxiety, generalized anxiety disorder, obsessive-compulsive disorder — or phobias spend most of their time in an anxious condition.

That can take an enormous emotional toll after a while, and depression sometimes sets in. According to the Anxiety and Depression Association of America, there's no definitive reason as to why anxiety and depression coexist so much. Still, you will receive relief from both with the right care.

WHICH ANXIETY CONDUCES DEPRESSION

Anxiety disorders are far more than simple nervousness and anxiety. They can trigger fear of things other people wouldn't give a second thought to. Many people with anxiety disorders realize that they have irrational beliefs, but they still cannot avoid them.

"It's a circle," says Sally R. Connolly, LCSW, a therapist with Louisville's Couples Therapy in Kentucky. "You seem to get this omnipresent anxiety about some concern or some problem when you get nervous, and you feel bad about it. Then you feel like you have failed, and you fall into depression."

The relation between the two conditions is complicated. In addition to an anxiety disorder, the likelihood of experiencing depression is high-about half of all people with significant depression often suffer from extreme and recurrent anxiety.

"People who are depressed also feel stressed and nervous, so one can cause another," she says. "Too often, anxiety comes before depression." Both depression and other anxiety disorders may have a biological pre-disposition. According to the National Institute of Mental Health (NIMH), people with post-traumatic stress disorder (PTSD), an anxiety disorder, are particularly likely to experience depression too.

"There is always a family background, particularly with anxiety, more so than depression, and so we think there might be a genetic predisposition to that," Connolly explains. "Most people just stress and move it on."

SYMPTOMS OF DEPRESSION AND ANXIETY

These are symptoms a person can suffer from an anxiety disorder as well as depression:

- Constant, unreasonable anxiety and fear
- Physical symptoms, such as rapid heartbeat, fatigue, hot flashes, nausea, abdominal pain, headaches, and breathing difficulty
- Ignorance
- Changes in food, too much or too little
- Remembrance, decision making and concentration difficulties
- Constant feelings of sadness or futility
- Hobbies and hobbies lost interest
- Feeling tired and nauseous
- Inability to unwind
- Blows of fear

PANIC ATTACKS

A panic attack is an extreme wave of anxiety marked by its unpredictability and weakening, immobilizing severity. You can't breathe, your heart pounds, and you may feel like dying or going insane. Sometimes, without warning, panic attacks hit out of the blue, often with no apparent cause. When you are comfortable or sleeping, they can also occur. A panic attack can be a one-time incident, but several individuals encounter recurring symptoms. A particular circumstance, such as crossing a bridge or speaking in public, often causes repeated panic attacks, especially if that circumstance has previously triggered a panic attack. The panic-inducing scenario is usually one in which you feel threatened and unable to flee, triggering the body's fight-or-flight response.

You may have one or more panic attacks, but you may be absolutely happy and healthy elsewhere. Or, panic attacks can occur as parts of another illness, such as panic disorder, social phobia, or depression. Panic attacks, regardless of the cause, are treatable. There are strategies you can use to mitigate or eliminate panic symptoms, regain your confidence, and take back control of your life.

Signs and Symptoms of a Panic Attack

Suddenly, the signs and symptoms of a panic attack intensify, and they typically reach their height within 10 minutes. They only last longer than an hour, with most coming to an end in 20 to 30 minutes. Panic attacks can happen anywhere and at any moment. You could have one while shopping at a supermarket, walking down the street, driving in your car, or even sitting at home on the couch.

Symptoms of panic attacks include:

- Breath shortness or hyperventilation
- Palpitations of the heart, or racing heart
- Pressure in the chest or discomfort
- Shaking or trembling
- Choking sensation
- Feeling disconnected from your world

- Sweating
- Nausea or tummy discomfort
- Feeling dizzy, faint, or light-headed
- Numbness or feeling of tingling
- Flashes that are hot or cold
- Fear of death, losing control or being mad

Is it a panic attack or a heart attack?

Much of the panic attack symptoms are physical, and these symptoms are so extreme at times that you might believe you have a heart attack. In reality, to get help for what they think is a life-threatening medical condition, many people suffering from panic attacks make frequent visits to the doctor or the emergency room. Although it is important to rule out potential medical causes of symptoms such as chest pain, elevated heart rate, or trouble breathing, confusion is frequently ignored, not the other way around, as a possible cause.

Panic condition signs and symptoms

Although many individuals experience only one or two panic attacks without more episodes or complications, certain individuals continue to develop panic disorder. There is no need to worry if that is you. Repeated panic attacks, associated with significant changes in behavior or intense anxiety about having more attacks, are characterized by panic disorder. You may have the panic disorder if you:

- Have frequent, sudden panic attacks that are not related to a particular situation
- Are worrying a lot about another panic attack
- Because of panic attacks, you behave differently, such as avoiding areas where you have already panicked.

Although a single panic attack will only last a few minutes, a permanent impression can be formed by the encounter's results. Recurrent panic attacks take an emotional toll if you have a panic disorder. Your self-confidence can be adversely affected by the experience of the extreme fear and terror you felt during the attacks and can bring significant damage to your daily life. This inevitably leads to the effects of the following panic disorder:

- Anticipatory anxiety - You feel nervous and stressed instead of feeling calm and like your usual self in between panic attacks. This depression results from a fear of experiencing potential panic attacks.
Much of the time, this "fear of fear" is present, and can be incredibly debilitating.
- Phobic avoidance - You start avoiding certain conditions. This avoidance may be based on the assumption that a past panic attack was triggered by the situation you're avoiding. Or if you had a panic attack, you should avoid areas where escape would be impossible or support would be inaccessible. Phobic avoidance, taken to its peak, transforms into agoraphobia.

Disorder of panic with agoraphobia
It has historically been thought that agoraphobia entails a fear of public places and open spaces. Agoraphobia, however, is now thought to grow as a complication of panic assaults and panic disorder. While it can occur at any time, within a year of the first chronic panic attacks, agoraphobia usually occurs.
You're afraid of getting a panic attack in a situation where it would be impossible or embarrassing to flee if you're agoraphobic. You might even be terrified of a panic attack where you can't get help. You start avoiding more and more circumstances because of these fears.

You can begin to avoid, for instance:

- Crowded areas, such as shopping centers or sports arenas.
- Cars, aircraft, subways, and other modes of transport.
- Social events, bars, or other instances where having a panic attack will be humiliating.
- Physical activity if panic is caused.
- Certain panic-provoking foods or beverages, such as alcohol, caffeine, sugar, or particular drugs.
- To go anywhere without someone's company who makes you feel comfortable. You could only feel secure at home in more serious cases.

Causes of Panic Attacks and Disorder of Panic

While the precise causes of panic attacks and panic disorder are unknown, there is a propensity to have panic attacks in families. A connection with major life changes such as graduating from college and entering the workplace, getting married, or delivering a baby also appears there. Panic attacks may also be caused by severe stress, such as the death of a loved one, divorce, or work loss.

Medical conditions and other physical triggers can also trigger panic attacks. If you suffer from panic symptoms, it's necessary to see a doctor rule out the following options:

1. Mitral valve prolapse, a mild heart condition that arises when one of the valves of the heart doesn't close properly
2. Hyperthyroidism (Thyroid Gland Overactive)
3. Hypoglycemia (low sugar in the blood)
4. Application of stimulants (amphetamines, cocaine, caffeine)
5. Withdrawal of Medicine

Tips for Self-Help in Panic Attacks

It's essential to remember that there are many things you can do to support yourself, no matter how weak or out of control you can feel about your panic attacks. To help you conquer panic, the following self-help strategies will make a significant difference.

Learn about anxiety and panic. It can go a long way to relieving your anxiety by actually learning more about fear. Read up during a panic attack on fear, panic disorder, and the fight-or-flight reaction encountered. You will understand that when you panic, the sensations and feelings are natural and that you are not going insane.

Stop consuming alcohol, caffeine, and Smoking. In prone individuals, these may all cause panic attacks. Often, be vigilant of stimulant-containing drugs, such as diet pills and cold drugs that are non-drowsy.

Learn how your breathing is regulated. Hyperventilation brings on many sensations during a panic attack (such as lightheadedness and chest tightness). On the other side, deep breathing can alleviate panic symptoms. You can calm yourself down by learning to regulate your breathing when you start to feel nervous. And if you know how to regulate your breathing, the same feelings you're afraid of are also less likely to develop.

Arse methods to relax. Activities such as meditation, yoga, and progressive muscle relaxation enhance the body's relaxation response when done daily, the opposite of the stress response involved in anxiety and panic. And these calming activities not only facilitate calming, but they also improve feelings of joy and serenity.

Connect with family and friends face-to-face. When you feel alone, anxiety symptoms can get stronger, so reach out regularly to people who care for you. Explore ways to meet new people and develop supportive friendships if you feel like you don't have someone to talk to.

Regularly workout. As mentioned in several instances, exercise is a natural anxiety reliever, aiming to move on most days for at least 30 minutes (three sessions of 10 minutes are just as good). It can be particularly useful to do rhythmic aerobic exercise that involves moving both the arms and legs, such as walking, running, swimming, or dancing.

Get ample restful sleep. Anxiety may be made worse by inadequate or low quality sleep, aiming to get seven to nine hours of restful sleep a night. These tips for having a good night's sleep will help if sleeping well is a problem for you.

Panic Attack and Panic Disorder

Therapy is the most successful form of psychiatric therapy to combat panic attacks, panic disorder, and agoraphobia. It will help to provide even a short course of treatment.

Cognitive Behavioral Therapy focuses on the patterns of thought and habits that prolong or cause your panic attacks and makes you look in a more rational light at your fears. For starters, what is the worst thing that would happen if you had a panic attack while driving? You may not be likely to crash your car or have a heart attack, but you may need to pull over to the side of the road. The sense of fear becomes less alarming as you learn that nothing completely catastrophic is going to happen. Panic disorder exposure therapy helps you to feel the physical sensations of panic in a healthy and monitored setting, allowing you the chance to learn healthier ways of coping. You may be asked to hyperventilate, to shake your head side by side, or to hold your breath. Similar to the signs of fear, these multiple exercises trigger sensations. You become less fearful of these internal bodily stimuli with each exposure and experience a greater sense of control over your fear.

Exposure therapy for panic disorder with agoraphobia requires medication that also requires exposure to the conditions you fear to avoid. As in exposure therapy with particular phobias, before the fear starts to go away, you face the dreaded scenario. You realize from this process that the situation is not harmful and that you control your feelings.

Panic Attacks and Panic Disorder Treatment

Medication can be used to control or reduce any of the symptoms of panic disorder temporarily. It does not, however, handle or fix the issue. In extreme situations, medicine may be helpful, but it should not be the only treatment sought. When paired with other therapies, such as counseling and behavioral changes, which resolve the underlying causes of panic disorder, medication is most effective. Used drugs can include:

Antidepressant drugs. It takes several weeks to start working with antidepressants, so you have to take them on an ongoing basis, not just during a panic attack.

Benzodiazepines. These are very fast-acting anti-anxiety medications (usually within 30 minutes to an hour). Rapid relief of symptoms is given by taking them during a panic attack. Benzodiazepines, however, are extremely addictive and have extreme signs of withdrawal, so they should be used with caution.

How to support those with a panic attack

It can be frightful to see a friend or loved one having a panic attack. They can breathe unusually quickly and shallowly, become dizzy or lightheaded, tremble, sweat, feel nauseous, or think they have a heart attack.

It's important to note that the danger seems very real to your loved one, no matter how crazy you think their desperate reaction to a situation is. It won't help to simply tell them to calm down or to alleviate their anxiety. Yet you can make them feel less afraid of any potential assaults by helping your loved one ride out a panic attack.

Keep yourself cool. Being calm, understanding, and non-judgmental will help the panic of your loved one subside faster.

Place your loved one's attention to their breathing. Find a quiet spot where your friend can sit and then direct them for a few minutes to take long, deep breaths.

Do the physical anything. Together, lift your arms or stomp your feet and lower them. It will help to burn off some of the tension from your loved one.

Get your friend out of their mind by asking them to name or speak soothingly about a common interest in five things around them.

Encourage the person you love to seek support. Your loved one may feel guilty about getting an attack in front of you until the panic attack is over. Reassure them of their fear and urge them to seek assistance.

Anxiety disorders may impair a person's capacity to work, study, and engage in other activities. With adequate care, recovery is possible. As introduced in the first chapter, different kinds of anxiety disorder exist. They include:

- Compulsive obsessive disorder
- Panic disorder (and agoraphobia-panic disorder)
- Disorder of social anxiety

- Unique phobias
- Post-traumatic stress disorder
- Pervasive anxiety disorder
- Trichotillomania / dermatillomania or repetitive behaviors based on the body)
- Hoarding

There can be distressing and crippling anxiety disorders. They may lead to a lack of educational and work opportunities and family and social relationship difficulties.

Recovery is possible with adequate medication that will help you control your symptoms, such as exposure therapy, attention training, and various anxiety management strategies. You can study the following methods yourself (for example, using books or taking courses), or you can consult a qualified specialist.

THE ROAD TO RECOVERY

One should treat both anxiety and depression together. Successful treatment methods include:

- Cognitive Behavioral Therapy (CBT) which is commonly used to treat depression anxiety disorder. CBT can teach people how to handle their anxiety, anxieties, and depressive symptoms by finding out what triggers them; people can also learn how to control their emotions. We will look at a few CBT techniques later in the chapter and throughout the book.
- Medicinal antidepressants, as seen earlier in this chapter, which can be used to help with both conditions. Often these medications are used in combination with CBT. According to the NIMH, selective serotonin reuptake inhibitors (SSRIs) are newer, commonly used antidepressants that provide fewer side effects than older antidepressants. An exercise can also benefit both anxiety and depression disorders. Exercise releases

hormones that make you feel good in your body, which can help you relax.

The Anxiety and Depression Association of America notes that taking only a 10-minute walk can relieve the symptoms for several hours. Relaxation techniques include meditation and awareness practice. According to a broad research review published in the March 2014 issue of JAMA Internal Medicine, both can relieve the symptoms of both anxiety and depression and improve the quality of life.

Organizations are providing mental health programs that can include in your community a hospital or support group. Check out America's National Center of Mental Health for more information, or the Anxiety and Depression Association.

YOU SHOULD NOT IGNORE WARNING SIGNS

Those who deal with anxiety and depression should look for these warning signs of a mental health crisis:

- Inadequate everyday self-care, such as denying personal hygiene practices, getting out of bed, or eating
- Severe and sudden mood shifts
- Getting angry, dangerous, or aggressive
- Substances Misuse
- Looks lost or has hallucinations
- Thinking about suicide or finding no reason to live

Treatment for anxiety and depressive disorders needs to be administered and handled by a doctor, says Connolly. "Having a clear evaluation to rule out bipolar disorder is especially important for people with both anxiety and depression," she said. Bipolar disorder, a disease in which emotions may range from very low to very high levels of mania and depression, is treated with depression much differently from an anxiety disorder.

No one, and not both, has to suffer from anxiety disorder or depression. People with anxiety disorder should talk about their symptoms with a doctor, therapist, or other health care provider and seek therapy before depression has an opportunity to set in.

HOW ADVICE WILL HELP YOU TO CONTROL YOUR ANXIETY

Anxiety is the number one reason to seek clinical help. Anxiety is on a continuum, and the symptoms can range from everyday anxiety to a persistent sense of distress and even full-blown panic attacks. If anxiety becomes a concern for you, then therapy will help you control your symptoms and improve your anxiety relationship.

Anxiety, however, is just as much a social problem as a personal one. We are living in a world full of restrictions, aspirations, and responsibilities. Your anxiety is also a symptom of something else: depression, morbid fears, or problems of identity.

The desire to monitor people and events in your life is what lies at the heart of the anxiety. If absolute control is not feasible, then everything fails here. Anxiety, with its worst-case – panic attacks – comes with a sense of not being a safe place for the planet. Thus, a therapy room may become an island of protection and peace, which in itself is healing. Anxiety is also commonly correlated with the "good girl / good boy" mentality and perfectionism. Here a therapist can help you become conscious of and note your repetitive behavior patterns in your daily life. When you start to know the habits, you don't get frightened anymore, and the burden is released. Learning how to ask for support and embrace it becomes an invaluable new ability.

You may see your anxiety as something in your mind that takes over your thought: "Why can't I stop thinking about it? "I can't stop worrying." If you recognize your thoughts there, then it can be helpful for you to work with a therapist who uses techniques to get you into your body, feelings, and emotions. These techniques may include visualization, working parts, sand tray, working cards, writing a letter to your body, or emotion journaling. The goal of this work is to achieve "grounding": to make you feel safe, relaxed, and focused once more. The purpose of therapy is to help you get out of the ever-worrying mind world and to learn the new skills of being in the present, not in the past or future.

While everybody may be anxious from time to time for various reasons, people usually seek counseling support when they feel their anxious thoughts or state is beginning to impact on their overall health, relationships, or life.

Counseling will also help people with anxiety by doing the following:

1. Offer yourself a supportive relationship and a healthy atmosphere and share your true feelings without bias or judgment.
2. Encourage self-consciousness to recognize the context and causes of the anxiety.
3. Establish a holding room where you can work through your problems. It can also include a new prism through which you can start looking at your problems from another, yet healthier viewpoint.
4. Empower yourself to help reduce or resolve your feelings of anxiety (including mindfulness and CBT exercises) through the application of various therapeutic strategies/techniques.
5. Provide practical tools and support to help foster a sense of agency and control within you in achieving your goals
6. Ultimately, therapy will make you feel less burdened and develop a sense of freedom to live your life optimally by conversation and active listening.

Earlier in the book, we talked about Cognitive Behavioral Therapy (CBT). One of the most vital aspects of CBT, essentially, is that it can give you hope. It is positive, fundamentally. It helps you to believe that change is possible and that in your life, you can affect change.

While it is recommended to start a CBT therapy with an experienced professional, Cognitive Behavioral Therapy tips can be used at home to help relieve anxiety. The goal is to gain abilities that you can use outside the therapist's office to solve real-life issues. The more you practice, the more CBT skills become a habit.

If you're someone who has good intentions but wants someone to be responsible for them, you could make an appointment with a therapist. You could also do it on your own if you know you're a person who is good at being self-taught.

Here are some tips for practicing the techniques at home (or wherever you happen to be).

Modify your perspective. Using a cognitive restructuring tool will help you adjust troublesome perceptions, which will help you modify your actions in turn. Ask yourself the next time you find yourself feeling anxious or depressed: What am I worried about, or what feelings am I dealing with that might cause me to feel this way? Note if some unique thoughts or memories trigger distressing physical symptoms, you may also make a chart. Doing this will encourage you to understand how your feelings and thoughts are related and what causes you to feel anxious.

Balance your ideas. Most mental health issues include painful, but fundamentally faulty, thoughts or predictions that impact actions. For example, if you get nervous when you're in crowds and so deliberately avoid them, you might convince yourself that you would panic, do something to embarrass yourself, and wouldn't enjoy it if you tried to go to a crowded venue, such as a sports game or concert. That belief then reinforces your avoidance.

But is it valid? You can't predict the future, so you can't know for sure that your nightmare scenario will happen, and you could miss anything you'd like.

Note how your brain rationalizes choices you make based on fear or avoidance, and then ask yourself: What is the proof of that thought? Is there some cold, hard truth about things going wrong, or am I just speculating about that? Consider if you might have any ideas that would be more balanced or beneficial. What new emotions would emerge if you changed your thought process slightly less anxious or negative? Your feelings and actions are likely to obey if you are trying to make your thoughts more controlled.

Be patient on your own. If you try CBT on your own (or even with a therapist to help you), improvement will not happen immediately, so don't expect that. Instead, developing your strengths should be your objective so that you feel more prepared to cope with whatever obstacles your mental health needs to throw your way.

Focus on setting yourself up for small wins, then build up your goals steadily over time. Be proud, no matter how insignificant it can seem, of any positive progress you make. Recognize that change is not linear; it will be easier for some weeks, more challenging for others, and that's natural.

Be kind to yourself, be kind. Without even noticing it, it is easy to get caught up in negative self-talk. But getting down on yourself continually isn't going to inspire the faith required to make you feel better.

"When you see adverse thoughts slipping into stuff like " Why can't I just get it together? or "Other individuals don't have this problem," substitute anything kinder for them. Question yourself if your friends will ever tell you the things that you say to yourself. Huh? No? So don't allow yourself, either, to say to them.

This doesn't mean that when you have already made a mistake or done something wrong, you should make excuses for yourself, but instead, you should allow yourself to cut the slack that you usually reserve for others.

Do what you're in love with. There is a way to eliminate the things that matter to you in life from anxiety, depression, and other mental health challenges, either because you become afraid of them or lack the desire you once had to follow them. You may have enjoyed reading, but now you feel exhausted all the time. Or you would have wanted to go out with your friends, but now you're afraid of being away from home at night. However hard it might be, even if you have to push yourself, try to do things that matter to you. Mental well-being needs to do something that makes you happy, links you with others, and offers you a sense of mastery or competence.

Make it a point to take time to do one or two things daily that have always been used to bring you pleasure and do your best to be present rather than overwhelmed by the past or concerned about the future. After that, ask yourself how you feel now that you've done that stuff. Has this made you feel better?

Be attentive. Maybe while you're trying to fall asleep or beat yourself about what you told a buddy when you should finish a vital work job, you're ruminating about work problems; either way, you're not concentrating on the present moment. Instead, if they are not associated with what is happening right now, try to change your feelings. Ask yourself: Do my feelings reflect what's happening right now? Focus on your senses, if not. What do you hear and see? In the world around you, what's going on? Learn to be aware of what is right in front of you instead of what's happened in the past or what's going to happen in the future that you're afraid of.

Chapter 4: THE INSECURE FEELING

It can be excruciating and upsetting to feel insecure in your relationship. It can manifest in all manner of ways. You may feel like your partner is always about to break up with you. You may have difficulty trusting them not to cheat on you. Or you might think that your connection has become weaker and weaker for a while and that the foundations are starting to fall away.

Feeling like this can make it hard to have a great deal of faith in your future together and can sometimes leave you wondering whether breaking up would be the easiest solution. Also, it can start having adverse effects in other areas of your life. It can undermine your self-esteem and confidence, and this can make it difficult to feel able to address any issues.

WHERE INSECURITY ORIGINATES FROM

A sense of insecurity can stem from several different places in your relationship. If you and your partner have not been effectively communicating about issues or making an effort to maintain your connection, you may start feeling as if you are drifting apart.

Insecurity can also be a consequence of changes in your relationship. For example, if you have moved in together or married recently, you may feel all sorts of new strains and pressures. If you can't discuss these together, then you can start feeling less confident about your ability to work as a team.

It can also come from self-image or self-esteem issues. For example, if you feel exceptionally low after having put on weight after a series of disappointments in your work life or less happy with your physical appearance, this could make you worry about your relationship.

Sometimes we can carry feelings from past relationships into our current relationship-including those with family members. If we weren't having very secure or loving relationships when we were younger with our parents or primary caregivers, we might be carrying that feeling with us as adults. Past romantic relationships where your trust has been broken can make it hard to trust anybody else. You may find yourself searching for 'patterns' or assuming history will repeat itself.

WHAT TO DO TO TACKLE INSECURITY

The first call is to talk things over together. This can be tricky, of course-especially if you haven't been talking correctly for a while or you feel hurt or angry with your partner.

If you do feel capable, however, you might find the following tips helpful.

Keep things laid back. Hearing the words 'we must talk' can make a defensive feeling even for the most laid back person! The more positive framing of things can get things off to a better start. You may want to try something like, 'I really would like to talk to you about our relationship when you have a chance.'

Choose the right moment. Try talking when things go well and not ill. Bringing things up amid an argument can only create more conflict. If you introduce the subject when you feel good about the relationship, both of you are more likely to move in a positive direction.

Tell how you feel, not how you think they're making you feel. If both of you are merely trading blows and blaming each other for everything, you probably won't get anywhere. To keep things under control, it can be useful to use phrases about 'I' ('I sometimes feel worried about that') rather than names about 'you' ('you always make me feel worried because').

Listen. Even if it's hard to hear what your partner has to say, try and stick with it. For it to work, a conversation needs to go both ways. Try to start by recognizing their perspective can be different from yours.

You might even plan. It may sound a bit clinical, but it may be useful to think about what you want to say in advance. That doesn't mean drawing up a shopping list of grievances but merely collecting your thoughts about what you want to talk about.

Come on to it again. Rarely in one chat are these things solved. Working on relationship issues takes time and effort, so you may need to revisit things in a month to see how you're getting on with each other. This kind of conversation will seem far less appalling after a while!

7 STEPS IN YOUR RELATIONSHIP TO OVERCOMING INSECURITIES

"The most common insecurity people bring into relationships is that they're 'not enough': not sexy enough, not pretty enough, not thin enough, not sufficiently successful, all have to do with not being sufficient," explains Terri Orbuch, professor at Oakland University in Michigan, Institute for Social Research.

That said, insecurities can – and do – run the gamut, some common ones:

- *Doubt that long-term relationships can be healthy and satisfying.* As in, you're worried that your partner won't love the "real you" once the shininess of a new relationship wears off (Or vice versa).
- *Worrying about goals, expectations, and values changing or in-*

consistent with the relationship. Thoughts you may experience: What if they decide they don't want to have children? What if we can't agree where we should be living?

- *Fearing your partner would suddenly give you up*. This one is more common if you have an edgy style of attachment that usually stems from what you observed about growing relationships and how your parents responded to your needs.

So yes, having insecurities in relationships is normal, but being obsessed with them will not do you or your partner any good. Instead, try this 7 step, expert-approved process to avoid sabotaging your bond by hang-ups:

1. Stop assuming you are to blame for your insecurities.
Or they are your partner. Insecurities aren't just pop-up from nowhere. According to Orbuch, they are often triggered by specific events, people, ex-partners, or even current partners. Because you can't control all of that (especially, you know, others), focus on what you can control: yourself. The first step to tackling your insecurities head-on is to let go of self-blame and self-bashing. Think you're the only one to have insecurity? Not even near. Celebrities also have them.

2. Curiosity tackles your insecurities.
Forget all the defense mechanisms that you used to survive the three-year middle school insecurity fest. Now you are an adult, meaning it's time to have your doubts. According to Squyres, a Ph.D. Clinical Psychologist, the best way to do that is by viewing them with curiosity and an open mind. Spend time specifying exactly why you don't think you're enough. ("My first boyfriend cheated me so; I don't have what it takes to keep people interested in the long haul.")
Evaluating where your insecurities come from (write them down so you

can see them as a third party if you need them) will help you figure out if they are truth-based or simply fear-based. You will see most (if not all) of the time, this is the latter one.

3. Let your partner know how you feel.

If your S.O. isn't a mind reader (spoiler alert: they aren't), you need to tell them when you feel insecure — and encourage them to do the same for you. "A safe emotional space creates a strong foundation for a loving relationship with your partner." "A safe emotional space with your partner, where you know you can directly but gently discuss worries, creates a strong foundation for a loving, trusting relationship," says Squyres. This can be harder if the behavior of your partner triggers your insecurities, of course, but that is when it's even more important to get everything out of the open. "You never want to go into attack mode, but when you're feeling insecure based on their actions, you also don't want to hold in and let it fester," she says. "The emotional pressure cooker that this creates will explode if you do so, and the results won't be pretty." Be super transparent about what is bothering you and why to prevent this whole mess. Is Flirting a Cheating Form? Maybe your partner has a flirty personality, and the second you see them chatting to another person, you go into the worst-case-scenario mode. "What one person often considers flirting, the other regards friendliness," notes Squyres.

She suggests explaining how each of you sees the difference between flirting and friendliness — or whatever discrepancy you may encounter — then discuss what you're willing to change.

4. Concentrate on the positive attributes.

If you don't love yourself, how do you love someone else? I know, said more easily than done. No one (not even the most confident drag queen) becomes an overnight self-loving master. You have to start small.

Orbuch recommends making a list of five things you like about yourself and then reading them whenever you start to feel in doubt about yourself. Make a list of your unique gifts while you are at it, too, she says. Perhaps you're doing Instagram-worthy acai bowls on the reg or tackling hills like a pro in your cycling class. Feast on them, whatever your talents.

5. *Build up those wins.*

Building on your self-confidence in one area of your life that is already going well — work, for instance — is a fabulous way to boost your overall self-image. Whatever you like about yourself as an individual can translate into your relationship, helping you to overcome your insecurities as a partner. After all, if you believe you're a total catch (which, btw, you 're ARE), then your other half will.

6. *Don't compare to others.*

Oh, Instagram: The inspiration apex and insecurity. The social media platform makes instant self-doubt all too easy to trigger, mostly because it can cause you to compare your life (with all its ups and downs) to the highlight reel of someone else.

Remember: The most common insecurity people bring in relationships is feeling "not enough," but you can't feel like you're "not enough" when you don't have someone to compare to, right? One (relatively) easy way to halt unfavorable comparisons is to take a break from social media, even if it's just a few hours or days. Or reduce your overall use of social media (Gasp).

Cutting back on scrolling will help you reset expectations for yourself and your relationship, and most importantly, those expectations will be based on your actual desires and needs, not on how you 'think' you measure up to others.

If you're still in a "she's X," "they have Y" mindset, consider muting or unfollowing people that spike that negative rabbit hole of comparison. Then go back to your talent list, or create one that spells out all the things you're grateful for in your life, so you're not only forced to leave the app, but you also remember that there's no one like you - I repeat, nobody.

7. Converse with a professional.

Real talk: Even if you've got the world's most supportive partner, sometimes you just have to get help from outside. Your history can result in insecurities, yes, but also just your general personality, Squyres says. "Some people are more anxious, more compulsive, more ruminant, or more self-conscious than others."

So if you've put in all of the above work and still don't feel better, it might be time to speak with a therapist or coach; you can then set goals together and figure out strategies to change.

THINGS YOU NEED TO DO BEFORE SEEKING FOR COUPLES COUNSELING

Even interacting with a therapist will help you see your insecurities in a different light. Perhaps you have already figured out, for example, that the root cause of your insecurity is a betrayal from a past partner. You're afraid that your current partner will do the same, but you don't necessarily want to tell them this.

Having an unbiased person, like a therapist or coach, listen to your concerns and immerse yourself in them can help you find connections that you wouldn't have if you just went to a nodding friend.

Finally, take heart in knowing that "a good relationship built on love, respect, communication, and commitment should help most people lose their insecurity," Squyres says. And remember this: you will discover a degree of trust that you might not have found on your own when people just remember your faults and love you anyhow.

Chapter 5: DOUBT CAUSED BY ANXIETY IN RELATION-SHIP

THE RELATIONSHIP DOUBT YOU SHOULDN'T IG-NORE

Even though we love our partners to the moon and back, it is always possible to find ourselves facing questions that make it challenging to communicate. From confusion about your shared objectives to a total contact divide — once our suspicions start to fester, letting them go can be challenging.

If we want to avoid the breakup of our relationships, we have to discuss our suspicions and the root causes behind them. Although some doubts come to any couple usually and naturally, others are signs of warning that should not be ignored. Don't wait for heartbreak and tension to come knocking at your door. Try to fix now to get to the root of problems surrounding your relationship before they overtake the affection you have for each other.

Doubts are a prominent part of the process

No matter who you are, and no matter how long your relationship has withstood the tests of time — you've faced questions about your partnership at one point or another. When it comes to our romantic relationships, items are a standard part of the process, but some are more detrimental to our peace of mind and health than others. When faced with questions, we've got to answer them and be truthful about where they're taking root.

Running from our questions leaves us nothing but afraid, weakened, and hanging on to something that might not be right. Although doubts are natural and come with the seasons of our relationships, some doubts are also critical red flags that need to be addressed to sustain and safeguard our inner peace and long-term wellbeing.

To overcome the questions, we have to answer them frankly and fiercely. That's not just about questioning our friends. It means facing ourselves and the burdens we are bearing, as well as the stuff from this life and our relationships that we want. Addressing those questions can be a moment of change for you and your family. Avoid running out of the items and reach out to learn. It's the only way you can find your way to the reality you must both know.

WHERE DOUBT COME FROM IN YOUR RELATION-SHIP

Romantic doubts are natural, and they come and go no matter what stage you find yourself in your relationship. However, they have underlying causes, and these causes may also be just as significant as the same doubts. To ensure that our fears are rooted in the right place, we must first consider where they come from.

Stressful Atmosphere

Stress is a major toxin in our surroundings, and it is one of the most probable. We are living in a chaotic world, and it creates utter chaos when the stress rains over our lives. We also get into a state of constant anticipation of the worst as a way of preparing ourselves for the challenges. The more tension we face, the more questions we find ourselves grappling within our personal lives. However, these suspicions are always our problems in disguise — so check your stress levels to see if there is something you do to self-sabotage.

Unresolved Baggage

Our unresolved emotional baggage is perhaps the most common cause of romantic doubts. Our past pain plays an essential part in our future, as it moves from relationship to relationship around us. You have to work through your past marriages' traumas and even your childhood to make sure you will later lead a safe, happy relationship. If you still hold your past baggage, this may lead you to doubt the legitimacy of your right here and now.

External Pressure

Often it's the outer world that contributes to the suspicions within our relationships that we experience. Society goes a long way to help us form our views on everything from how we dress up to how we create relationships. If your relationship has a lot of pressure from friends and family (or even your career) to deal with — then it may lead to some serious questions that follow you around. To prevent such problems, we need to be clear about what we as individuals want, rather than simply falling in line with the herd.

Off-mark Validation

Are you anyone who gets approval from outside sources? Besides being a significant indicator of vulnerability, it can also become a source of severe doubts about the relationship. The more you base your worth off the people and interactions around you, the more unpredictable and dysfunctional you will become. You will doubt your inner self, your ability to make eroding decisions, and you will come to doubt everything ... including your ability to make decisions on the most basic levels.

Bad Partner Choices

Like it or not — we always question our partners because we choose the wrong guy/gal. At times, our reservations are the way our subconscious brain tells us that the relationship (and the person who shares it with us) is a bad match. It's up to us to wake up in those moments and decide if this is the actual reality we're missing. Everything else may seem right in your relationship, but if something still feels wrong — it is wrong. More often than not, listen to your gut.

Lack of Nurturing

Although you may be with the right person, you might still find yourself grappling with doubts — even if you may have both worked hard to overcome your baggage. It may mean a lack of nurturing that feeds an increasing divide when things are still not working out (or the doubts are creeping in). Relationships are living beings breathing in and of themselves, and they take a great deal of energy and commitment for all interested parties.

Doubts, you can never forget

So, is there a seething of doubt in your relationship? Don't forget these. Of course, as they might be, whether you stop them or disregard them, they always bear implications. Stop running from those worries and face them in the back of your mind. These are the questions you can never in any conditions ignore about your relationship.

Am I being drawn to them?

One of the most common relationship doubts to experience deals in our level of physical and emotional attraction. For a connection to succeed in some long-term sense, all partners need to feel a general attraction to each other. This draw can fluctuate through the physical and emotional planes, but it should still have its available pull in place. Although it's normal to challenge your attraction from time to time, you should always take serious doubts... well, really.

Am I Humiliated?

If you have to ask yourself if your partner is manipulating you — some questions need to be answered. We should be able to trust our partners, and we should be mindful that even though we are out of the picture, they have our backs. If your partner makes a fool out of you whenever you're not around, or you're humiliated continuously by foolish behavior, then you have to fix your questions about them and make sure they're a person you can live around.

Is she/he loyal?

Loyalty is crucial in every relationship, but it becomes particularly important when it comes to our romantic relationships. The incredibly critical thing is to question the loyalty of your partner. In comparison to confidence, commitment implies the other individual's willingness to stand by your side through hardship. In contrast, it may also indicate their ability to hold you back from the attacks of others. It's hard to trust your partner without commitment. It's also challenging to make sure you'll always be there to help each other when the chips fall where they can.

What if the beliefs that we carry are too different?

Values form who we are and direct us towards people and experiences that can bring value and pleasure to our lives. We are rudderless in a stormy sea, without our principles. Without ideals in a relationship, we can find ourselves clashing with frustrated expectations and not balanced behaviors. Doubting your partner's principles is something we can never ignore. It is a warning sign that things are not what they look like.

Want the same stuff?

While many of us have been brought up to believe it's the similarities that have sustained good relationships, the real glue in a long-term partnership wants the same things out of life. It makes it easier to resolve challenges and concentrate on one another and our dreams when we want the same things from our futures as our partners do. But it becomes easier to find disappointment when we seek different things. Do you want something the same as your partner does? This is a grave doubt to carry in your heart.

Are they honest with me?

Honesty in a relationship is vital, no matter what age or stage you are in. We need to be truthful with each other to trust each other, and we need to be honest in ensuring integrity and transparency.

A partner who isn't honest with you is one who gives their personal interests priority over your own. It's natural to distrust someone you can't trust, but it shouldn't be a regular part of your relationship.

How big is it that they make me feel?

Our friends and spouses need to pick us up and inspire us while we are down or dealing with life's difficulty. Besides that, they should always treat us with compassion and reverence. Without that, keeping a just relationship is unlikely. If your partner makes you feel weak, inferior, or otherwise insignificant — then soon, the doubts begin to fester. You're going to doubt yourself, but you're going to challenge them as well as someone else's thoughts on the world around you.

Then what you have to do

Did you decide the doubts are simply too much to bear? These are the steps that you need to take next to resolve your concerns and find peace. The longer you run out of receiving the answers that you need, the greater the pain.

Don't wait until the conflict is getting bigger. Face your fears to rediscover your truth, and address your doubts.

1. Consider which source

In addressing your doubts, the first step is to consider the source. While some of our doubts are well-founded or justified, others are simply projections of our doubts. We have to dig deep and be brutally honest about where our concerns come from. We need to look at the source of our doubts and get real about the reasons we have come to see our partner in another light.

Break down your doubts one by one, and work backward to get to the root of your relationship's arrival. Don't shy away from past pain and baggage, and don't lie when you make comparisons that don't exist. Know that your partner isn't your dysfunctional parent; they aren't the ex who broke your heart into a million pieces. Analyze the comparisons you make and know when to spot the projection signs. Ask critical questions for yourself. Doubts about my partner? Or do I put my past in doubt? Is this a behavior that they have shown to me? Or am I looking back for yesterday's troubles? Once you are aware of where your doubts come from, you take steps to correct them.

2. Get yourself clear about what you want

Once you've identified your doubts and sussed out what's real and what's not, you need to be clear about what you want so you can create an action plan. Consider what it means most to you in this world and what you hope to build 5, 10, or even 20 years from now before you open up to your partner or make any dramatic moves.

Take yourself a few quiet moments each day and spend some time journaling about what you want from your life. Consider every aspect of your life, from your career to where you want to live, to your family. Look at your relationship and compare it with your dream partnership. Is this that person with whom you can build tomorrow?

Don't hurry the process and avoid any truths that are required. If you're standing on the edge of a cliff looking at a relationship with more questions than advantages, you need to be sure about what you want to do before you cut any cords that you don't want to. Accept your needs at face value and see you need them to be happy.

3. Open up to each other

It's time to open up to your partner with your truths to hand and have an honest discussion of your concerns. Again, this is a process that cannot be hurried and one that should be carried out with special care. That means you have a grasp on what you want, what you need, and the emotions that surround the issues you have. With little less than the facts, there's no point running into a big conversation.

Find a safe space where you and your partner can securely open up to each other, without fear of being overheard or disrupted. Choose the time you carefully talk to each other and make sure it's not in the midst of a lot of emotional distress or chaos.

Open to your partner. Explain to them your doubts and explain the work you have done to get to this point. Leave off any accusing language and try (as much as possible) to keep your emotions out of it. Give them space and time to answer once you have had a chance to express yourself. Remember that this is not necessarily a one-and-done conversation, too. If you need to, walk away but don't stop talking until both of you get answers.

4. Check your space

Now that all is out in the open, it's time to lean into the room, separating you and your partner. With your new information, you both need time to process how you feel, and you need time to weigh the information against your needs and action plans. How you feel when you give up your doubts can differ significantly from how you feel after expressing your partner's needs and hearing their answer.

Make yourself comfortable spending time and get back into the routines and pastimes that bring you joy. Investigate who you are more thoroughly and re-engage with life in a way that gives you a more in-depth, more compassionate viewpoint.

Our doubts can be natural moments of fear and passing, but they can also be important indicators that we are moving in the wrong way. If your doubts are yet to subside, then you need to spend some time in your world — to decide if that's preferable to a world shared with someone else. Once again, the key here is honesty... uncomfortable as it might be. Explore who you are, and actively and without hesitation, explore what you want from your life.

5. Talk the patterns

Sometimes, our doubts arise because of concrete patterns that repeatedly rear their heads. These patterns manifest as self-sabotage, in which we drive away people who might otherwise fit well into our lives and futures. To stop them, we have to address these patterns, and then quench the originating fire that feeds them. This means digging through our pastures and hearts to let go of the pain that lurks in the shadows.

It is time to address any patterns that might feed your negative emotions and thoughts after you have both addressed your concerns and given yourself time and space to explore and process them. You need to be brutally honest here, once again. Do you doubt the ability of your partner to be there for you? Or are you pushing away someone you don't believe deserves?

Look at the way your past relationships have played out. What stopped you opening up? What's broadening the divides? Is it old wounds from your childhood, playing your heart's stage time and time again? Do you prove right to your dismissive and narcissistic parents by failing in love, just as they have? Go back as far as necessary to get to the root of your patterns. Stop shooting yourself in the foot and begin to let go of the baggage that pushes love out of your life.

Putting everything together

Our relationships are a significant cornerstone of our lives, but they can fill us with fear and doubt as well. When these doubts appear in our partnerships, we need to address them so that we can see them for what they truly are. The more we approach the next steps with compassion and understanding, the better for our relationship, after all, the only way to tackle your doubts is by opening to your partner and taking action. Take some time to consider the source of your doubts or fears before making any bold moves. The way we feel about a situation, sometimes, is justified. But other times, it's just a manifestation of our baggage from the past. Get clear about where your worries come from, then (once you know their source) spend some time familiarizing yourself with what you need and want from life. With this knowledge to hand, you can approach your partner and open yourself to some honest dialogue, which will help both of you find the resolution you need. Once both of you have said what you need to say, take some time (and space) to process your feelings and next action plans. Address whatever negative patterns come into play. Take charge and stand up for the things you want and need. You are the only one that can be, after all.

DEALING WITH FEAR OF RELATIONSHIP: HOW TO HEAL HEALTHY RELATIONSHIPS

Romantic relationships can sometimes be the cause of depression. There's a good explanation that romantic relationships are one place where we don't have much influence, as opposed to certain aspects of our lives. We have an organization on how we connect with the person we are dating, but we can't regulate how they feel about us. We may feel like "all the right things" are being done, but we can't make someone like or commit to us. Romantic relationships also put us in a position of vulnerability. We open up to our partners in intimate relations rather than other forms of relationships and reveal aspects of ourselves that we are afraid to let the world see. This combination of complexities combined with the desire for others to like us and the pressure we feel to find and marry the right partner make relationships a powder keg for anxiety. Thankfully, by developing understanding and practicing the techniques taught in this book, we can emerge more relaxed and grounded in ourselves and be much less insecure in a relationship. Instead of suddenly being overwhelmed and leaving the relationship or continuing to blame the partner in reaction to our anxiety, we can learn to soothe ourselves, learn to recognize when we have to fix a problem and when we should let it go.

Below, I illustrate some of the most significant difficulties that people face in romantic relationships related to anxiety, along with methods to begin handling your anxiety effectively so that your relationship is not ruined.

Interpreting it as a sign that you don't like the person you're dating. We prefer to view something as an indication that our partner or future partner does not like us if we are nervous about whether our relationship will work out and is uncertain about ourselves. Haven't they replied immediately to your text? They must have been losing interest. Do they want to hang out on a Friday night with their friends instead of spending time with you? They've got to like their mates better than you like them. Don't they continually confirm your physical appearance? They've got to think you're mean. Some of this stuff may sound ridiculous when you read them here, but these possibilities feel all too real when we are in the throws of anxiety. It feels like we are being rejected, and in our efforts to gain reassurance, unless we know how to soothe ourselves, we can cause relationship issues.

We could assume our concern over whether or not we like a partner is related to our self-worth. When we see that our worth is not connected to being in a relationship but is unchangeable, our anxiety in romantic relationships decreases dramatically. I urge you to build a sense of your worthiness that is not linked to your rank, profits, or achievements in your relationship. Work to appeal to the part of you that is still deserving of it. Also, I would advise you to focus on liking yourself; when we like ourselves, we seem to be much less concerned about whether other people like us.

Waiting for your partner to get rid of your depression.
Anxiety also encourages us to try to manage things, which may involve the person we are dating. We can try to regulate how and when a partner interacts with us, how and when we spend time together, or what kinds of things our partner does when they are not with us. It may all be an effort to quiet our fear. You wouldn't be nervous if your partner replied quickly to your text messages. If they never associate with people you think they might be drawn to, then you're going to be good. Unfortunately, it also erodes the love and intimacy in a relationship to try and dominate your partner. When they are worried that something they do could make you uncomfortable, it is difficult for people to feel free to be

themselves.

I want to be clear that it is always important to set limits and have standards for your partner's actions. There is a difference between constructive boundaries and setting expectations and reactive attempts to regulate another person's behavior in response to anxiety. My essential advice for resolving the issue of expecting your partner to get rid of your anxiety is to learn when you feel nervous about soothing yourself. This could include going to counseling to focus on your anxiety-related underlying problems.

When you are nervous, ground yourself at the moment, try to be kind and gentle to yourself and take some time to relax before acting out of your fear. This doesn't mean that when you are nervous, you can't ask your partner to help you calm down; I think it's incredible when partners support each other through tough emotional experiences. If you want your partner's help, see if you can tell them how you feel (not what you think of their behavior) and just ask them to listen and maybe hold your hand or hug you. It will help you understand that your stuff is more connected to your anxiety than their actions.

Trying to quickly move the relationship forward.

We search for something safe and stable to hold on to while we are nervous. That typically implies a commitment in the sense of a relationship. Before the person we are dating, and we are fully ready for it, we can press for a commitment because we hope that the committee will relax. The challenge is that it can trigger tension and problems in the relationship to press for a commitment before both partners are ready. Additionally, it is not valid to commit to a relationship because you want to feel less insecure about being with your partner. The good feelings you have for your partner and the shared sense that you know each other well enough to take your partnership to the next level should be about committing to a partnership, moving in, getting engaged, or getting married. I advise you to concentrate on the moment to avoid pushing the relationship forward too fast because of anxiety. Pay attention right now to what the relationship is like for you. What are you going to like? What would you dislike? Sometimes, in the expectation of things going better, we strive to move our relationships forward. We think that the person we are dating would treat us how we want to be handled if we are in an exclusive relationship.

The truth is that you should come from within and be strengthened by a commitment as a partner treats you; if someone doesn't treat you well, that's an indication that you should not pursue a more profound commitment. It will help you appreciate the relationship just as it is right now by concentrating on the moment. I believe our culture's emphasis on marriage makes us forget the excellent dynamics in the early stages of romantic relationships that we witness. Without the added burden of living together, planning a wedding, or having children, I encourage you to enjoy dating and getting to know a new partner, learning about each other as your relationship grows over time, and soaking in the lightness of the relationship.

Trying to be flawless.

In the sense of a relationship, experiencing anxiety may also drive us to conceal our shortcomings in the hopes that our partner will think we are flawless and thus choose us forever. There are many issues with this: first, when we strive to be excellent, we still have the feeling that they would stop loving us if our partner were to see our faults. Essentially, we end up feeling only conditionally loved and accepted in our effort to be unconditionally loved and accepted. Another problem related to trying to be perfect is that we don't allow the individual to see the real us, to know our quirks and funny ways.

I urge you to accept your full self to fix this and let them get to know you as you know the person you are dating. It's much easier to let go of striving to be perfect and encourage a partner to see your shortcomings when you build an unconditional relationship with yourself. The only way to get it is to give it to yourself if you are yearning for unconditional love and acceptance. This will provide you with the protection that you need in your relationships to turn up as your whole self. If your relationship does not turn out as you hoped, it will encourage you to be there for yourself.

Getting disproportionate concerns.
The last thing I want to stress related to anxiety is that it may cause us to make irrational allegations about our partners and relationships. We may be projecting our insecurities on how we looked at past partners and felt. We wanted them to make us feel worthy, and when they did not, we blamed their actions on our feelings of indignity. Although some of the things we want from our partners are rational, our anxiety might turn irrational requests into understandable desires.

It is necessary to sort through what is causing your grievances and demands to fix this issue and decide whether they sound fair. Taking the time to talk with someone you trust could help you recognize when the issues are stemmed from fear and insecurities and not explicitly correlated with your partner's actions. This clarification could help you determine what issues you should let go of and what problems you should address with your partner. Also, taking the time to think about what you are worried about can help you calm down enough to deal with things in a positive manner rather than start an unnecessary war.

Chapter 6: NEGATIVE THINK-ING IN YOUR RELATIONSHIP

WHAT IS NEGATIVE THINKING? HOW IT CRIPPLES YOUR MENTAL HEALTH

Negative thinking is something we all indulge in from time to time, but your mental health can be ruined by persistent negativity, leaving you depressed and anxious. Science suggests that positive thinking can boost mental wellbeing, decrease stress, and even contribute to improved cardiovascular health, but many of us are stuck to negative thinking habits. Looking for ways to break the loop, let's discuss the impact of stress on mental wellbeing.

If you're someone who analyzes your emotions, differentiating negative thinking from everyone's daily concerns can be difficult. It's natural to feel depressed about an upsetting case, just as worrying about financial pressures or relationship problems is something we sometimes all do. However, it is when those feelings are persistent and widespread that issues occur ("Why Am I So Pessimistic, Angry, and Depressed?").

The Rethink Mental Disorder concept of negative thinking stipulates that "Bad thinking refers to a negative thinking pattern about yourself and your environment. While everyone encounters negative thoughts over and over again, negative thinking that significantly affects the way you think about yourself and the world and even interferes with work/study and everyday life can be a sign of mental illness, like depression, anxiety or personality disorders.""

Not everybody who engages in suicidal thinking has a mental disorder, just as not everyone with a mental illness has persistent depressive thoughts. Negative thinking, however, can detrimentally affect your mental health and quality of life, mainly when you cannot stop. Fortunately, there are ways to stop negative thoughts, but first, you have to look at what triggers them.

There are several possible reasons for negative thinking. Intrusive negative thoughts may be a symptom of obsessive-compulsive disorder (OCD), generalized anxiety disorder (GAD), or any mental illness. Depression is also symptomatic of negative thinking. While negative thinking can be a sign of mental illness, it can be a normal part of life, too. However, negative thoughts can have a severe effect on your life, so it's best to get to the bottom of them, whatever the cause.

There are three leading triggers of negative thinking, according to the Power of Positivity.

1. *Fear of the future:* People always fear the unknown, and they are worried about what the future will bring. Sometimes this leads to "catastrophe," which often means anticipating failure and catastrophe. Whichever way you look at it is a waste of time and resources to think about the future. The trick to letting go of these negative feelings is realizing that there is a limit on what you can do in the future and just try to concentrate on the moment.

2. *Anxiety about the present:* There is reasonable anxiety about the present. All of us are concerned about what people think about us, whether we're doing an excellent job at work and what the traffic on the way home will be like. Negative thoughts always come up with the worst-case scenario: nobody in the workplace likes us, our boss is about to tell us that we have done horrible work, and the traffic will make us late to pick up the baby. Once again, this stems from the

fear of losing power. Organization and practice may help banish negative feelings, but you will still need to use practical therapy methods.

3. *Shame on the past:* have you ever been waking up to think about something you did last week or even last year? Everyone does and says things they feel guilty about, but negative people tend to focus more than others on past mistakes and failures. Of course, recognizing that the incident happened and contemplating how you could keep it from happening again in the future is a more positive way to handle mistakes.

HOW TO STOP BEING NEGATIVE ONCE AND FOR ALL

You shouldn't succumb to a life of negative thinking. You can learn to get rid of negative thoughts by intercepting them with some simple combat strategies until they become all-consuming. The trick is to perform counter-exercises if you have negative thoughts, and not give up if you have a blip.

With this in mind, the next time negative feelings emerge, here are five questions to ask yourself. You can do this in your head, or write down your comments in a journal.

1. Is the observation true? Is there a foundation for the negative belief?
2. Is the thought of giving you strength, or is it taking away your power?
3. Can you bring this thought into a constructive context, or benefit from it?
4. If you didn't have these opposing views, what will your life look like?
5. Is the thinking glossing over a matter which needs to be addressed?

Know it takes time and effort to fight negative thinking.

The Damaging Negative Effects

You make assumptions that a disease or illness causes your tired body or constant aches, but have you ever considered that thinking negatively could be the reason for that? Pessimism has more impact than just mental wellbeing. Doctors have found that people with high levels of depression are more likely to suffer from degenerative brain disorders, cardiovascular issues, digestive problems, and to heal far slower from illness than those with a positive attitude.

What are the causes of Negativity?

Negativity is also a result of fear or depression. It can be triggered by sickness, incidents in life, personality disorders, and drug abuse. Negativity, like so many things in life, can become a habit too. Frequent criticism, negative thoughts, and denial can build neural brain pathways that promote sadness. These negative patterns can cause our brain to misinterpret reality and make breaking the negative cycle much more difficult. Fortunately, most customs can be broken. Experts also said breaking a habit takes 21 days.

WHAT ARE THE TYPES OF NEGATIVITY

Negativity can manifest in many ways:

- *Cynicism:* A general lack of faith in people and their intentions.
- *Hostility:* intransigence towards others; inability to establish relationships.
- *Filtering:* Just seeing the negative about what good events or memories might be.
- *Polarized Thinking:* The idea that if something isn't great, then it must be wrong.
- *Jumping to Conclusions:* Believing that something negative occurs regardless of the present circumstances.

- *Catastrophic:* The idea that tragedy is imminent.

- *Blame:* blame others for personal problems, and believing you are a victim of uncontrollable incidents in life.

- *Emotional Reasoning:* Determining what is right and what is not using your emotions.

- *Change fallacy:* Assuming that if people or situations shift, then you will be happy.

- *Heaven's Reward Fallacy:* a form of cynicism that implies hard work and effort will always be rewarded. You get cynical and sad when the reward isn't coming.

HOW NEGATIVITY AFFECTS THE BODY

Sad thoughts and feelings are a common reaction to heart attack and tragedy. However, prolonged periods of depression can lead to serious health issues. Negativity is putting our body into a state of tension, or 'fight or flight.' Our bodies are engineered by releasing cortisol into the bloodstream to cope with stressful conditions, making you more alert and centered. Although some stress is good for us, too much can harm your health. Extended negativity cycles delay digestion and decrease the capacity of the immune system to combat inflammation. This is also why losers are more likely than optimists to get sick.

Among the common effects of negativity:

- Headache
- Fatigue
- Upset stomach
- Chest pain
- Sleep problems
- Depression
- Anxiety

- Social withdrawal
- Dramatic metabolic changes (i.e. overeating or under-eating)

Often, constant depression affects mental health, making people more likely to resort to smoking or drug abuse as a way to cope.

OVERCOMING NEGATIVITY

Much as negative thoughts build neuronal pathways in the brain, so too can positive self-talk and affirmation become a habit. Research indicates satisfaction and optimism are more of an option than situation factors. Here are some strategies for reducing negativity:

- *Learn to acknowledge True*. See the universe both for the good and the poor. The more practical optimist you become, the more you can concentrate your attention on the positive.
-*Work right now*. Concentrate on the job at hand and stop worrying about past failures or possible worries. If a negative thought enters your mind, instantly respond with at least three positive affirmations. Positive thinkers can control their minds and are mindful of the emotions going into their heads.
- *Be favorable*. If it's a habit to be optimistic, then you must practice happiness every day! Take part in activities that foster positive thoughts – like hobbies, spend time with loved ones, and meditation. Engage in uplifting discussions and newspapers.
- *Turn on your anger*. It's likely to encounter negative feelings and perceptions, but optimistic thinkers know how to turn those negative words into effect. For example, a positive thinker may look in the mirror and see that she has gained a little weight over the holiday season. Instead of focusing on her look, she uses it as an opportunity to live a healthy lifestyle.

- *Spend time being uplifted.* Poor thinking is infectious. Don't catch another body's gloomy bug! Instead, spend time talking to people who care for you and make you feel enlightened and fulfilled. People are social beings, and the maintenance of a healthy family and friends network will help you see the glass half-full.

Negative thoughts can affect your mood and mental health. However, you can break the cycle. We can find ourselves harboring unhelpful thoughts all too often. You can concentrate on what lies behind them with some easy exercises, reframe your problems, and take back control. Occasionally you may think of yourself as an issue that isn't as burdensome as it may seem. Getting "unhelpful feelings" is very normal, and it's not something that ends with puberty; even relatively mature adults do get them. Many people will use the same unhelpful positive thought style again and again.

Unfortunately, not everyone becomes conscious of their patterns of thought, and they perpetuate types of thinking that are not helpful. Being mindful of some unhelpful feelings is a big step in making some significant life changes. Learn through examples of unhelpful forms of thought. Ask yourself why they may influence anyone. Consider also if you are familiar with any tone, and whether you appear to overuse any of these.

Types of unhelpful thinking

- *Labeling:* attaching rigid labels on oneself or others, e.g., "I'm so dumb;" "It's great." Our search for success harms our mental health.
- *Should/must:* Using these terms for ourselves or others leads to high expectations (sometimes very unreasonable ones).
- *Catastrophic:* Imagining the worst of a situation, blowing things out of all proportion, not viewing items rationally or reasonably.
- *All or nothing:* Also known as "black and white thought," this is an inability to see ambiguity or the "dark" complexities of life, e.g., "If this test

fails, my whole life is over."

- *Mental filter:* pay attention to only a few of the facts but forget the whole picture. Naturally, our minds appear to ignore the positive and to remember the negative, so we might be more likely to see our mistakes but overlook our achievements.

- *Mind reading:* Thinking we know what someone feels, e.g., "I know he hates me."

- *Personalization:* Blaming something wrongly on yourself or others.

You are likely to have noticed a lot of the thoughts mentioned above as the stuff you do, and that is to be expected. What is crucial, though, is to consider how much you choose to use anyone thought style, and how well (or not) it fits you in your daily life.

Luckily there are ways to help the outlook turn around. These strategies require practice and will not change things immediately for you. In our case study below, Susan found that she was able to break out of her rumination loop every day by using defusion strategies (see below) so she could have thought, but only consider it from a distance instead of getting caught up in it.

Case studies

Rumination is a common unhelpful type of thought. It defines a situation in which you are trapped in a loop and repeat the same ideas or feelings. Let's take the example of Susan, who found that she dwelt on stuff she was thinking about, so much so that she could barely think about anything else.

Of course, almost everyone thinks about problems. If we want to fix them, we need to. The most effective approach that leads to a resolution is by asking ourselves "how" questions, like "how can I change this situation?" Often there is nothing we can do to alter a situation, in which case acknowledging the problem as it is, is a positive step.

Unhelpful rumination comes when people ask "Why" questions like "Why does this happen to me?" These thoughts can cause high anxiety levels if they get caught in a loop, which can lead to negative thinking, inactivity, and even depression.

Susan figured she'd become depressed and concerned about how little she'd slept over the past three months. Her mood and sleeping habits seemed to have changed quite quickly, so she began a "Thoughts Log" that could be addressed in future sessions with her therapist.

Anxiety may be overwhelming, but you can take control back

It was through reading back through her journal that Susan could see how much she ruminated in her life on the same topics, without either agreeing or changing her situation. She could see on reflection how these thoughts caused her to lose sleep and made her feel low as she felt trapped in her condition and unable to break out of her thinking cycle. Break this cycle of rumination; here's how to do it:

1. Analysis

You may want to try out what Susan did and start a journal of thoughts. Through doing so, you will start realizing that if you have a specific thought style that keeps cropping up, it is not beneficial to recognize it. Another choice is to consult with a counselor or psychologist to determine with their guidance what thoughts are helping you and not.

2. Challenge

Just because you've got a thought, that doesn't mean that's valid. If you have a feeling that might be negative or unhelpful, list the proof for it to be accurate. First, list the facts that it's fake. What could be more rational thinking or more beneficial thinking? Considering what you'd say to a friend or someone you respect if they had the thought can also be helpful.

3. Neither resist nor fight.

Having negative or unhelpful thoughts is perfectly natural, and we all have them every day and every day, several times. Seek to defuse them instead of running away from unhelpful thoughts or distracting yourself from them (which can be useful, but only really in the short run).

Defusion is a profoundly useful technique that helps us to understand our emotions and bring them into context without getting drawn into them.

Imagine your hands as your emotions, as an experiment to understand why we should defuse unhelpful thoughts. Now put your hands before you, about 30 cm from your face. Moving your open hands towards you slowly, until they cover your eyes. What about the edges of your hands? What would life be like if your hands constantly made you miss out on seeing things around you and engaging in them?

Switch your hands off your face now. Your hands still belong to you but do not block your vision or prohibit you from communicating with the world. They can rest your hands before you need them next. Your feelings should be a part of you in the same way without trying to barge in on any aspect of your life.

Some feelings are worth giving in, here's where they can be found. So how do we stop our thoughts hampering our lives? A choice is laughing at the idea, putting it in its place. By doing this, we will take away some of the influence that negative thinking will have over us. So say it in a stupid voice with the thought "I'm bad at all" (try various voices to attain their full comedic potential). Singing it in a melody like Happy Birthday diminishes and ridicules the thought, which was, in the first place, a very absurd idea when you think about it.

4. Be aware of what else is around you

It can be hard to be present in the moment when we get sucked into a negative thought. As well as using defusion strategies, meditation and grounding exercises can be useful in ensuring that unhelpful thought patterns don't wholly take up the concentration.

5. Beware of sensations

Thoughts can affect our emotions, which, in turn, may physically affect us. For instance, when we feel scared, we often tense up, and maybe our breathing patterns change.

You can take immediate stress relief anytime, anywhere. Rather than attempting to drive away those feelings, make room for them. Notice when you feel a shift in your body, and imagine breathing into that space. Feel a knot in the stomach, triggered by fear and worry? Try to close your eyes, and imagine you're bringing fresh air to that part of your body when you inhale. This behavior is very soothing and nurturing and will benefit you both physically and mentally.

Essentially, we take back control of our thoughts by making space for challenging feelings and let them live without allowing them to take over and harm us.

Additional help

If you're looking for a counselor or psychologist to support you with your unhelpful feelings, you might want to ask them a little bit about what kind of therapies they're using and training in. Take, for example:

1. *Cognitive Behavioral Therapy (CBT)* may be effective at questioning unhelpful ways of thought.
2. *Mindfulness therapy* will enable us to be at the moment and be mindful of our truth beyond our negative thinking.
3. *Acceptance Commitment Therapy (ACT)* uses (among others) defusion strategies to unhook us from powerless feelings.

7 WAYS TO STOP TOXIC THOUGHTS FROM SABOTAGING YOUR RELATIONSHIP

All sorts of things can ruin a perfectly good relationship. The hacking and incompatibility, for example, are two big ones. But according to experts, there is one thing that can ruin a relationship more than anything else. "The ultimate relationship killer can be negative thoughts," says Bustle licensed psychologist Nicole Issa, Psy. D. "There's a very close loop of feedback between the thoughts, feelings, and behaviors of a person, so getting negative thoughts can take you down the rabbit hole."

According to Dr. Issa, it is essential to know that your patterns of thinking can lead to significant issues regarding relationships. Early childhood experiences with your parents, for example, can cause you to think you're unworthy of love. Because of that, you may go into any relationship fearing your partner would abandon you at some stage, and you may be afraid to speak up.

"The truth is we're making our reality," coach Joann Cohen, matchmaker and dating, tells Bustle. "When we believe we have a good relationship, then we work through things believing things will always be Fine. But when you enter a relationship with negative thoughts, you always expect the worst not only of your partner but of the result of your relationship." You need to find ways to turn them positive and stop negative thoughts. Thus, according to experts, here are some things you can do to keep toxic thinking from sabotaging your relationship.

1. Think of the first time you fell with your Partner

Relationships endure ups and downs. It is easy to let that cloud your judgment when you're going through a rough patch. When doubt about your partner's "real" feelings for you starts to invade your mind, think about the first time you have fallen in love with them and think about how you felt. "If you close your eyes and see the bright-eyed guy with whom you fell in love, life will look much more hopeful and doable," says Cohen. Often we need only a little reminder of the good days to conquer the bad ones.

2. The Past from the Present

To be honest, it is easier said than done to let go of the past altogether. "We all keep with us a piece of our history to somehow 'protect' us from getting hurt again," says Cohen. "But if you keep bringing your old relationships into your new and the pain along with it, then you are self-sabotaging and creating the fact that things just don't and won't work." Try separating your past from your present to prevent your past from producing negative thoughts. No matter how much they look, speak, or act the same, your ex is not your current partner. If you can separate your past relationship from your current one, being more present would be a lot easier for you.

3. Find alternative ways to channel your energy

Toxic thoughts have a way to make you do things unreasonably, sabotaging relationships, such as breaking into your partner's phone or putting yourself down. Dr. Issa says to consider what your emotions are leading you to do to curb this habit. Why, for example, do you feel the need to email your partner twenty times in a row just to "check-in?" Chances are, you're looking for some affirmation or reassurance that you still care for your partner. "If you feel the urge to do these things, take some time out for yourself and practice some skills to help you like counting down to ten and breathing," she says. Seeking ways to lower your negative emotions so you won't be acting out in ways you'll only regret later on.

4. Never assume that you know what your partner thinks

More often than not, negative thoughts come from beliefs that are not always real-life focused. "If we place our negative feelings on someone else or project them onto your significant other, what you can read is the other person's negativity," Cohen says. Here the secret is never to presume. Don't leap to conclusions. If you can't help it, don't just mull yourself over it. Get to the bottom, and get in touch with your girlfriend. "Try taking their statements on face value or demanding clarification," she says. "Never take for granted that you know how they feel."

5. Have one go-to-person to fix your issues of relationship
When you're angry about your girlfriend, it's not unusual to bring all your problems out to everyone listening. But as Cohen says, "When you do that, you're creating a divide between your significant other and your universe. That's going to create more misery than you realize." If you've got to wind up, just pick one go-to-person and stick to it. "Reporting your hideous business to others isn't helpful and would only encourage more resentment and hurtful feelings," she says.

6. Make a list of your harmful thoughts and use positive alternatives
It'll take some self-reflection to keep negative thoughts from sabotaging your relationship. One of the easiest things to do when you're thinking is to write all of your usual thoughts down that contribute to fights or even break-ups. Take it one step further and write down rigorous proof for or against any thought. Then come up with an alternative idea that is more valid and efficient after you do that. For example, if you think your partner is no longer interested in you because they have not replied to your text, make a list of all the other things that they might be doing. "Think of other occasions it took them a while to react or show they are still interested in," says Dr. Issa. "The alternative thinking here could be as simple as 'just because I haven't heard of them yet, that doesn't mean they aren't interested.'" According to her, the more information you are, the more successful it will be.

7. Take Breaking up away entirely from the table

Whatever your toxic thoughts are, they typically come from the same place — fear. More precisely, the partner's fear of going out. "I use the analogy, you're 'burning the fire' when you commit to," Cohen says. "Once you're burning the ship, there's no way to get off the island, so you need to work together to make things work." If there's no other choice, you're beginning to see the positive in a scenario. Taking the opportunity to break up from the equation (i.e., "burning the ship") will help you approach the relationship from a position of love and not fear. When your words and actions come from a loving place, remaining optimistic will be far more comfortable for you.

A thought is only a thought at the end of the day. The truth is not always so. If you don't allow that to overtake you, your relationship is going to be much better.

TIPS TO STOP HAVING NEGATIVE THOUGHTS
A gradual habit can become a mighty mental weapon

Treatment is usually pretty straightforward with most outside wounds. For example, you can use antibacterial cream and a bandage when cutting your finger, and after some time, the damage will close. You are pretty good to go.

It's not as easy or prescriptive to express thought processes, especially if they arise from general anxiety, depression, or another mental health disorder.

Negative thought patterns are like a cut of paper that you keep getting because you only have a vague idea of its causes. Or perhaps you don't feel the cut until it begins to sting.

A person may require different approaches to treatment, psychotherapy, and lifestyle changes depending on their condition and triggers. And when therapy is out of reach, quick treatment can be hard to get.

One incremental pattern which could aid is mental changes

Shifting the way you think means that you are deliberately halting an existing pattern of thinking. You re-evaluate how you feel about a situation, or even what you think about, to focus on something else. It's like flipping gears in your brain, so not just looping and looping your train of thought. This is about undoing many unhealthy habits and behavioral conditioning that you might have absorbed from others, in several respects. For starters, if you've grown up believing you must be the best in school and life, you're probably primed for stressful perfectionism.

Having a mental change is a way of battling the anxiety and stress or snapping out of winding thinking. Learn the most popular patterns of thought, how to identify unconscious negative thinking, and ways to re-orient yourself and offer the kind and favorable consideration you need.

If your feelings are "should," then take a break.

"I should be doing it, acting or feeling better."

"Every day, I should be going to the gym."

"I need to eat better."

"I am expected to avoid thinking like this."

It's not like there's evil intent behind those feelings. Depending on the case, eating more whole meals and going to the gym can be better. The word "should" is potentially harmful. This can cause remorse and send you down a painful road of spiraling negative thoughts.

Stop leading your thoughts with "I should"

If statements may lead to nervous patterns of thought since they impose a demand on you, that is often difficult to live up to. Everyone makes mistakes.

Instead of...	Try...
I should go to the gym every day.	I will try my best to go to the gym every day. Here's how...
I should eat healthier.	I can eat healthier today by doing these things...
I should stop thinking this way.	I see that I'm having anxious thoughts right now. What's a more credible opinion? What would I tell my best friend?
I should be able to get on a plane without anxiety.	I wish I wasn't so afraid of flying, but I accept that I'm working at a solution. What can I do at this moment?

And sometimes, feeling like you're supposed to do, behave, or feel a certain way adds just enough pressure to end up procrastinating or entirely evading a duty or task. This, for others, just contributes to more nervous thoughts.

Listen to your reflections, then. You tell yourself you're going to do things? What is a childlike way to keep yourself motivated to stay on track without spiraling into a destructive path of thought?

Reminder: There is no way to do anything right. Faults form a part of development. Try to understand other, unconscious negative thinking patterns. There may be a form of cognitive distortion known as automatic negative thoughts (ANTs) behind those "should" statements. When you have a strong feeling or reaction to something, like a reflex rather than free-thinking, ANTs are your first thought. They are consistent and experienced, and sometimes repeat themes like anger or fear. It is common in anxiety and depressed thoughts.

Identify and combat ANTs by keeping a record of your thoughts

You can do this by breaking down a situation into three pieces according to the "Mind Over Mood," a hands-on Cognitive Behavioral Therapy (CBT) workbook:

- Situation
- Their moods
- A thought or an image that springs to your mind spontaneously

You need to consciously turn the thinking into a more positive, beneficial, or wiser one after you recognize those.

What condition triggers your anxiety?

Keeping a record of your thoughts is simply putting your ideas to the test. First, ask yourself who, when, where, and when. This will help you explain what happened when you are sticking to the truth rather than your emotions.

- Who were you with?
- What was it that you did?
- Where were you?
- At what time?

What is your mood in a situation like this?
Describe your moods in one word, and then score these moods on a percentage scale equal to 100. For example, if you hand in a work project, your moods may include:

- Irritated
- Nervous
- Guilt, maybe if handed in late

In this situation, if your prevailing mood is nervousness — which falls into anxiety — you'd score it about 80 percent. The remaining 20 percent will then be packed with frustration and remorse.
The percentage need not be perfect — just go with the gut. The main point of evaluating them is to see how much of your emotions, for example, have been affected by a particular form of mood — an optimistic attitude versus a guilty one.

What automatic thoughts do you think go through your mind?
This is the most critical step in your record of thinking: List the thoughts and images that have arisen in your mind about this situation. Try to recall what you felt about it back then.

Might include automated thoughts:

- I am just too stupid.
- I am going to screw this up.
- No one likes me anyway.
- The planet truly is a bad place.
- I cannot do this.
- I will end up alone.

If you find yourself stuck with ANTs like these, breaking the situation down into "tasks" can help move your attitude away from the prevailing mood that dominates your thoughts. Before you start, for example, determine why the situation causes you to think, "I'm going to screw this up."

If it's a job situation, ask if you're scared of past ventures that went awry? How different is the case from previous projects? Play the worst-case scenario and see how it feels. Break down your feelings and moods and see whether there are legs and stand on in your anxiety or unconscious thinking. When you dig into the specifics, you will find this job situation is different from your background and future. Identifying your unconscious thoughts is the first step in keeping your feelings under control. What is it that you say yourself? How do you alter it now?

How do you change your outlook on the negative?
When you have found out about your unconscious feelings, it's time to put them to the test. Is there any evidence to support that thinking? Why does this apply to this new experience, if this proof is based on the past?

You want to rely on objective facts — not thoughts or theories. Then it's time to reflect on facts that don't back up your theory. Let's have one run through to show you how it works.

Thoughts: I'll screw up on this.

Reliable proof for my thinking:

- I made an early error that set this project back by a couple of weeks.
- I don't have good presenter skills.
- I have never done a major project myself before.

Credible evidence, in my opinion:

- My boss and I discussed the project schedule and got to an agreement.
- I've been doing my presentation for over two weeks, and I've been practicing in front of a colleague who gave me positive feedback.
- I know the subject, so I should be able to answer any questions that arise.

Now is the moment to find an alternative to your initial thinking. On both sides, you have your evidence, so now is the time to be a judge. A good technique is to behave as though you are assessing a friend's opinion rather than your own.

Now you will find a more rational, different way of thinking. This new thinking will take all the facts for and against you into account and will give your wiser mind a shot at running the show. Take, for example:

"I made mistakes, but I work hard in general."

"I'm honestly doing my very best."

"So far, I have had positive reviews, and my boss trusts me to do so."

Reminder: It will break down anything into smaller, more manageable tasks. Find a place to stop and check-in with your thoughts and see if you may be able to give yourself a break in the process. Recognize the emotional roller coaster or pressure when you sense it.

Like recognizing ANTs, simply realizing that you feel overwhelmed also has the strength. Don't put yourself immediately in defensive mode and whirl into a tailspin of fear. If it's because of stress, anxiety, or another illness, embracing it is the first step in overcoming mental pressure. I know what you're thinking: why would I ever accept all my brain and body shakes and jitters? Because it can take a lot less energy to accept than to fear it. Realize that this reaction means you are experiencing something important to you, rather than using additional energy to actively fight back. It also means that you do not need to continually push yourself to work at 100 percent. It is frustrating.

Understanding the anxiety and what it means to handle the tension that comes with it is one of the first steps. You can find there's a trigger in there. You should act to stop this when you encounter it, or you may discover yourself spending less time dreading it.

Spend more time asking yourself, "Oh, hi fear, what must we do to work together today?" And you may end up competing for less with yourself during this traumatic experience.

Reminder: There is always a different choice — even if it means saying no or opting out. If a situation is built on your anxiety or tension, ask yourself if you should opt-out. You could have chances!

Challenge yourself to take small measures, rather than pushing positive thinking

Mind changes are not about turning "I feel sad" into "I feel good." First of all, if this worked, it would be much easier to handle general anxiety and could be thought of as being out of existence.

There will be moments when you can't change your thinking pattern, no matter how hard you try to change it. And during those moments, it is necessary to note that it is enough simply to recognize the thinking or accept it — as described above.

Feeling sad is Good. Feeling nervous is Good. Take a break and have another day. If you do have the ability, you may slowly work towards getting beyond initial "I feel sad" thoughts to realize there might be an issue and consider a solution.

The more you consider these things, the more you untangle your emotions so that you can reach the next level of development and power.

AVOID BEING NEGATIVE WITH THESE 5 STRATEGIES

One of the biggest challenges you may face is overcoming negative thinking. After all, while you're harnessing all these incredible new resources that help you think positively and look to a brighter future, you're still grappling with unhelpful limiting beliefs from earlier in life. Many of those beliefs can crawl into unbidden and start undermining your vision of a better life.

Luckily though, there are plenty of practical things you can do to help you break negative thought habits. Here are five of the most potent forms of preventing negative thinking.

1. Stopping Thought

When you realize that your mind is beginning to enter negative thoughts or pictures, immediately try to say "stop!" to yourself. If you're alone, you can try to say this out loud, but when you just say it in your head, it can be mighty too.

If you prefer, you can use more persuasive language than "stop" (such as "Get out of my mind!" or something a little more colorful). The pictures can be more powerful for people who aren't as moved by words.

The classic example is a bright red stop sign that you imagine when distracting thoughts start to surface in your mind's eye.

There are also a few more straightforward approaches to stopping thinking. For example, you can try the old technique of splashing your face with water or simply change your thought path. Some people want to count 100 to 1 backward.

2. Positive Affirmations

Strong affirmations may be used in various ways. Next, they can be applied in the same manner as strategies for stopping thinking. In other words, as soon as you sense a negative thought coming your way, you might say an affirmation.

For example, if you're working using the Law of Attraction to find a new partner and catch yourself thinking you don't deserve love, you might say, "I'm a good, lovable person, and I'm going to find a great relationship."

Second, however, saying affirmations daily begins to reshape your mind, making them a strong weapon even if you're already in a good mood. Carefully plan the affirmations and strive to make eye contact in the mirror as you recite them. In the last chapter of the book we will look at 10 positive affirmations that can change your life.

3. Strengthening borders

If you've lived for a very long time of negative thoughts, you may think it's crazy to just instantly expect yourself to change approach. In this case, even statements and strategies to avoid thinking can tend to merely postpone negative thoughts until a later date.

If this sounds familiar, you may want to spend at least a few weeks imposing restrictions when it comes to negative thinking. The idea here is to choose a set, limited duration to allow your mind to entertain negative thoughts, and to actively avoid or battle them any other time of the week. You will find they seem less strong and have less ability to control your mind when you are told that you will have time to consider these thoughts. Moreover, many people find that when they arrive at their scheduled time to encourage reflection of negative thoughts, they can't even think of something and that this helps them break their cycle.

4. Destroying and Writing

If your negative feelings are connected to a particularly strong emotion such as anxiety, rage, or envy, try to let it all out in writing. Use a pen and paper and show all the pent-up frustration. Then you can choose a way to kill this paper, which symbolizes your determination to move forward. You might, for instance, rip it up, crumble it into a ball, burn it or scribble it over.

Those who aren't as keen to use words to describe themselves may have similar effects on creative endeavors. For instance, you could sculpt or paint a representation of your negativity, and then kill it (or alter its shape). The point of this technique is just to get some form of physical representation of your negativity, so you can banish it symbolically in some satisfying way.

5. *"Just Because"*

When you feel you are beginning to descend into depression, you should also try to reason with yourself. This method involves identifying a sentence that you can repeat to yourself to remember that you have control over your bodily reactions and raise that power over time.

Practice this approach by taking a deep, clean breath and saying something like "Just because I have had some bad relationships doesn't mean I've got to do this to my body" or "Just because I've been struggling to find a good career doesn't mean I'll never find one in the future."

Tell "Relax Now" after your chosen expression (letting the word "relax" be your excuse to exhale, letting out stress and negativity).

Chapter 7: THE NEGATIVE EFFECTS OF ANXIETY ON INTIMATE RELATIONSHIPS

The substance of pop songs and poetry has long been the wonder, fear, and curiosity that is so much a part of meeting somebody new: what are they doing right now? Do they want to think about me? But once a bond is formed, and two lives merge, such anxieties are typically replaced by the comforts and intricacies of understanding and trusting one's partner and of, yes, even some form of predictability and routine. But when such thoughts are not tempered by a large, healthy view of one's own life, they can start to take over, unleashing a powerful and destructive emotional force that can have catastrophic consequences for both partners.

Naturally, individuals look to their intimate partners for physical closeness. They seek their consolation or help; they may rely on them, and a separation saddens them. During infancy, the defining features of an individual's attachment to their caregivers may affect the way they perceive intimate relationships.

Appendix Theory Explained

According to British psychologist John Bowlby's theory of attachment, the quality of care received during infancy, including sensitivity and responses to a child's signals, affects the nature of an individual's attachment later on in life. The perceptions of parents and other sources of attachment and their ideas affect the internal working model, which is the mental representation of self or themselves and others by a person. Research with children by the psychologist Mary Ainsworth endorsed Bowlby's claims by suggesting three distinct patterns of attachment: stable, anxious-avoiding, and anxious-ambivalent.

- Securely attached children feel confident that their carers will meet their needs; they feel comfortable exploring new environments, and they have faith in others.

- Anxious-avoiding children perceive their caregiver as indifferent and insensitive, so they do not tend to be distressed to avoid dealing with a caregiver who is rejecting them.

- Anxious-ambivalent children are handled by carers who are often incoherent and erratic. They continue to assume that the only way to get attention and closeness is to exaggerate their expression of discomfort; when separated from their caregivers, they begin to become highly distressed and exhibit trouble moving away from them in discovering new surroundings.

THE SYMPTOMS OF ANXIETY

Individuals who are anxiously attached appear to experience more extreme negative emotional responses and cognitions, such as rumination and downplay, and deny positive life events and experiences. Findings from a study studying individuals with a social anxiety disorder and attachment types found that those with nervous attachment reported more extreme social anxiety and avoidance, greater disability, higher depression, and lower life satisfaction than participants with a stable attachment.

Anxiously Attached Adult and Romantic Relationships

Stable adults are known for having optimistic feelings regarding interpersonal relationships while considering the influence of adult commitment on romantic relationships, and they are not afraid of closeness. By comparison, avoiding adults can become uncomfortable if someone comes too close, pretending to be independent and having no one. Anxious adults are clingy types and sometimes feel jealousy; they usually worry a lot about their partner being rejected, so they try to impress and win their approval.

Fear of infidelity may become an overarching concern for those anxiously attached. In a recent study, anxiously attached participants showed themselves to be more hypervigilant regarding their partners' rejection signals, and more likely to interpret certain behaviors—sexual, romantic, and causal interactions—as cheating.

Fears of infidelity and breakup may also affect the actions ("mate preservation behaviors") of adults seeking to minimize the likelihood of infidelity and the relationship breakdown. Findings from a study in 2016 found that women and men who score higher in nervous romantic attachment display more frequent partner retention behaviors.

Holding Friends in Partnership

Men appear to exhibit such behaviors more often, and in general, they scored higher on tests showing nervous romantic commitment than women. From an evolutionary perspective, it could make sense to increase the frequency of mate retention behaviors because the specter of cuckoldry and ambiguous paternity was an important problem for men. Men registered higher scores on behaviors such as direct guarding, vigilance, time monopolizing, envy-inducing, punishing a partner's threat of infidelity, manipulation of emotions and loyalty, negative acts, aggression against rivals, obedience and degradation, and public signals of ownership. In comparison, women seem to use a distinct range of mate retention strategies — meaning to improve their beauty, affection, and care.

ANXIETY IN CLOSE RELATIONSHIPS

While much of this discussion focuses on the aspects of anxious attachment to the self, it is not difficult to find a relationship that is impaired by this problem. Many individuals who are anxiously attached may appear clingy, controlling, or even aggressive. Their anxieties reflect their over-dependence for support and reassurance on their partner to give their lives meaning and intent. Paradoxically this puts a strain on relationships and leads to lower satisfaction in relationships.

And while this type of attachment slices through the fabric of one's most intimate connections a damaging course, the termination of such a relationship does little to relieve the situation. People who are anxiously attached will respond to break-ups with angry protests, an all-consuming obsession with the former partner, a heightened sexual attraction to win back the individual, and often self-medicating with alcohol or drugs.

Chapter 8: OVERCOMING ATTACHMENT ISSUES

When it comes to the state of their interpersonal relationships or other relationships in general, nervous individuals will be well-served to accept ways of resolving attachment problems as a major step towards enhancing the social aspects of life.

A clinician will help them to understand their internal models of practice, how they relate to others, their early experiences, and their relationships with other people. The adjustment of their working models to reflect the complexities of new experiences and relationships may be a significant therapy goal.

UNDERSTANDING VARIOUS ATTACHMENT STYLES

Attachment Classification

As introduced in the previous chapter, Bowlby, with Harlow and Lorenz demonstrate through their Evolutionary Theory of Attachment that children bind themselves predominantly to one individual during early infancy and childhood (ages 0-5). Typically it's the mother (or replacement mother), and this relationship is a blueprint for all future relationships. If the relationship between parent and child ends, is broken, or otherwise is dysfunctional, it can have a detrimental effect on future ties. It is these encounters (or lack of them) that lead humans to form one of the following types of attachment

1. Stable mounting type

While Hollywood and current popular culture can categorize secure attachment as "boring" or "mundane," it is from this attachment style that solid, healthy ties are born. A stable attachment ensures that every person in the relationship feels safe, looks after, and understands. Kids who are firmly attached also develop into strong, healthy adults.

The variations in attachment styles and how they affect our lives are becoming ever more evident when assessing the success and happiness rating of securely attached children versus unsafely attached or avoiding forms.

Interestingly, this is not perfect parenting or even a lack of parenting skills, which determines the style of attachment. When a caretaker can make a child feel safe and secured via nonverbal communication, stable attachment grows. Factors which prevent attachment protection from forming include:

- Abuse or maltreatment
- The only concern when doing poorly or behaving badly
- Occasionally or inconsistently, getting your needs addressed
- Separation from parents (e.g., hospitalization, a departure from home)

Children who are tightly attached to their parents during their infancy:

- They choose to be with his/her parents over others.
- They should isolate themselves from their parents without being too angry.
- If they're scared, look for support from their parents.
- They are happy when they return to see their friends.

Similarly, people who have been securely attached as children to their parents appear to have long-term relationships in which they trust their partners and display a high level of self-esteem. Not only are these folks comfortable sharing with their partners their thoughts, hopes, and dreams, but they can also seek support when needed.

Stable people are also able to support and console their friends when they're suffering. Individuals with a stable style of attachment appear to become great partners.

2. Anxious-preoccupied form of attachment

If you can't relate to the first form of attachment when it comes to explaining discrepancies in attachment types, you possibly developed an insecure style of attachment during childhood or the fourth style of attachment, which is nervous.

There is an anxious attachment style among about 15 to 20 percent of people. Many people in this state of mind are seeking therapy because of the difficulties they face when trying to develop stable adult attachments. Many stressed carers are distracted or otherwise unable to consistently meet the needs of their children. People who form this kind of connection were not abandoned as children, and in most cases, their parents showed some care and concern for them; however, they did not fully establish their inner feelings of security as children. The inconsistent treatment has meant that they cannot rely on their parent or another caregiver. This incoherence creates an emotional storm inside the anxious child, which translates into adulthood and can contribute to relationship-avoiding types of people.

Like those individuals with a stable attachment style, people with the attachment style of an insecure child desire affection and intimacy but also experience a lack of self-worth. This negative self-esteem is directly linked to their attachment protection to their attachment figure.

Attachment types in early childhood maintain themselves, the attachment theory says. Their deep-rooted insecurities can lead to behaviors that seek attention (or antisocial actions for types that avoid it). While many good people are caring, friendly, all-around, their clinginess, neediness, envy, and ability to nag many drives loved ones away. Popular characteristics of the type of relationship an anxious child has included:

- A need for reassurance from friends and consistent affirmation.
- A desire from partners or potential partners for continuous contact, interaction, and focus.
- Serious High and Low Partnerships.
- A sensation of distress or fear when separated (even temporarily) from a partner.
- A propensity to use blame, guilt, shame, and other types of coercion to hold the partners close.
- A propensity to ignore duties because of an interest in relationships or personal interests.
- A propensity to overreact when the partnership is considered to be under pressure. These risks could, in some cases, be imagined.

If the above characteristics reflect your habits, obviously you are not alone. While an insecure attachment style can make building and maintaining stable long-term relationships challenging, it is important to remember that attachment styles are complex and can be changed with understanding, self-acceptance, and function.

3. Removable attachment
A sort of dismissive-avoiding attachment is the polar opposite of the type of attachment that is anxiously worried out above. Though the two types have one similarity — both are vulnerable — these styles of attachment couldn't be any different. Emotionally detached and avoiding, people with a sort of dismissive relationship don't desire love; in reality, they run away from it.
Interestingly, several forms of nervous attachments are associated with

dismissive-avoidant partners in relationships and marriages. The more the insecure partner strives for love and approval, the further it separates him or herself from the insensitive partner. The non-evitable partner, upset by this lack of intimacy, will threaten to end the relationship, which will have little impact on the dismissive partner.

Capable of detaching themselves from others, shutting down completely, and living their lives inwardly, folks with a dismissive attachment style give off a pseudo-independence that implies that they need no relation. That is, of course, simply untrue.

You have noticed a pattern by now. The avoidance of intimate relationships is the consequence of childhood events in which a caregiver was unable to build a secure connection to the parent.

Parents were physically present in some cases, but they were unable to fulfill the emotional needs of their children for one reason or another. In this situation, the child learns to suppress the feelings and repress them. When looking at contrasting variations in attachment styles — securely attached kids usually show a higher level of satisfaction with their adult lives than precariously attached kids.

This dysfunctional attachment style for avoiding forms brings adulthood, and the grown person avoids the need for love and connection. Typically the following characteristics occur when a person has a form of avoiding attachment:

- Intense emotions and personal circumstances make them anxious
- They set emotional and/or physical limits to extremes
- It can conceal information from its partners
- They send out mixed messages and ignore the feelings of partners
- They are selfless and enjoy casual sex
- Past partnerships are idealized

While avoidant types may have a deep desire for close relationships and intimacy, they are usually unable to satisfy their desires due to their deep-seated internal challenges. Avoidant forms are more likely to indulge in sexual affairs and divorce themselves.

According to attachment theory psychology, people with an avoiding attachment style need to transition to a stable attachment style to form and sustain healthy relationships. Like any form of attachment, this change is possible if directed by a mental health professional who understands the attachment process.

A licensed therapist will work with your primary relationship figure — and yourself to address unresolved problems. Adults and children who are safely attached experience considerably less pain in their lives. If you want to learn more about how your relationship with your primary attachment figure has changed your life, speak to a licensed therapist specialist focused on attachment theory and attachment technique, who is trained in counseling.

Since it's challenging for avoidant types to express their emotions, seeking counseling can be a daunting process. Still, it's a vital and essential step to help them move towards stable attachment.

4. Disorganized form of attachment

The final form of attachment is not based solely on frustration or anxiety but on extreme fear as well. The attachment figure of children with a disorganized form of attachment typically manages the trauma themselves. The attachment figure is unable to bind itself firmly to the child because of unresolved trauma, pain, or loss. Eighty percent of those exploited as a child have this kind of attachment.

Since their primary attachment figure's actions were always unpredictable and fear-driven, adults with that kind of attachment style have never learned to soothe themselves. Their history is marked by pain and loss, and they may become violent, look upon the world as dangerous, and otherwise have psychological problems. Signs of that type of attachment include:

- A hot/cold mentality concerning relationships.
- Antisocial conduct and inadequate remorse.
- A tendency towards selfishness, self-control, and lack of personal responsibility.
- The recreating of dysfunctional behaviors in adult relationships from their youth.
- Drug and alcohol misuse and criminal acts of violence or devastation.

If you think you may have some sort of disorganized attachment, don't be discouraged. With the aid of a licensed counseling specialist, you will learn how to become safely attached. Information is crucial once again. Education, motivation, and counseling will help you move towards a stable relationship style, so you can develop good, healthy ties.

Additional Resources
The ambivalent type of attachment is debated less regularly. It's akin to the nervous attachment. When a carer is seen as unreliable, ambivalent attachments form. It may be they are disinterested in the development of the infant, or they are interested but not always present. Whatever causes attachment formation, adults with an ambivalent attachment pattern can lack attachment in adult relations. They may be disinterested in forming new relationships, but they may experience love development, sensitivity, and attachment to individuals with whom they spend a great deal of time.

The protection of attachment in infancy may result in adult persons being securely attached. However, as with the outcomes of adult relationships, the role of attachment can shift, as can the types of sensitivity and attachment.

For example, avoiding attachment styles appear to evolve in adults who may have had stable attachments in childhood and then experienced problematic relationships.

You've heard in this book that counseling can be life-changing for people with non-secure forms of attachment. Online therapy can also provide a comfortable place to address your problems, and best of all, you can enjoy the benefits without leaving your home comfort.

In the next pages we will go through some commonly asked questions about Attachment patterns and styles, and how these influence adult relationships and behaviors.

What does Attachment Patterns mean?

As just discussed, attachment patterns demonstrate that people as adults develop relationship styles based on attachment patterns from early childhood. In the pre-school years, we are told to start practicing learned attachment when we start communicating with others outside our family. According to the attachment theory, our main attachment styles secure themselves in place in early infancy and childhood.

When it comes to the various forms of attachment and the roots of attachment theory, people with children who are securely attached usually see these children develop into adults who are firmly attached to them. As a result, people with stable relationship styles will possibly feel more positive in themselves and their surroundings. The theory of attachment works based on the assumption that securely attached infants (and securely attached children) become secure adults.

Safe forms have an air of trust and certainty, which seems to lack in the other attachment styles. People with unsurely attached styles are less self-confident and distrustful of their world. It is assumed that firmly attached infants do better than adults. The mental health professionals, such as psychologists and therapists' main attachment approach are to help people who formed unstable attachments in early childhood, learn how to develop more stable attachments.

How are attachment forms evolving?

The attachment patterns and attachment types are formed in early childhood according to attachment research and attachment theory. The theory of attachment works under the assumption that children securely attached to it can develop to become adults securely attached. The attachment model used in attachment theory research is focused on attachment style and relationship research being carried out using a mother, a stranger, and a child.

Could you change your type of attachment in adulthood?

Experts in psychology say people who are firmly connected tend to do better in life. But not everyone in early childhood was able to firmly connect themselves to their primary attachment figure. The good news is that in early childhood, adolescents who formed an unstable relationship with their primary attachment figure have opportunities for improvement.

Attachment theory teaches us it's possible to alter one's type of attachment in adulthood. By seeking professional support from a licensed therapist, you can learn how to alter unhealthy attachment behaviors and build a healthy attachment style. A therapist will help you learn about the origins of the attachment philosophy and the four ways of attachment.

These four types of attachment (created by our interactions with our primary figure of attachment) set the stage for how our emotional connection and relationship ties will develop over time. Conversing with a mental health professional will help you explore how the forms of attachment impact your life. In counseling, you will discover how childhood trauma still affects you today. You and your therapist will work together to develop an attachment plan that can help you develop a healthy attachment style — considering your past attachment behaviors.

It's possible to change your attachment styles once you start to understand the differences in attachment styles and attachment protection. Adult attachment styles like anxious-evitating attachment, avoiding attachment forms, and unstable attachment styles can be modified using a personalized attachment approach based on the principles used in attachment theory.

Unfortunately, both ways swing the door, so as to speak. Children who have formed stable attachments may develop other attachment types, such as rejecting attachment styles, if they have challenging experiences in relationships later in life without the support networks to function healthily through their emotions and experiences.

What are the examples of behaviors about attachment?

Securely attached infants have a preference for their attachment figure when it comes to attachment protection and the prime attachment figure. Safe forms display earlier flexibility and greater self-confidence when exploring their surroundings. In comparison, insecurely attached children are less confident in their actions when interacting with others and their environment, and less and more negative.

The variations in attachment types are reflected in the variations in the study of children's self-confidence levels and behaviors. Anxious-avoidant attached infants are oblivious to their attachment figure, or a stranger, being present.

The attachment figure can display disdain or disinterest in insecurely attached infants. Because of this detrimental infant attachment experience, these habits are likely to pass into infancy and eventually adulthood. If you have trouble with a dysfunctional child attachment-related relationship, talking to a licensed counseling professional will help.

What is an attachment figure?

An attachment figure is an early caregiver that serves as the basis for an attachment to a child. Attachment statistics are known to have a lasting impact on our lives. In attachment research, contact with the attachment figure focuses primarily on the mother's attachment to the child. However, if there was no mother present (or if the mother was not the primary attachment figure), the infant's attachment theory and attachment patterns are looked at about the caregiver present.

Attachment figures are thought to play a significant role in whether or not children develop secure attachments. Attachment styles of a child are developed in response to the affection and care the attachment figure gives. The attachment figure gained more affection, support, attention, and care from people with stable attachment styles than avoiding forms of unstable forms of attachment styles.

A child needs to feel comfortable and secured to build a stable relationship with the primary attachment figure. Attachment types are shaped about the mother or other attachment figure, based on the child's sense of protection and security.

What would you behave like in a relationship?

In their adult relationships, a person may be a bit insecure, they might be insecure, very dependent, concerned about a partner going out with friends or having different interests. Unfortunately, what happens is that they cause arguments over these things in relationships. In extreme situations, they might end up being quite controlling, possessive and jealous. They might start doing many check-ups and covert surveillance like placing cameras in a partner's car.

This is someone who displays no kind of jealous or possessive behavior, that's the couple where they don't do anything together, they have their own interests, they go out with friends as well as each other, they aren't jealous of each other, they aren't possessive, they don't keep checking in with each other, they don't have to keep calling or phoning to see where the other is.

What makes the attachment look insecure?

Depending on the type, an unstable adult attachment can look similar to a precarious infant attachment. For example, if an adult is affected by ambivalent attachment, they may be nervous the majority of the time. They can also be seen as in a relationship involving a lot of emotional support. In a relationship, that could make people feel insecure.

What are the symptoms of Adult Attachment Disorder?

Signs of adult attachment disorder include influence, frustration, urges, and confidence issues. Also, people feel like they don't belong, can't be affectionate, and have difficulty in all kinds of relationships. The theory and research on the topic suggest that treatment is needed to move beyond this kind of condition regardless of age.

What are the Attachment Disorder Symptoms?

Attachment disorder symptoms are similar to signs of attachment disorder. Other signs include aversion to people who love them, withdrawal from circumstances, and feeling hollow.

Do avoidant partners cheat?

An evasive partner could likely cheat. This means that if someone shows an avoiding adult attachment style, they may lie, which could be used as a coping strategy to prevent themselves from getting hurt or other people being close to them emotionally. Attachment theory and research have explored adult attachment forms to see how people act like adults when they have not received treatment formed as children for potential attachment problems. This is how they know how evasive partners will respond to certain romantic relationships between adults.

How do I know when I have problems with the attachment?
You may be able to tell if you have signs of a reactive attachment disorder that you have attachment issues. Some signs include having anger problems, manipulating, not trusting, not feeling you belong, or avoiding contact with others. If you have any of those symptoms, especially when it comes to romantic relationships, you can have attachment problems. You should learn more about social psychology and adult attachment when you believe you have attachment problems that were a result of your childhood. You will then be able to decide for yourself whether you need to reach out to a therapist for assistance. This can translate into insecure attachment in adults, particularly if largely overlooked if a child does not develop a secure attachment with their caregivers.

How do you break an attachment?
Generally speaking, if you want to sever somebody's bond, you'll need to focus on it. To do so, you may also need a support system and counseling. If you're trying to break an unstable childhood connection, this might include clinical applications to assist you in the process.

Ways to resolve attachment issues in an insecure relationship
If you think you are uncertainly attached and it has a detrimental effect on your love life, here are a few steps you may take to make the transition to stable attachment.

Get to know the pattern of attachment by reading up the theory of attachment. Trust me: Information is authority. If you don't have a great therapist now with the experience in attachment theory, find one. It could also be worth asking if they've ever had a patient or client in their adult romantic relationships that they've seen make the transition from vulnerable to stable attachment.

Find partners that have stable types of attachment. If you are trying to overhaul your attachment style, the last thing you need is to be undermined by someone who can't help you. Research shows that about 50 percent of adults with secure attachment style, have pretty good chances of finding someone out there who rocks the world AND is secure in their attachment style. Studies say that a positive encounter with a person who is certainly attached will overcome your insecure instincts in time. If you haven't met a partner like this, go to couple therapy. If you are, say, anxious-concerned and you are already in a loving relationship with, say, someone who is fearful-avoiding, I would encourage you to find a couple therapist who can motivate both of you to become safer together. Even if you feel your relationship is going well, consider taking this measure as a pre-emptive strike to solve trouble.

Exercise. Isn't pillow talk just your thing? Do it yourself, even though you have to start talking to an animal that is stuffed up. Hate asking about your relationship's future? Try worrying about your relationship's next few months if you can't deal with worrying about the next few years. It is also important to bear in mind that stable connection in intimate relationships not only makes such relationships more fulfilling; there is proof that it can connect you with someone you are even not near to. Research suggests that "boosting" one 's protection in some way ("safety priming" in psychology circles) makes people overall more generous and compassionate. This study by leading attachment researchers indicates that "whether formed in a person's long-term relationship background or nudged up by subliminal or supraliminal priming, the sense of attachment security makes altruistic caregiving more probable."

My impression is that it's just like riding a bike for those trying to up-grade their attachment style from vulnerable to stable, as the saying goes: once you've got it, you've got it. You can always push yourself over time to become a "better biker" a stronger one, a quicker one, a more agile one — but once you've mastered looking forward and pedaling at the same time, you're still good to go.

Chapter 9: HOW TO HANDLE JEALOUSY IN YOUR RELATIONSHIP

Nobody likes to feel jealous. Yet envy is an unavoidable emotion that we feel pretty much anyone of us. The problem with envy is not that from time to time it shows up, but what it does to us when we don't get hold of it. Experiencing what happens when we allow our envy to overtake us or influence the way we feel about ourselves and the world around us can be scary. This is why knowing where our jealous feelings come from and learning how to deal with envy in positive, adaptive ways are crucial to so many areas of our lives, from our interpersonal relationships to our jobs to our personal goals.

Why are we so insecure, then? Studies have shown predictably, that increased envy correlates with lower self-esteem. "Most of us are also unaware of the underlying guilt that resides inside us, for it comes so naturally to think of ourselves with self-critical thoughts. But the degree to which we feel jealous and insecure in the present can be highly affected by guilt from our experience," said Dr. Lisa Firestone, a Ph.D. clinical psychologist; the "powerful inner voice" is a form of negative self-talk, as Dr. Robert Firestone (Lisa's father) describe it. It perpetuates negative thoughts and emotions, with great scrutiny pushing us to compare, assess, and evaluate ourselves (and sometimes others). That is one reason why it's so important to learn how to cope with envy.

This voice will intensify our feelings of envy with negative and suspicious comments filling our heads. In reality, what our vital inner voice tells us that our situation is always more difficult to cope with than the actual situation. A rejection or alienation from our partner is painful. Still, all the negative things our critical inner voice tells us about ourselves after the event are what sometimes hurts us even more. "You're such an insane person. Have you ever felt you could truly be happy?" "You're going to end up alone. You can never again trust anybody."

To explain how this inner enemy feeds our negative feelings about jealousy, we will discuss two forms of jealousy more closely: romantic jealousy and competitive jealousy. While these two forms of jealousy sometimes overlap, considering them separately can help us understand better how jealous feelings can affect different areas of our lives and how we can best cope with jealousy.

ROMANTIC JEALOUSY

It is a fundamental reality that relationships become better when people don't become excessively competitive. The longer we can hang onto our envy feelings and make sense of them apart from our partner, the better we'll be off. Note, our envy also stems from our fear – a sense that we are doomed to be misled, harmed, or rejected. Until we deal with this feeling inside ourselves, in any relationship, no matter what the circumstances, we are likely to fall victim to feelings of jealousy, mistrust, or insecurity. These negative feelings about ourselves derive from very early life experiences. Sometimes we take on emotions that our parents or significant caregivers have had about themselves or us. In our current relationships, then, unconsciously, we replay, recreate, or respond to old, familiar dynamics. For instance, if we felt set aside as children, we might easily interpret our partner as ignoring us. We could choose a more elusive partner or even adhere to behaviors that would drive away from our partner. The degree to which we, as adolescents, assumed self-critical attitudes often shapes how much our critical inner voice will influence us in our adult lives, especially in our relations. And yet, no matter what our particular experiences might be, to some extent, we all hold this inner criticism. Most of us can relate to having a feeling that we are not going to be selected. The degree to which we believe this insecurity influences the way we feel insecure in a relationship. Dr. Lisa Firestone wrote, "Lurking behind our partners' paranoia or questioning a perceived third-party threat is also dismissive of ourselves. Thoughts like, "What is he seeing in her?" Can easily turn into "She is so much more pretty/thinner/successful than I am!" Even when our worst fears come to fruition when we hear about the affair of a partner, we always respond by transferring frustration to ourselves as being foolish, unlovable, destroyed, or unwanted. Our vital inner voice, like a sadistic coach, advises us not to believe or to be too weak. It tells us that we are unlovable and that we are not fit for romance. It is that whisper which spreads doubt, suspicion, and uncertainty. "Why does she work tardy?" "Why choose his friends over me?" "What does she do while I'm away?" "Why is it that he pays so much attention to what she says?" Many of us who are familiar with how envy works know that all too frequently, these feelings will eventually begin to sprout and grow into even larger, more engrained assaults on ourselves and/or our partner.

"She's not trying to be around you. Somebody else has to be there." "He is losing interest. He needs to get away from you." "Who would listen? You're all too dull" At any point in a relationship, from a first date to the 20th year of a marriage, this jealous feeling may emerge.

We may listen to our inner critic to protect ourselves and pull back from being close to our partner. And yet, in an absolute 22nd trap, we also appear to feel more selfish when we have withdrawn from doing what we want. If we know at any level that we don't make our relationship a priority or consciously follow our aim of being close or caring, we appear to feel more insecure and jealous. That's why learning how to deal with jealousy is even more important, and not acting blindly on jealous feelings by driving our partner further away.

COMPETITIVE JEALOUSY

Though it can feel futile or illogical, wanting what others have and feeling competitive is completely normal. But how we use these emotions is important to our degree of happiness and satisfaction. That is simply a destructive pattern with demoralizing consequences if we use these feelings to support our inner critics, to bring down ourselves or others. But if we don't let these feelings fall into the hands of our vital inner mind, we can actively use them to understand what we want, to be more goal-driven, or even to feel more self-acceptance of what affects us.

It's all right, even safe, to let ourselves have a competitive mind. When we just let ourselves have the momentary feeling without judgment or action plan, it can feel good. But if we ruminate or distort this thinking into self-criticism or an assault on another human, we end up getting hurt. If we find ourselves being overreacted or haunted by our feelings of jealousy, we may do a few things.

1. Be conscious of what is caused. Think of the different incidents that make you feel worked up. Is it a boyfriend who has financial success? An ex who dates someone else? A colleague who talks her mind in meetings?

2. Ask yourself what critical voices come up from inside. What kinds of thoughts spark jealous feelings? Do you use those envy feelings to bring yourself down? Do they make you feel weak, incompetent, ineffective, etc.? Is there a pattern or theme that seems familiar to those thoughts?

3. Think of the deeper meanings and roots of these thoughts: Do you feel the motivation to do something? Is there something that you think you should be? What does that mean about you having this thing? Does this apply to your past?

Once we have raised these questions to ourselves, we may understand how these feelings may have more to do with unresolved issues within us than with our present life or the person our envy is directed at. For ourselves, we can have more patience and try to suspend the prejudices that lead us to feel insecure.

HOW TO HANDLE JEALOUSY

This is what you should to overcome and deal with jealousy.

1. Consider what's being stirred up – The SIFT acronym (Sensations, Images, Feelings, and Thoughts) explains how we can sift through the emotions, pictures, feelings, and thoughts that come up as we focus on some issues in our lives. When we feel jealous, we should try to do just that. We should understand what envy brings forth from perceptions, pictures, feelings, and thoughts. Is the current scenario causing something old – a complex or long-held negative self-perception in the family? The more we can relate certain feelings or overreactions to past events that first produced them, the better we can feel in our current situation.

2. Calm down and remain relaxed – We should find ways to come back to ourselves and relax, no matter how insecure we can feel. First, we can do this by compassionately acknowledging our feelings. No matter how strong we feel, our feelings tend to pass through waves, first develop, then subside. Our Envy can be recognized and understood without acting on it. For example, by taking a walk or a series of deep breaths, we can learn strategies to calm ourselves down before we respond. In this way, it is much easier to calm down when we fail to accept or engage in our inner critic's angry words, so it's essential to learn steps to resist. When we do, we can stand up for ourselves and the people we care for and stay transparent and open to how we relate to each other.

3. Do not act out – Our vital inner voice continues to warn us to take long-term decisions that can harm us. If it spirals us into a state of envy, it may tell us to abandon or avoid doing what we want. It could lead us to self-sabotage, blow up, or punish someone that we admire. If we're in a relationship, it could tell us to the ice at our partner or to lash out. Everything we do when we do this is to build the situation we are scared of. We may harm and weaken our partners' love feelings for us and stir up their feelings of mistrust and fear. We may unconsciously allow them to become more closed, less transparent about their emotions, thoughts, and acts, which then adds to our feelings of envy and mistrust.

4. Find our sense of security – the most we can do is concentrate on feeling safe and comfortable inside ourselves. To conquer our inner critic, we have to do the work and believe we're all right, even on our own. We do not need the love of one single person to believe we are lovable. Human beings are full of mistakes and shortcomings, and no one can give us 100 percent of the time that we need. That is why practicing self-compassion and learning to stand up to our inner critics is so necessary. That doesn't mean shutting out people or cutting us off from what we want. It simply means wholeheartedly accepting our lives while acknowledging that we are strong enough to fail or lose. We can handle the feelings that come up, no matter what.

5. Keep competitive – plenty of people sneer at the thought of winning, but what we're talking about here isn't a desire to be the best, but a personal ambition to be at our best. That means that we feel like ourselves and accept the qualities that will motivate us to achieve what we want. Instead of making the green monster transform us into monsters, we should encourage ourselves to feel empowered, connect with who we want to be, and take action to get us closer to that. If we want the respect of everyone around us, we need to be careful of our interactions and considerate. If we want to feel our partner's constant affection, we must dedicate ourselves to daily acts of love. If we retain a willingness to act with dignity and follow our ambitions, we will win the most critical fight we face, the struggle to understand and become our true self — apart from everybody.

6. *Talk about it* – It's important to find the right person to speak to when something like insecurity takes over and a safe way to convey what we feel. The kind of friends we want to chat about our jealousy are the ones who embrace a better side of us and help stop us from ruminating or falling deeper into our sorrows. We all have friends that get a bit too worked up when we bring up those things, and these might not be the best friends to look for when we feel irritated and riled upon ourselves. We should try to find people who can help us stay on track and be the kind of people we want to be. Venting to these friends is good as long as it's a matter of getting our emotional thoughts and feelings out while knowing that they're excessive and unreasonable. This method only works if it relieves us from the feeling and helps us to step on and take positive action. If we struggle with envy feelings, it is also very wise to seek a therapist's support. This will help us make sense of our emotions and get a grip on them while behaving in a better, more resilient way. It's crucial to keep open, honest contact with our partner in a relationship. If we want to gain their confidence and have ours for them, we need to listen to what they say without being defensive or jumping to judgment. This open communication line is not about unloading our insecurities on

our partner, but rather encouraging us to be compassionate and linked, even if we feel unsafe or jealous. This makes our partner, of course, do the same.

No doubt, coping with the many emotions surrounding envy requires a certain degree of emotional maturity (In Chapter 21 we will go deeper into analyzing Emotional Intelligence and how it can help in relationships). Challenging our vital inner voice and all the insecurities it creates requires a willingness to. It also needs the willpower to step back and avoid acting on our jealous, impulsive reactions. But when we nurture this force within ourselves, we know that we are far stronger than we think. We become more comfortable in ourselves and our relationships by learning how to cope with envy.

TIPS TO OVERCOME JEALOUSY

"Good relationships are based on confidence and loyalty," tells Bustle Carolina Pataky, a Love Discovery Institute relationship therapist, and co-founder. "Jealousy can disrupt and sometimes destroy the love that occurs in a relationship and manifest itself in negative habits such as possessiveness and dependency. It is not conducive to a stable relationship and can grow old and stressful over time."

According to Pataky, there are typically underlying problems that occur when envy comes into the picture, such as insecurity, low self-esteem, and feelings of inadequacy. So finding ways to tackle these is crucial before it becomes a bigger problem.

The biggest problem is that people don't know how to get over the envy several times. But there are ways around the anger, and it begins by being honest by yourself as to why you feel white-hot rage over an Instagram like this.

1. Consider the insecurities you have

Our insecurities lie underneath the feelings of envy, which may look like self-esteem questions or the doubts you have when you compare yourself to others. As clinical psychologist Paul Greene, Ph.D. tells Bustle that fear of rejection is also focused on insecurity. So try to tackle the fear if you're feeling jealous.

"Consider all the qualities that you bring to the partnership and all the stuff that your partner says they appreciate about you," says Greene. Try to note you want your partner to be with you.

If in your S.O.'s life there's a particular person you're always feeling jealous of, consider blocking or muting their Instagram, so you have fewer chances to compare with them. Not only are the continuing parallels needless, but they'll also only make you feel even worse.

2. Consider where your faith comes from

Jealousy in a relationship can help bring the underlying problems to the surface, according to Shannon Chavez, licensed psychologist and intimacy expert for K-Y. For instance, if you haven't recovered entirely from a past relationship through childhood insecurities or infidelity, it may show up in the way you act in your current connection. Identify where the emotions come from before you converse with the partner. "Be responsible for your actions and commit to tackling your insecurities or past problems that contribute to envy," says Chavez.

3. For your relationship, create more reasonable expectations

It is entirely natural from time to time to find other people attractive. It doesn't have to be a concern unless your partner is rude about their attraction or actively flirts with others. According to Chavez, establishing reasonable expectations in the relationship is crucial, and note that you cannot influence someone else's actions. "You should share your concerns with your partner, speak freely and frankly, and aim for mutual understanding with one another's objective of empathy and compassion," she said. "Don't just try to monitor what they are doing."

4. Using the Technique of Rubber Bands

Put a rubber band around your hand and snap the rubber band every time you start to feel yourself falling into envy. As Danielle Maack, Ph.D., a licensed clinical psychologist and associate professor at the University of Mississippi's Department of Psychology, tells Bustle, the rubber band strategy is a beginner's method associated with learning how to properly handle uncomfortable feelings or thoughts. "It is typically called a pain management strategy, one that allows you to regroup at the moment. More precisely, people are asked to 'snap' with the rubber band while feeling intense feelings as a cue to pause, take a step back, and analyze what's going on."

5. Be transparent and honest about your feelings

Lately, if you've been overwhelmed with envy, it might be time to have an open and frank talk with your partner about how you feel and why you may feel this way. "Say, talk, talk!" says Pataky. "I know it may sound repetitive, boring, and cliché, but it's that important. In many situations, envy is an internal struggle, so take action to get to know and work on yourself. Then share those findings with your partner. Explain to them how you feel, what makes you insecure, and build boundaries for yourself and your relationship."

6. Talk it out with a therapist or a friend

While it is essential to have a conversation with your partner about how you feel, it can be especially helpful to talk about your jealousy problems with someone who can have an objective viewpoint on what's going on. If something, then your friend may be there to listen to you as you wind up.

It is also essential to get support from a trained therapist to help you work through and overcome the emotions that keep you stuck. "To dive into sensitive, insecure emotions requires strength and bravery, but it can be rewarding and allow for healing, change, and personal development,"

7. Practice Appreciation

Learning appreciation and gratitude for what you've got will help you concentrate your relationship on the positive. As transformational relationship coach John Kenny tells Bustle, think about what your partner does for you rather than what they don't do, or all the moments when they're there for you or when they aren't. If you can find something useful, then maybe it's time to move on.

8. Consider how jealousy affects you negatively

It is worth your time to think about how negatively your jealousy affects you as a person. Being always on the verge, for example, because your partner is talking to or texting someone is not good for you or your relationship. By completely coming to terms with how the jealousy is affecting you or making you feel and act, you will be more likely to find out how to conquer and let go of the jealousy.

Regardless of how you handle your emotions, it's crucial to note that it's not your spouse's responsibility to comfort you or to "fix" the issues that trigger envy. "Your emotions are your duty, and they're about you, not your circumstance or family," according to Ortiz.

9. Write it down

A diary is a perfect place to keep track of your jealousy-related insecurities and grievances since it is suitable for venting. Certified relationship coach Nina Rubin recommends you think about your relationship and ask yourself questions like, is your partner the right person for you? Have they done something unusual to trigger the jealousy? "If so, then this is a dealbreaker, too," she says. "If not, ask yourself if you need to look into your ways of being in a relationship. Are you bringing your past into this new relationship? Are you sabotaging yourself? It might be time to try something else to save your relationship!"

10. Focus on the bad vs. the good
One way of getting over your jealousy feelings is to shift focus. As licensed clinical psychologist Kim Chronister, PsyD, says to Bustle, "The most empowering thing you can do in a relationship is to let go of fears about what could go wrong and concentrate on what's going well." Chronister recommends concentrating on the things your partner does that you're grateful for and reminding yourself that you're more than enough for your partner every day.

11. Avoid holding onto jealously
When you're not sure your partner's cheating, your best bet is to try to let go of the jealousy that weighs down you. Chronister recommends using self-care strategies to improve self-esteem, such as exercise and outings with friends. "The better you feel about yourself, the more you can let go when you're not looking at what others do," she says.

Instead of making yourself wallow in envy, in your relationship, you may choose to take action to feel less of the hated emotion. Next time you feel jealousy creeping up, try some of these tactics, and you may find it much easier to control the feelings.

SIGNS OF JEALOUS MEMBERS OF THE FAMILY AND HOW TO DEAL WITH THEM

There's a phrase that says, "Blood is thicker than water." In my opinion, blood is even more jealous. It's so sad to know that envy can drive your aunts, cousins, or even your friends to hurt you. And when it comes from family members, the hurt is more profound. Plus, they can create a lot of needless tension in your life.

Strangely enough, I've had terrible luck in my life dealing with jealous families. It may be worse, but it's always a shame that envy exists inside the family. I think we might claim it's only human nature, but it's so needless.

What Are Suspicious Family Members Signs?

You may think it's easy to detect jealousy in others, but some people are very subtle in their acts or language. According to Frances M. Bledsoe, a licensed social clinician at the Nashville Relationship Center, signs of a jealous relative can include things like, "Criticism, overt, or behind one's back, passive-aggressive conduct (like "forgetting" to make good on a commitment, intentionally sabotaging)."

They weren't impressed

Do you ever feel that your cousin or sister is never impressed by your achievements? Jealous relatives prefer to downplay your successes by telling you that a lot of people can do that. They're going to say something like, "If they just work hard enough, everyone can get a promotion. It's not that big of a deal." Certainly, this is a sign of their insecurities.

You try to "One Up."

It seems every family has that one person who is always trying to be the best. If your 16-month-old child said their first term, theirs did so at 12 months. If you share the news of your big raise, they already have one six months after starting their new job. Try not to get yourself trapped in their desire to compete and concentrate on you.

When you give them suggestions, they get angry

Now, most people don't like unsolicited advice, but insecurity is the driving force of envy, as I stated above. People who are loaded with jealousy easily become insecure and don't want to be pointed out about their "flaws." Even if the suggestion is well-intentioned, they do not see it this way. They think instead that you are trying to prove that you're better than them.

You feel bad for yourself when you see them

You should feel good and enjoy seeing your family. If you still leave a family feeling worse than you did when you arrived, this is a warning that something is wrong. Your family should support your dreams and be proud of your achievements.

They are highly critical

If your aunt or cousin regularly telephones your mistakes or tells you derogatory things, this is a warning that they are jealous. People who are self-insecure tend to put others down to make themselves feel better. They can find almost everything to blame. Try not to let them come over to you.

How to Treat Dangerous Relatives

Keep your mouth shut. While you can't remove yourself from the family tree, you can handle any jealous family members that you have easily. The most crucial step is to keep them away from your personal affairs. They don't have to know you are buying a new house, waiting for a promotion, or even dating a new partner. Only share those stuff with people who will support you.

You don't want to have your ambitions or current events at their dinner table as the main discussion. They're all going to devour it and talk about your life negatively. Don't fuel their gossip and negative talk on the flames.

Avoid the Guilty Feeling

Do not feel guilty by not sharing your life story with them, that you are pulling away. You just have to love people from afar sometimes. It is easy to feel that you are the bad guy when you are trying to protect yourself.

Limit Interaction

You can still attend if they invite you to family functions. You just got to be careful of what you're sharing with them. Enjoying their business is no bad thing. In most instances, though, you can find that certain relatives who harbor envy usually won't invite you to their activities. You should not despair, and neither should you push your way into their culture. Probably better to restrict your interactions with them in-person. Why hang out with someone who doesn't affect your life positively? And note, for some people, it's all right to set limits. You will love them from a distance anyway.

Avoid Confrontation

Some say a person should schedule a family meeting to address the issue of envy, but it just makes the drama last longer a lot of times. Bledsoe says, "Occasionally, a healthy relative may have to say out loud how uncomfortable or overwhelmed she or he feels, and be treated with compassion, but not everyone jealous is willing and able to be truthful and vulnerable."

The most important thing is to remain a loving, compassionate person and not cause you to get upset by jealous family members' actions. This may sound odd, but it's the peace you're getting from your family. Compliment them and concentrate on becoming a supportive family power. It's hard to be the larger person, but it's going to be easier in the long run. You will understand the positive things that happen in your life by ascribing them to hard work and/or chance. Try not to get across as judgmental because their jealousy is most definitely driven by their fear that they are not good enough.

Pay attention to yourself first

The envy and negative emotions that accompany it can be easy to dwell on. However, to remain emotionally stable, it is necessary to practice self-care. If you start feeling angry or sad, try journaling or meditation. Have compassion, and be strict with yourself. They're all right to be annoyed by their behavior, but try not to let them overtake you.

Why do people become jealous?

These same jealous relatives may often feel conflicted on the inside. They might be proud of you, but they're just jealous that they haven't been able to accomplish what you do. They struggle with perceptions of inadequacy.

That's sad though it's not your problem. This is a matter they need to resolve on their own, so you should not feel burdened by their feelings. You shouldn't be too shy and ashamed of your achievements either, so you don't offend family members. Learn to be self-confident and proud of your accomplishments! Don't let these individuals affect your self-esteem and make you lose faith.

In time, either you will find that your absence has made your heart develop into a foundry or that nothing has changed for you. Find it in your heart to forgive them, so the anger doesn't overwhelm you. Find what their frustration is driving and try to put yourself in their shoes. They might be jealous of your new relationship because they have been single for several years, or maybe they resent your new work because they cannot find anyone they love. This may help you become empathetic about their condition in life.

But remember, you can only do what you do yourself. Only that is the way to find happiness. This can trigger some jealous feelings and a sense of competition when one sibling gets engaged first.

Sibling Envy Triggers

The rivalry between siblings is extremely common, particularly if you are the same gender or about the same age. They're one of the few people you've met all your life, and you've shared every single milestone. In adulthood, however, childhood sibling rivalry can quickly turn into envy if not handled. Here are some explanations of why it happens.

Parental influence - Many parents place high expectations on their children, and if one child lives up to those expectations, and the other does not, it is particularly difficult. Bledsoe says, "Families often foster unhealthy competitiveness among children. For example, a parent may raise awareness of a child who is more academic, athletic, artistic, etc. than another child." These competitive feelings may persist and trigger adult problems.

Knocking Milestones at Various Times - When you reach maturity with your brother or sister, you can start accomplishing different things and leading different lifestyles. This may trigger some rivalry as to who first gets married, who first has children, who first buy a home, and so on. Marriage can be particularly difficult if you don't approve of your sibling's significant other, or you feel that this person is compromising your relationship with them.

What if I'm the One Jealous?

Maybe you are the one who is jealous of a relative. It's all right to be envious of someone but do your hardest not to let that show up. Recall that this stems from your vulnerability and has little to do with the other person. Don't let those emotions ruin what a very lovely relationship is otherwise! And don't let them build up either — you'll probably start resenting this family member, and the relationship worsens.

Here are some safe ways of handling yours

Acknowledge your jealousy: Just knowing that you have these feelings opens the door to let them go. Bledsoe recommends asking yourself the following questions: "What am I most afraid of in this situation?" "Why have I come to believe that there is not enough to go around (love, acceptance, etc.)? Are those acquired beliefs/feelings really important to the current circumstances? Am I able to recognize the old fears and let them pass?"

Expose up to a friend or trained professional: It's important to speak to a friend or even a qualified professional, such as a counselor or therapist, about your jealousy. They'll help you discover the causes of your anger and how to cope with it.

Remember your positive qualities: Just because somebody else's better than you are at doing something, that doesn't imply they're better than you. Everybody has their strengths and weaknesses, so remember the things you're good at or the positive attributes you have. It may also help you write these attributes on a post-it note and tape it into your mirror so that you can get a regular reminder.

Chapter 10: EXERCISES TO HELP YOU RELAX ANXIETY

A normal human response to stress is anxiety. But too much anxiety can interfere with how to live a safe, happy life. Try a few of the following exercises anytime and anywhere to find relaxation if you feel caught up in your anxiety. The aim is to execute activities that will help you relax quickly.

1. Relax by breathing

You will also see that your heart rate and breathing are getting a little faster if you feel nervous. You might also begin to sweat and feel light-headed or dizzy. Having your breathing under control will calm both your body and mind when you're nervous.

Take these steps to get your breathing under control when you're anxious:

    I.   Sit down in a place that is quiet and relaxed. Place your chest in one of your hands and your stomach in the other. When you breathe in deeply, your stomach can shift faster than your chest.

    II.   Take a slow breath through your nose. Monitor and feel your hands as you inhale. Although the hand on your stomach will move slightly, the hand on your chest should remain still.

    III.   Breath out slowly through your mouth.

    IV.   Repeat this process at least ten times or until you start to experience a drop in your anxiety.

2. Relax by visualization

Have you ever used the phrase 'seeking your happy place'? In reality, painting a mental image of a location that makes you feel comfortable will calm your brain and body.

Sit in a quiet and relaxed position when you start to feel nervous. Think of your dream spot to relax. While it can be any real or imaginary location in the world, it should be a picture that you find relaxing, happy, quiet, and safe. Make sure that it's easy enough to think about it so that you can return to it in your mind when you feel nervous in the future.

Think of all the tiny things that you would notice if you were there. Think about the smell, feel, and sound of the place. Imagine yourself in that spot, happily enjoying it.

Close your eyes and, once you have a clear vision of your happy spot, take long and frequent breaths through your nose and out of your mouth. Be mindful of your breathing, and once you feel your fear lifting, continue to concentrate on the position you've pictured in your mind. Whenever you feel nervous, visit this location in your mind.

3. Have the muscles relaxed

You could experience pressure or stress in your muscles when you feel anxious. This muscle tension will make it more difficult to control your anxiety at the moment you feel it. You will normally decrease your anxiety levels by relieving the tension in your muscles.

In moments of fear, to easily alleviate the muscle tension:

I.   Sit down in a place that is quiet and relaxed. Close your eyes and concentrate on breathing. Breathe into your nose and out of your mouth slowly.

II. To make a tight fist, use your hand. Tightly squeeze your hand.

III. For a couple of seconds, hold your clenched palm. Note in your hand all the stress you experience.

IV. Turn your fingers open slowly and be mindful of how you feel. A sensation of stress can be found, leaving your body. Your hand will feel lighter and more comfortable finally.

V. Continue to tense your hands, legs, shoulders, or feet and then release different muscle groups in your body. You will want to work your way up and down your body to different tense groups of muscles. In any part of your body where you are injured or in pain, stop tensing the muscles, which may further aggravate the injury.

4. Relax by counting

Counting is an easy way for your anxiety to be relieved. Find a quiet and relaxing place to sit when you sense anxiety running over you. Close your eyes and count towards ten slowly. Repeat and count to 20 or an even higher number if appropriate. Continue to count until you find as the anxiety subsides.

This relief happens quickly sometimes, but other times it could take a while. Keep patient and cool. Counting will calm you because, aside from your anxiety, it gives you something to concentrate on. It's a perfect technique to use in a crowded or busy space like a store or train where it may be more difficult to do other anxiety exercises.

5. Relax by holding yourself present

As mentioned earlier, mindfulness is the practice, kindly and without judgment, of being present in your current state and environment. When you feel your thoughts spinning and anxiety rising, remaining present will help you establish a relaxed state of mind.

To get yourself into the present outside of your thoughts:

I. Find a nice and quiet place to sit and close your eyes.

II.   Note how it feels in your breathing and body.

III. Now transfer your focus to the sensations in your world you experience. Only ask yourself what's going on outside of my body? In your area, note what you hear, smell, and feel.

IV.   Move your mind from your body to your surroundings multiple times and back again until your anxiety begins to fade.

V.   Relax by disrupting your nervous thoughts

When you are feeling nervous, it can be difficult to think clearly. Anxious thinking can also make us believe that negative thoughts are true or make us do stuff that worsens our anxiety. Breaking or interrupting your nervous thoughts may be beneficial to think better and respond to your thoughts appropriately.

Here's how to break the loop of your nervous thinking: ask yourself if the constant concern is an issue for you. It's nice to be conscious of that if the answer is yes.

Try various ways to disrupt the nervous process of thinking, such as:

Sing a silly song to an upbeat tempo about your anxiety, or talk in a funny voice about your anxieties.

Pick a pleasant thought instead of your fear of concentrating on it. This could be a person you love, your place of happiness, or even something you're looking forward to doing later that day, like having a nice dinner.

Listen to music or read a novel. When you move your attention from your anxiety to a task at hand and note how you feel, be aware.

Relaxation is an ability that you acquire. It takes practice, just like physical exercise. Choose an exercise for anxiety and pursue it before you feel less nervous. Try a different one if one exercise doesn't work.

THE 3 BEST ANXIETY AND DEPRESSION EXERCISES

You know that in certain particular moments, the last thing you can feel like doing is moving your body if you suffer from depression or anxiety. Still, exercise may play a key role in controlling your symptoms due to the powerful relationship between your physical and mental health. Ben Michaelis, Ph.D., an evolutionary clinical psychologist and author of The Next Big Thing: 10 Small Steps to Get Going and Get Satisfied, says, "We know that the old distinctions of body and mind are wrong. The body is the soul, and the body is the spirit. You support the whole system when you take care of yourself."

Though you should still consult a doctor about medical choices (and before you initiate some form of an exercise program), the U.S. Department of Health and Human Services suggests that adults should get a regular amount of exercise every week. The organization recommends a moderate-intensity exercise of 150 minutes (2 hours and 30 minutes) to 300 minutes (5 hours) a week. These guidelines are reduced to 75 minutes (1 hour and 15 minutes) to 150 minutes (2 hours and 30 minutes) if the workout ramps into high intensity exercise.

It's certainly necessary to integrate some form of exercise into your routine, but certain workouts can better help mental wellbeing than others. Research indicates that, in particular, the following three behaviors may help relieve symptoms of depression or anxiety.

Running

There's a reason why you've learned time and time again that running is one of the best activities for your health: it can burn calories, decrease cravings for food, and reduce the risk of heart disease. According to studies from 2014, running for only five minutes a day could also help you live longer.

But, Michaelis notes, it's also been shown to boost mood in several ways.

"During and after exercise, running induces permanent improvements in our 'feel good' neurotransmitters serotonin and norepinephrine," he describes. What's more, repeated running movements seem to have a meditative effect on the brain.

For people who suffer from depression, mental benefits may be particularly strong. Researchers found evidence in a 2006 study published in the Journal of Psychiatry & Neuroscience that exercise can function similarly to antidepressants, alleviating major depressive disorder by stimulating the development of new brain neurons.

Also good: Running will make it easier for you to fall asleep at night, says Michaelis, which improves your overall mental health by improving memory, decreasing stress levels, and protecting against depression.

Hiking in the mountains

To optimize your sweat session's mental health benefits, consider hitting the trails. Nature," says Michaelis, "has a soothing effect on the mind. There is evidence that it can help reduce anxiety by being around plants, trees, and particularly dying trees because these plants emit chemicals to slow the process of their decay, which also seems to slow us down." Japanese researchers sent participants to either a wooded or urban area in a 2009 study published in Environmental Health and Preventive Medicine. They found that those who had taken a "forest bath" (A.K.A. a walk in the woods) for 20 minutes had lower stress hormone levels than the participants who had been in a town.

The belief that being immersed in nature is beneficial for your mental health seems validated by newer studies. For example, a 2015 study published in the journal Landscape and Urban Planning showed that they felt less stressed and had better memory performance when young adults went on a 50-minute nature walk.

Yoga

All of the research participants who had taken yoga classes recorded "major" reductions in depression, frustration, anxiety, and neurotic symptoms in a small 2007 study published in Evidence-Based Complementary and Alternative Medicine. The results prompted the researchers to suggest yoga as a supplemental therapy for depression.

A study of studies published in Alternative Medicine Study explored yoga's impact on anxiety and stress in 2012, conducted by another group of researchers. In 25 of the 35 studies, after beginning yoga, subjects experienced a substantial decrease in stress and anxiety symptoms.

"The best thing about yoga is that there is a huge emphasis on meditation, in addition to relaxing and core strengthening, which helps to slow down and relax the mind," says Michaelis. Experts agree that yoga's emphasis on the breath is particularly helpful for mental well-being because when you are concentrating on peacefully breathing deeply, it is hard to feel anxiety, he says.

TIPS FOR BEGINNING A RELAXATION EXERCISE

It's not difficult to learn the fundamentals of these relaxation methods, but it takes daily practice to fully harness their stress-relieving strength. For your relaxation practice, consider setting aside at least 10 to 20 minutes a day.

In your routine, set aside time. Schedule a certain time once or twice a day for your work, if possible. If your day is already complete, try meditating when riding on the bus, taking a yoga or tai chi break at lunchtime, or practice mindful walking while exercising your dog.

Making use of mobile and other aids for smartphones. Many people find that it can be useful for mobile apps or audio downloads to direct them through various relaxation activities, create a daily routine, and keep track of progress.

Expect downs and ups. It may also take time and practice to start reaping the full benefits of relaxation techniques like meditation. The longer you stick with it, the quicker there will be results. Do not get frustrated if you miss a couple of days or even a couple of weeks. Just get started again and build on your old momentum slowly.

14 WAYS TO ALLEVIATE ANXIETY AND STRESS

1. Practice. We mentioned it a few times throughout this book, and we repeat it: one of the most important things you can do to reduce stress is exercise.

It may seem contradictory, but it can alleviate mental stress by placing physical stress on the body through exercise. When you work out regularly, the advantages are greatest. People who are frequent exercising regularly are less likely than those who don't exercise to experience anxiety.

The reasons behind this are a few:

- *Stress hormones:* In the long term, exercise decreases stress hormones in the body, such as cortisol. It helps to release endorphins, chemicals that boost the mood and serve as natural painkillers.
- *Sleep:* Exercise will also boost your sleep's consistency, which can be influenced negatively by stress and anxiety.
- *Confidence:* You can feel more capable and secure in your body when you exercise regularly, which improves mental health.

Try to find a sport or workout routine you enjoy, such as walking, dancing, rock climbing, or yoga.

Activities requiring repeated movements of large muscle groups, such as walking or jogging, may be especially stress relieving. By releasing endorphins and enhancing your sleep and self-image, daily exercise will lower stress and anxiety.

2. Think of supplements

Several supplements encourage reducing stress and anxiety. Here is a list of some of the more famous ones:

- *Lemon balm:* Lemon balm is a member of the mint family investigated for its anti-anxiety effects.
- *Omega-3 fatty acids:* One study showed that medical students who received omega-3 supplements reported a 20 percent reduction in anxiety symptoms.
- *Ashwagandha:* Ashwagandha is an herb that is used in Ayurvedic medicine to alleviate stress and anxiety. Several studies suggest that it is effective.
- *Green tea:* There are several polyphenol antioxidants in green tea that have health benefits. By raising serotonin levels, it can lower stress and anxiety.
- *Valerian:* Due to its tranquilizing influence, valerian root is a popular sleep aid. It contains valerenic acid, which, to relieve anxiety, changes gamma-aminobutyric acid (GABA) receptors.
- *Kava kava:* Kava kava is a member of the pepper family who is psychoactive. Long used in the South Pacific as a sedative, it is progressively used for treating moderate stress and anxiety in Europe and the US.

Most supplements can interfere with drugs or have side effects, so you may want to see a doctor if you have a medical condition.

3. Light up a candle

It can help reduce your feelings of stress and anxiety by using essential oils or burning a scented candle. Particularly calming are some scents. Here are some of the most calming scents:

- Lavender
- Rose
- Vetiver
- Bergamot
- Roman chamomile
- Neroli
- Frankincense
- Sandalwood
- Ylang-ylang
- Orange or orange blossom
- Geranium

Aromatherapy is called the use of scents to treat the mood. Many studies suggest that aromatherapy can alleviate anxiety and improve sleep. Aromatherapy can help lower stress and anxiety. To gain from soothing scents, light a candle, or use essential oils.

4. Lower your intake of caffeine
Caffeine is a stimulant used in beverages made from coffee, tea, chocolate. High doses can raise anxiety. As for how much caffeine they can handle, people have different thresholds.

Consider cutting back if you find that caffeine makes you jittery or nervous. Although several studies suggest that coffee in moderation can be safe, it isn't for everybody. In general, a moderate sum is known to be five or fewer cups per day.

High levels of caffeine can exacerbate stress and anxiety. The sensitivity of people to caffeine, however, can vary greatly.

5. Note it down
Writing things down is one way to relieve tension. While one solution is to document what you're worried over, another is to jot down what you're

thankful for. By concentrating your attention on what's good in your life, gratitude will help alleviate stress and anxiety. Keeping a journal, particularly if you concentrate on the positive, may help alleviate stress and anxiety.

6. Gum Chewing

Try chewing a stick of gum for a super fast and straightforward stress reliever. One research found a greater sense of well-being and lower depression in people who chewed gum. One potential explanation is that chewing gum induces equivalent brain waves to those of relaxed individuals. One is that blood supply to the brain is encouraged through chewing gum. Additionally, one recent study showed that when people chewed more intensely, stress relief was highest.

7. Spending time with family and friends

Friends and family social support can help you get through difficult times. Being part of a network of friends gives you a feeling of belonging and self-worth, supporting you in difficult times. One research found that spending time with friends and children, particularly for women, helps release oxytocin, a natural anxiety reliever. This effect is called "tend and befriend," and the fight-or-flight response is the opposite. Bear in mind that friendship helps both men and women. Another research showed that depression and anxiety were more likely to occur in men and women with the fewest social interactions. It will help you get through difficult times and lower your risk of anxiety by having close social links.

8. Laugh to Relax

When you're joking, it is impossible to feel nervous. It's good for your health, and it can help alleviate stress in a few ways. Laughter will also help strengthen the immune system and mood in the long term.

Research of people with cancer showed that individuals reported more stress relief in the laughter intervention community than those who were distracted. To help alleviate tension, find humor in daily life, spend time with funny friends, or watch a comedy show.

9. Learn how to say no

Not all stressors are under your jurisdiction, but some are. Take care of the components of your life that you can alter and trigger stress. Saying "no" more frequently could be one way to do this.

If you find yourself taking on more than you can handle, this is particularly true, as balancing multiple duties can leave you feeling exhausted. Your stress levels can be minimized by being careful with what you take on and saying no to stuff that would unnecessarily add to your load. Try not to take on more than you can accommodate. Saying no is one way your stressors can be managed.

10. Avoid procrastination

To stay on top of your goals and stop procrastinating is another way to take care of your tension. Procrastination will lead you to behave reactively, leaving you to catch up with scrambling. This can cause tension, which adversely affects the quality of your health and sleep.

Get in the habit of making a priority-organized to-do list. Give yourself practical deadlines and work down the list to work your way. Work on things that need to be completed today and allow yourself bits of uninterrupted time, as it can be difficult to move between tasks or multitasking. Prioritize, and make time for, what needs to be achieved. Staying on top of your to-do list will help fend off tension linked to procrastination.

11. Cuddle

Stress management can all be improved by cuddling, kissing, embracing, and sex. The release of oxytocin and lower cortisol can be helped by positive physical touch. This can help reduce blood pressure, both of which are physical signs of stress, and heart rate. Interestingly, humans aren't the only ones cuddling for relief from stress. Chimpanzees often cuddle stressed relatives. Releasing oxytocin and reducing blood pressure, positive contact from cuddling, embracing, kissing, and sex will help lower stress.

12. Listen to music that is calming
Listening to music can influence the body in a very calming way. By helping heart rate and lower blood pressure and stress hormones, slow-paced instrumental music can trigger a relaxation response. Some forms of classical, Celtic, Native American, and Indian music can be particularly calming, but it's also successful to simply listen to the music you love. Sounds from nature can also be very soothing too. That is why they are also mixed into the music of relaxation and meditation. A good way to alleviate stress would be to listen to music you enjoy.

13. Deep respiration
The sympathetic nervous system is triggered by mental tension, signaling the body to "fight-or-flight" mode. Stress hormones are released during this reaction, and you feel physical symptoms such as a quicker heartbeat, rapid breathing, and constricted blood vessels. Your parasympathetic nervous system, which regulates the calming response, can be triggered by deep breathing exercises.

Several types of deep breathing exercises are available, including diaphragmatic breathing, abdominal breathing, paced breathing, and belly breathing.

Deep breathing aims to concentrate on your breath with your consciousness, making it slower and deeper. Your lungs completely expand as you breathe in deeply through your nose and your belly grows.

This helps slow down your heart rate, making it easier for you to feel more relaxed. The relaxation response is triggered by deep respiration. Several techniques will help you learn how to breathe deeply.

14. Spend time with your pet

Getting a pet will help decrease tension and raise your mood. It can help release oxytocin, a brain chemical that encourages a positive mood to communicate with pets. Getting a pet can also help alleviate stress by providing you with meaning, keeping you busy, and providing companionship, all attributes that can reduce anxiety.

Exercise, mindfulness, music, and physical intimacy will all help to alleviate anxiety, and they can also strengthen the balance of your overall work-life.

Chapter 11: OVERCOMING ANXIETY IN RELATIONSHIP

The most prevalent medical illness in the US is anxiety disorders, which affect 18 percent of the adult population. Social anxiety disorder (SAD) is the third most common medical illness, affecting 15 million men and women in the US.

The DSM-5 (Diagnostic and Statistical Manual of Mental Disorders 5th Edition by the American Psychiatric Association) describes social anxiety as the "persistent fear of one or more situations in which others are subjected to the individual's possible criticism and concerns that he or she will do something or act in a way that will be embarrassing or humiliating." If not socially nervous, many who are anxious tend to experience social situations in a more reserved, tense, and awkward way, particularly when it can take longer to open up and connect, affecting one's ability to develop close relationships.

Usually, dating is a circumstance where individuals feel scrutinized, meet new individuals, and may be worried that they may do something humiliating. In this way, dating just adds fuel to the fire of anxiety. Will she turn up with chances for uncomfortable interactions and countless unknown variables? Is he going to like me? What am I saying? What if too much, I say? What if I spill my beverage? Get dismissed? Dating is also seen as overwhelmingly terrifying and extremely unattractive. This form of anxiety and shyness and a sense of loneliness and hopelessness about the prospect of finding a compatible partner contribute to avoiding meeting new people.

Adults also don't seek care until years of living with the condition have passed, considering the high prevalence of anxiety disorders, if they seek treatment at all. Since anxiety disorders usually occur in early adolescence or pre-teen years, anxiety disorders may be difficult to identify. And anxiety left untreated also causes comorbid conditions, such as depression, to develop. People can believe that feeling the kind of anxiety they experience is natural or think that anxiety cannot be handled. Since social anxiety is such a common issue, psychologists have been working hard to establish functioning therapies. Cognitive Behavioral Therapy (CBT) is effective in treating SAD in four distinct meta-analyses. Noting that CBT was successful in some patients but not others for social anxiety, or did not completely relieve symptoms, in the form of Acceptance and Commitment Therapy (ACT), they tried to pursue more treatment options. ACT's cornerstone is learning to understand that anxiety and internal struggle are part of truly living. Leading a life driven by personal beliefs and desire to experience life, instead of anxiety-based prevention and decision-making, is essentially what frees one from the anxiety constraints. The researchers found that the participants reported improved quality of life, decreased avoidance, and decreased anxiety after monitoring a 12-week ACT and exposure program. In 2009, another study focused on acceptance and group therapy based on mindfulness also reported similar improvements for socially anxious people.

I have so often seen incredible people in my work, and my life in general, who deserve love and companionship, but who have been crippled by fear, struggling with depression and hopelessness rooted in anxiety. I felt inspired to write a book about the skills that help people get through social anxiety, recognizing some therapies could (and did) help them build confidence and a new perspective. Here are some of the most successful forms of addressing dating anxiety by integrating ACT with conventional exposure and cognitive approaches rooted in CBT.

Practicing self-disclosures

Shy and nervous individuals are less likely to communicate and self-disclose about themselves. Dating advice books can prescribe pick-up lines or deceptive, gamey tactics to win over a date. But on sharing who you are with your date, real relationships are based. The gateway to intimacy is self-disclosure, as it helps you to get closer to someone when you both disclose more and more. But the last thing that a shy or nervous person can feel comfortable doing is letting their guard down, which is why a crucial element is to practice sharing. Self-disclosure activity might include letting your date know about a story or something specific to you, sharing how you feel about a recent case, or letting your date know that you think they look fantastic. Self-disclosure is about telling people what you think, how you feel, and letting them know what you think counts.

Reducing the possibility of judgment from others and yourself

For fear of being criticized, one of the reasons why people may not reveal anything about themselves is the risk of negative appraisal by others. This is the source of social anxiety, amplified in a dating environment, such as being negatively viewed by your date. Anxious daters strongly overestimate, most of the time, how negatively their partner views them. They immediately blame themselves if a social situation goes awry. They beat themselves up for hours or days afterward if they make a joke that comes out wrong. They presume that the other person thinks most of them and concentrate on their shortcomings and errors. This is generally because socially insecure individuals appear to have lower self-esteem and make automatic negative judgments about themselves. They presume others do, too, so they judge themselves harshly. And it does not make them want to communicate, to be available, or to be vulnerable.

Acceptance

An alternative to being guarded is accessible. It feels less daunting to share with others by reflecting on one's sense of self-acceptance and self-worth. It bolsters them against judgment when a person feels good about who they are, their beliefs, what they have to give, and sees their own experience in a caring way. It opens the door to stronger relations with others by soothing their harshest critic, their inner judge.

Reframing disastrous expectations

Reframing catastrophic thoughts is the second way to handle the danger of judgment from others and oneself. Because anxiety may cause catastrophic thoughts to take over, identifying, pointing out, and contradicting these catastrophic thoughts is an effective technique. Thoughts like "if I'm rejected, it's the end of the world," "I'm never going to meet someone," or "it was a total disaster," are typical in anxiety. Gently remind yourself that these views are exaggerated by fear, and then list why the feelings are not true. This will help to quell the catastrophe predictions that can be so damaging to the love finding process.

Mindfulness and the intelligence of emotions

By reflecting on the future and the past, anxiety thrives, creating uncertainty for what will go wrong, how the future is going to turn out, or how past events have gone wrong. Mindfulness is the alternative. Mindfulness is a deliberate attempt to concentrate on the here-and-now, the present moment. Instead of judgment, connecting to the present moment with acceptance contributes to greater emotional sensitivity inside oneself. And emotional awareness is one essential aspect of Emotional Intelligence (EI), or being able to distinguish the emotions and tailor actions of one's own and other people accordingly.

A recent meta-analysis of research found a clear correlation between EI and satisfaction in relationships. This suggests that in their love life to-gether, couples with high EI appeared to be happier for both men and women. The emphasis should be on learning to reap the benefits of EI in dating and new relationships. More on this in Chapter 21.

8 WAYS TO CONQUER THE FEAR IN RELATIONSHIP

1. Ask yourself, 'Is it worth the relationship'?

Behavior psychologist Wendy M. Yoder, Ph.D., advises individuals to begin by sincerely leveling themselves to relieve relationship anxiety. Is it worth the relationship? This is not an easy issue to take lightly or one to take. But, is this individual right for you at the end of the day? Bear in mind, there is no ideal partner, as Esther Perel tells us. Humans are de-fective, and that's OK! The problem is not, "Are they perfect?" The ques-tion is, "Are we good for one another?"

Pro tip: Begin with small steps if you don't know the answer to that ques-tion (indecision is a major factor in the anxiety equation). Try any of the below-mentioned strategies. Whether or not this is the individual for you will become much clearer as you advance.

2. Face it head-on, face it

Without looking at the signs, you can't solve a riddle; you can't cure re-lationship anxiety without calling it what it is and talking about it to your partner. Romantic relationships (although we want everybody to uncon-ditionally love themselves!) are not solo projects. To tango, it takes two, and your partner must be included in this activity.

Self-Discovery lessons to help you get the love you deserve maintain that there must be difficult conversations in person. According to Solomon, texting "is devoid of subtlety, non-verbals, and ambiguity." During diffi-cult talks, being in the same space as another person is crucial to more productive conversations.

Pro tip: If you are not sure that the relationship is worth fighting for, the response of your partner to your anxiety will be a good indicator of whether they are in it for the long term (and deserving of your time, energy, and love) or not.

3. Speak to each other about it

In the relationships and references research carried out by Dr. Carmen Knudson-Martin and Dr. Anne Rankin Mahoney on the subject, Solomon talks a lot about power dynamics. Think about who has control in your relationship while considering your anxiety or raising fears for your partner. Unbalanced power can fuel anxiety, like one partner always giving in to the other's needs at the cost of their own.

The wrong way to navigate a relationship is to try so hard to be cool about your rocky feelings or not stir the pot. We often avoid confrontation in an attempt to appear totally cold and put together, particularly at the beginning of something new. It's a blueprint for a catastrophe.

Pro tip: Even though there are just signs of relationship anxiety prickling here and there, quickly bring it up. If things get more complicated later (which, eventually, they will, in long-term relationships), the vocabulary already exists to discuss new anxieties, start discussions now about both of your fears, desires, and wants so.

4. Invest in therapy

Therapy is a place you go to vent, but that your therapist lets you speak about ways in which you can avoid negative thoughts from taking over instead of your best friend nodding and pouring you another glass of pinot. That's tremendously significant. Yes, relationship anxiety may have much to do with one's partner, but it is really important to look inward to discover personal demons as well. Therapy cannot only help you better understand, perceive, and control your feelings; it can also provide you with tools to better understand and manipulate other people's emotions. Pro tip: Before deciding on one that gets you, it's OK to browse around for a therapist.

5. Consider counseling for couples

All that has just been listed, except for couples. Therapy for couples can strengthen communication and establish relationship goals, which can create confidence and give both individuals more opportunities to express themselves in the future. Therapists also seem to be pretty good at asking questions that encourage debate about important subjects. With comprehensive psychology and relationship preparation, a third person would be able to make recommendations on strengthening the relationship based on studying the way you and your partner relate to and handle each other. This is also a good place to bring up trickier subjects that you might need to better discuss face-to-face. Professionals have seen such issues before and are here to help you overcome them.

Pro tip: Going to counseling for couples is not exclusively for couples on the verge of divorce. It is for all couples who want to get the best out of their relationship, including safe ones.

6. Date yourself

We're not talking about ending it with your girlfriend and just dating yourself, but we mean believing in your passions. Esther Perel says people are always trying to find the right combination of freedom and security, and it can trigger anxiety when we lose one or gain too much of the other. Until the person rediscovers and reinvests in themselves (harnessing their liberty), relationship anxiety that arises from feelings of inadequacy or isolation can also be diverted. You have to have a life away from your partner. Sign up for the class you were supposed to take! Set a personal objective and outline the necessary steps to achieve it! You are 50 percent of a partnership; carry to the table the best version of yourself. Pro tip: Think about being an aggressive partner rather than a reactive one. Your life is not meant to revolve around your partner's, nor should theirs revolve around you. Without stifling growth, you should be there for one another (security).

7. Rewrite your ideas

A big part of conquering anxiety is improving how we speak about ourselves (and many mental health disorders). Fixing on negative feelings ("He didn't call. He's cheating on me obviously.") fuels anxiety. Instead, first, train your brain to consider other possibilities ("He didn't call. His phone might be out of battery. He may still be in a work meeting. He's transfixed by Fortnite's game."). First, train your brain. It's not safe to leap to conclusions, nor is it to imagine what your partner would say when you confront them with what you think they have been up to. Instead of constructing a tall tale in your head, the next time you are together, check-in with your partner.

The same goes for how you speak about yourself. Try using the "Call It to Tame It" approach of Dr. Dan Siegel. Many individuals with anxiety return over and over to the same negative thinking patterns (in relationship anxiety, this may be "I'm useless, she'll leave me, of course."). Dr. Siegel says that being able to mark something allows us to choose how we react to it. So, as soon as you begin to fabricate a tale about the infidelity of your spouse, stop yourself, call it what it is ("I feel nervous" or "I feel insecure"), and make a firm decision about your next step.

Pro tip: The next step may be to convince yourself that you're a catch and that your partner is fortunate to have you (even though at the moment you don't believe it). It might be a list of positive times in your relationship being written down. It might be saying things you like out loud about yourself. It could be calling a friend or reading a book or whatever makes you feel good about yourself.

8. Exercise

Speaking of feeling healthy, an exercise in the land of mental wellbeing is a superhero! Again, anxiety in relationships is a type of anxiety. Exercise, particularly yoga, has been shown to decrease levels of cortisol (the stress-responsible hormone). In individuals who exercised regularly, a recent study found a 27 percent lower incidence of new anxieties arising than in those who did not. So, while exercise cannot overcome the anxiety of relationships independently, it is a vital part of a well-balanced lifestyle.

Pro tip: Even one yoga class will change your attitude positively. If your thing is not an exercise, start tiny.

Take a deep breath if you find yourself amid a nightmare of relationship anxiety. You're not alone. There are lights at the end of this tunnel, and you just have to start walking.

THE RIGHT CALMING TECHNIQUES

Relaxation for many of us means flopping on the sofa and tuning out at the end of a long day in front of the TV. But this does nothing to reduce stress' adverse effects. Instead, your body's normal calming answer needs to be triggered, a state of deep rest that puts tension on the brakes slows your breathing and heart rate, reduces your blood pressure, and brings your mind and body back into equilibrium. By practicing calming methods such as deep respiration, meditation, rhythmic exercise, yoga, or tai chi, you can do this.

For example, while you can prefer to pay for a professional massage or acupuncture session, most relaxation techniques can be performed on your own or with the help of a free download of an audio or a cheap smartphone app. However, it's essential to note that there is no single relaxation method that works for everybody. We're all distinct. The best strategy is the one that resonates with you, suits your lifestyle, and can concentrate your mind to evoke the reaction of relaxation. That means that finding the technique (or techniques) that works best for you can require some trial and error. Daily practice can help minimize daily stress and anxiety, enhance sleep, increase energy and mood, and boost your overall well-being if you do so.

Deep breathing
With its emphasis on absolute, cleansing breaths, a simple but effective relaxation technique is deep breathing. It is easy to read, can be practiced almost anywhere, and offers a quick way to manage your stress levels. Deep breathing is also the foundation of many other relaxation techniques and can be combined with other calming components, such as music and aromatherapy. Although apps and audio downloads can direct you through the process, a few minutes and a place to sit quietly or stretch out are all you need.

How to practice deep respiration
With your back straight, sit comfortably. Place your chest in one hand and your stomach in the other.
Through your nose, breathe in. Your hand on your stomach should be raised. The hand can move very little on your stomach.
Exhale through your mouth, forcing as much air out as you can when your abdominal muscles are contracting. The hand on your stomach should shift in when you exhale, but there should be very little movement of the other hand.
Via your nose and out through your mouth, continue breathing in. Try to inhale enough to rise and fall down your lower abdomen. When you

exhale, count slowly.

Try lying down if you find it hard to breathe from your abdomen while sitting up. Place your stomach in a small book, and relax so that the book rises as you inhale and falls as you exhale.

Gradual relaxing of the muscles

A two-step method to gradually tense and relax various muscle groups in the body is progressive muscle relaxation. Through daily practice, it gives you an intuitive knowledge of what discomfort feels like in various parts of your body, as well as total relaxation. This will allow you to adapt to the first signs of stress accompanying muscular tension. And so will your mind as your body relaxes. For additional stress relief, progressive muscle relaxation may be paired with deep breathing.

Practicing gradual relaxation of muscles

If you have a past of muscle spasms, back pain, or other severe conditions that could be exacerbated by muscle strain, contact your physician first. Begin at your feet and work your way up to your face, trying to tense just those intended muscles. Loosen your hair, take your shoes off, and be cozy. Take a few minutes for long, deep breaths to breathe in and out. Move your focus to your right foot when you are set. To reflect on the way it feels, take a moment.

The muscles in your right foot relax slowly, gripping as tightly as you can. Keep the count to 10. Relax the legs. Reflect on the stress flowing away and how limp and lose the foot feels as it becomes. Last for a moment in this comfortable state, respiring deeply and slowly.

Have your focus shift to your left foot. Opt the same muscle tension and release sequence. Slowly travel up through the body, contracting the various muscle groups and relaxing them. At first, it could take some practice but try not to tense muscles other than the expected ones.

Body Scan Meditation

This is a type of meditation that concentrates your focus on different parts of your body. You begin with your feet and work your way up, just like progressive muscle relaxation. But you simply concentrate on the way that part of your body feels, without marking the sensations as either "good" or "evil" instead of tensing and relaxing muscles.

Lay on your back, legs uncrossed, arms on your sides relaxed, eyes closed or open. Focus for about two minutes on your breathing before you begin to feel relaxed.

Convert your attention to your right foot's toes. Note any feelings that you experience while still concentrating on your breathing as well. Imagine every deep breath that runs down your toes. For three to five seconds (or more), stay focused on this area.

You are moving your attention to your right foot's sole. In that part of your body, tune in to any sensations you experience and visualize each breath streaming from the sole of your foot. Shift your attention to your right ankle after one or two minutes and repeat. Switch to the calf, knee, thigh, shoulder, and then repeat the left leg series. Step up the torso from there, through the lower back and belly, the upper back and chest, and through the shoulders. Pay careful attention to every part of the body that produces pain or discomfort for you.

Relax for a moment in silence and stillness after finishing the body scan, noticing how the body feels. Then open your eyes slowly and, if possible, stretch.

Visualization

Visualization is a classic meditation twist that involves imagining a scene where you feel relaxed, free to let go of all anxiety and tension. Visualization or imagery is guided. Whether it's a tropical beach, a favorite spot for children, or a quiet wooded glen, choose the most relaxing setting for you.

For example, suppose you have chosen a beach. In that case, you can also choose to quietly do your visualization or use listening aids, such as relaxing music or a sound machine or a recording that fits your chosen environment: the sound of ocean waves.

Visualization practicing

Close your eyes and imagine your place of rest. Picture everything as vividly as you can: you see, hear, smell, taste, and feel everything. It is not necessary to just "look" at it in the eye of your mind as you would a photograph. If you add as many sensory information as possible, visualization works best. If you are dreaming, for instance, of a dock on a quiet lake:

- See over the water the sun sets
- Hear the birds singing
- The pine trees smell
- Feel the water on your bare feet cool
- Taste the clean, fresh air

As you slowly explore your restful spot, enjoy the feeling of your worries floating away. Gently open your eyes when you are ready and come back to the moment. Don't worry if, during a visualization session, you often zone out or lose track of where you are. It's usually here. You can also experience sensations of heaviness, muscle cramps, or yawning in your limbs. These are, again, natural responses.

Self-massage

You're probably already aware of how much a professional massage at a spa or health club can help alleviate stress, alleviate discomfort, and reduce muscle tension. You may not be aware that you can reap some of the same advantages at home or work by practicing self-massage or sharing massages with a loved one.

To help you relax before sleep, consider taking a few minutes to massage yourself at your desk between activities, on the couch at the end of a hectic day, or in bed. You may use herbal oil, scented lotion, or combine self-massage with mindfulness or deep breathing exercises to increase relaxation.

A self-massage of five minutes to alleviate tension

To ease muscle tension, a combination of strokes works well. With the edge of your fingertips, try soft chops or tapping with fingers or cupped palms. Place fingertip pressure on the knots of the muscle. Knead and try deep, light, gliding strokes through the muscles. These strokes can be applied to any part of the body that falls within your reach easily.

Try concentrating on your neck and head for a short session like this: start by kneading the back of your shoulders and neck muscles. Easily make a loose fist and drum up and down the sides and back of your body. First, work for tiny circles around the base of your skull using your thumbs. Massage the remainder of your scalp gently with your fingertips. Tap your fingertips against the scalp, then shift from the front to the back, then to the sides.

Massage your face now. With your thumbs or fingertips, make a pattern of tiny circles. Pay careful attention to the muscles in the temples, forehead, and jaw. Massage the bridge of your nose and work outward through your eyebrows to your temples using your middle fingers. Lastly, shut your eyes. Loosely cup your hands over your face and quickly inhale and exhale for a brief while.

Mindfulness Meditation

In recent years, mindfulness has become widely popular, attracting headlines and endorsements from business leaders, celebrities, and psychologists alike. What is mindfulness, then? Instead of thinking about the future or focusing on the past, mindfulness changes your attention to what's going on right now, helping you to be completely interested in the present moment.

To relieve stress, anxiety, depression, and other negative emotions, meditations that promote mindfulness have long been used. By concentrating your attention on a single repetitive movement, such as your breathing or a few repeated phrases, some of these activities carry you into the present. Other ways of meditation on mindfulness allow you to obey and release internal thoughts or feelings afterward. It is also possible to extend mindfulness to things such as driving, exercising, or feeding. It could seem easy to use mindfulness to remain concentrated on the moment, but it takes practice to reap all the advantages. You'll find that your mind keeps wandering back to your concerns or regrets when you first start training. Don't get disheartened, though. You reinforce a new mental habit every time you draw your attention back to the present, which may help you break free from thinking about the past or worried about the future. Using an app or audio download, especially when you're starting, can also help focus your attention.

A meditation on simple mindfulness

1. Find a calm place where you won't be disturbed or disrupted.
2. With your back straight, sit on a comfortable chair.
3. Close your eyes and find a focal point, such as your breathing, or a meaningful phrase that you repeat during the meditation, the feeling of air flowing through your nose and out of your mouth or belly rising and falling.
4. Don't think about intrusive thoughts that go through your mind or how well you do. If thoughts interfere with your relaxation session, do not

combat them, only gently turn your attention back without judgment to your point of emphasis.

Mindfulness exercise and rhythmic movement

The exercise concept does not sound especially relaxing, but the relaxation response can be generated by rhythmic exercise that gets you into a repetitive movement flow. Examples are:

- Running
- Walking
- Swimming
- Dancing
- Rowing
- Climbing

Add focus to your workout for full stress relief.

While engaging in rhythmic exercise will help you alleviate stress, you can benefit even more by adding a mindfulness aspect.

As with meditation, mindfulness exercise involves being completely involved in the present moment, instead of your everyday worries or problems, paying attention to how your body feels right now. Focus on your muscles' sensations and how your breathing complements your movement, rather than tuning out or looking at a TV while you exercise. For instance, as you walk or run, concentrate on the feeling of your feet hitting the rhythm of your breath, the ground, and the feeling of the wind against your face. Focus on matching your breathing with your movements while you are strength training and pay attention to how your body feels when you raise and lower the weights. And gently return your attention to your breathing and movement when your mind wanders into other thoughts.

Yoga

We have already talked about it. Yoga includes, together with deep breathing, a sequence of both moving and stationary positions. Yoga can also promote flexibility, strength, balance, and endurance and reduce anxiety and stress. It is better to learn by attending community classes, hiring a private instructor, or following video instructions, because accidents can occur when yoga is performed improperly. If you've learned the basics, you can practice alone or with others, tailoring the practice as you see fit.

What form of yoga is best for tension? For stress relief, classes that highlight slow, steady movement, deep breathing, and gentle stretching are best, although nearly all yoga classes end in a relaxation pose.

Satyananda is a popular form of yoga. It features deep relaxation, gentle poses, and meditation, making it ideal for both beginners and those who are specifically seeking to alleviate stress.

Hatha yoga is also a fairly gentle way of relieving stress and is ideal for beginners. Alternately, when choosing a yoga class, look for labels like gentle, for stress relief, or beginners.

Power yoga is ideally suited to those looking for enhancement and relaxation, with its vigorous poses and emphasis on fitness.

Call the studio or ask the instructor if you are uncertain if a particular yoga class is ideal for stress relief.

Tai Chi

You've probably experienced Tai Chi if you've seen a group of people in the park moving slowly in synch. A self-paced sequence of slow, fluid body motions is Tai chi. You keep your concentration on the moment, which clears the mind and contributes to a calm state, by keeping your mind on the motions and your breathing.

Tai Chi is a safe, low-impact option for individuals of all ages and fitness levels, including older adults and those recovering from injuries. As with yoga, it is best learned in a class or from a private instructor. If you've learned the fundamentals, you can practice alone or with others.

HOW TO CONQUER ANXIETY IN RELATIONSHIP

It's maybe the simple part to find the root causes of your relationship anxiety. Although it can be gradual and daunting to conquer your fear, it can be achieved if you are consciously conscious, thoroughly committed to change and be kind to yourself as you walk the road ahead.

"Take some time to understand better how your early experiences have influenced your relationship style and remain mindful of ways you can replicate early experiences with your new partner," Zayde suggests. "Pay attention to how much you leap to conclusions, and whether or not you have enough evidence to support your concerns; sometimes, our concerns are focused on past experiences, not our present relationship." Follow these expert tips to remain in control and help relieve anxiety as anxious thoughts begin to grab hold:

Running. We already mentioned it, and we repeat it. Forshee suggests hitting the gym to help alleviate the tension at the moment. Various studies have shown that exercise improves the development and release of serotonin. The two worst things you can do are isolating yourself and being physically stagnant, so get going.

Healthy self-talk. "Engage in constructive self-talking rather than negative self-talking, and help a friend remind you of happier days and what the good things are now in your life," Forshee says. "This act helps to increase the development of serotonin in the anterior cingulate cortex, which is a part of your brain right behind the frontal areas responsible for treatment, judgment, and impulse control."

Take a step back. In feeling nervous, Forshee emphasizes the importance of not acting on your emotional impulses. She says your brain won't let you make wise decisions in the heat of the moment, and you're most likely going to regret your actions soon afterward.

Find ways to unwind. "If you are unable to get assistance from your support team or are unable to move, it could be useful to engage in a calming technique such as diaphragm breathing. This can help with physiological de-escalation so that you can think more clearly and feel less worked up, "says Forshee.

Take aid. "Finally, if you notice that your relationship anxiety has taken over in a way that you believe is beyond your control — or has wrought havoc in your life — it's likely to be helpful to pursue professional therapy."

Ultimately, managing relationship anxiety depends on gaining control of the feelings and mental process. There's a strong connection between your wellbeing — and the quality of your relationship — and the level of knowledge you have about yourself, your attitudes, and your feelings. Take action to recognize the causes of anxiety and re-route the cycle it incites today, and you might just be able to create a new path for your brain to follow around next time.

Relationships can be one of the planet's most pleasurable things, but they can also be a fertile ground for negative thoughts and emotions. Anxiety about relationships can occur at almost any stage of the courtship. Just thinking about being in a relationship will bring up stress for many single people. The early stages will present them with endless worries if and when people start dating: "Does he/she like me?" "Is this going to work out?" "What is this serious?". Unfortunately, in the later stages of a marital relationship, these issues do not appear to subside. Indeed, as things get closer to a couple, anxiety can become even more severe. Thoughts rush in like this: "Will this last?" "Do I like him/her?" "Should we hesitate?" "Am I ready for this kind of engagement?" "Does he/she lose interest?" All this thinking about our relationships can cause us to feel very lonely.

It can give us reason to separate ourselves from our partners. Our anxiety at its worst can even drive us to give up on love altogether. Knowing more about the causes and consequences of stress about relationships will help us recognize the negative thoughts and behaviors that can undermine our love lives. How do we keep our fear in check and get vulnerable to those we love? What triggers anxiety about Relationships?

Simply put, falling in love surprises us in ways we don't expect. The more we love another, the more we are to lose. We become scared of getting hurt in several ways, both conscious and unconscious. To a certain extent, we all have a fear of being close. Ironically, this anxiety always shows up when we get exactly what we want when we experience love like we never have or are handled in different ways. When we move into a partnership, it's not just the things that happen between our partner that make us anxious; it's the stuff about what's going on that we say ourselves.

The "powerful inner voice" is a phrase used to describe the mean coach we all have in our heads who criticizes us, imposes bad advice on us, and fuels our fear of intimacy. It is that which tells us:

"You are too ugly/fat/boring to maintain an interest in yourself."

"You are never going to meet anyone, so why even try it?" "You can't believe him."

"He is looking for a better guy" "She has no real love for you."

Get out before it hurts you. This vital voice inside makes us turn against ourselves and the people who are close to us.

It can encourage aggressive, pessimistic, and suspicious thinking that lowers our self-esteem and induces unhealthy levels of mistrust, defensiveness, envy, and anxiety. It effectively feeds us with a steady stream of thoughts that ruins our happiness and makes us worry about our relationship, rather than just enjoy it. When we get into our minds, dwelling on those worrying feelings, we get too disconnected from our partner's real relationship.

We can begin to behave in negative ways, to make nasty comments, or to become childish or parental towards our significant others. Imagine your partner staying at work late in one night, for instance. Seated alone at home, your inner critic begins to tell you, "Where is she? Could you believe it? Possibly she wants to be separated from you. She is trying to avoid you. She no longer loves you." These feelings will snowball in your mind until you feel nervous, angry, or anxious by the time your partner gets home. You could be acting angry or cold, then set off your partner to feel irritated and defensive. Soon, you changed the dynamic between yourself completely. Instead of enjoying the time you have with each other, you might be wasting a whole night feeling distant and angry. Now the gap you initially feared was effectively forced. The culprit behind this prophecy, which fulfills itself, is not the situation itself. It's that vital inner voice that warped your thought, skewed your perceptions, and eventually led you down a destructive path.

We are much more robust than we realize when it comes to all of the things we worry about ourselves in relationships. In reality, we're able to cope with the hurts and rejections we fear so much. We can feel pain and ultimately cure. But our vital voice inside tends to terrorize and catastrophize reality. It can stir up severe anxiety spells about non-existent complexities and risks that are not even observable. Even when important things happen, someone breaks up with us or has an interest in somebody else; our vital inner voice is going to tear us apart in ways that we don't deserve. It will distort reality entirely and weaken our power and resilience. It is this pessimistic roommate who is still offering lousy advice that you cannot survive. Just put your guard up and never make someone else weak.

We form defenses and hear influential voices based on our own specific experiences and adaptations. Some of us tend to become clingy and insecure in our acts when we feel nervous or uncertain. In response, we may feel possessive or controlling towards our partner. Inversely, some of us in our relationships would feel easily intruded on. We withdraw from our partners and detach ourselves from our feelings of desire. We may act aloof, distant, or guarded. These relating trends may come from our early styles of attachment.

Our pattern of attachment is formed in our extensions to childhood and continues to serve as a working model for adult relationships. It affects how each of us is reacting to our needs and how we are going to fulfill them. Different types of attachment may cause us to feel different degrees of anxiety about the relationship. You will learn more about your kind of passion and how it affects your romantic relationships here. What thoughts are perpetuating tension in the relationship?

The unique critical inner voices that we have about ourselves, our spouses, and relationships are created by the early attitudes to which we have been exposed in our family or society at large. Cultural assumptions, as well as behaviors our influential caretakers have about themselves and others, will invade our perspective and shade our current perceptions. Although the inner critic of all is different, some familiar critical voices within include:

- Relevant Voices inside the Partnership.

- Never do marriages work out.

- Your Partner Voices.

- Men are so arrogant, incompetent, and egotistical.

- Women are so delicate, so weak, and so indirect.

- He only wants to be with friends of his.

- Why get so excited? What's so sweet of her anyway?

- Possibly, he cheats on you.

- You can't believe her.

- He just can't get it right.

- Voices for Yourself.

- You'll never find anyone else who knows you.

- Don't get too hooked on her.

- He doesn't care for you.

- She's too good for you.

- You have to maintain an interest in him.

- You're better off alone.

- She will ignore you until she gets to know you.

- You have to have the leverage.

- If he gets angry, it is your fault.

- Don't be too weak, or actually get hurt.

Chapter 12: 7 MOST COMMON DISAGREEMENTS IN RELATIONSHIPS AND HOW TO RESOLVE THEM

You know that you love someone special to you, and you know that they love you. You also know how to argue the right way (or at least practice the right way!) and how to get the partnership you want exactly. So why does the same claim keep rearing its ugly head over and over again? You know the argument - maybe it's because your partner forgot to stop again at the grocery store, or maybe they nag you about constantly being on your phone - the argument that just keeps coming, particularly in times when one or both of you stress you out. Maybe it's a tiny tiff, or maybe it's a blow-out fight, but either way, it's not helping to support each other, to be there for each other, and to be as comfortable together as possible. Once and for all, get out of your relationship rut and fix those fights; here's how to fix 7 of the most common relationship problems, so you never have to argue about it again.

1. Either of you feels misunderstood (or both)
Although practically all relationship disagreements have to do with miscommunication (or lack of communication altogether), when you or your partner don't feel listened to or heard, some disagreements turn into long-term resentment.

The Correction: Although it might sound crazy, make an actual appointment to speak about every issue with each other. A formula for miscommunication and feeling ignored is attempting to express hurt feelings before bed after a long, busy day or bringing up irrelevant concerns when the partner forgets to unload the dishwasher. During the week, make an appointment to sit down, put your mobile phones away, and discuss how you feel. Often take turns talking, and if you can't speak without getting too hot, try to have a conversation in a public place such as a restaurant or park.

2. Splitting up household tasks

If you live together, there's been at least one "never" dispute over your partner unloading the dishwasher or how they put out the garbage for the third week in a row when you manage to forget. The shouting match or two may even have been over the sometimes empty toothpaste tube at 10 pm, or the forgotten grocery store may have run to get milk for the cereal of tomorrow. It's essential to break up household chores to avoid resentment, whether you both have jobs outside the home or only one person has one (or multiple) jobs.

The Correction: Write down all household tasks (everything from frequent grocery shopping to adjusting the air filter occasionally), and then divide them equally, taking into account preferences. Let them cook dinner five nights a week if your partner likes to cook, and promise that you clean up. They should do the laundry for the week if you hate laundry, but your partner doesn't mind it, and you pick up the dry cleaners. If you both do not like housework, see if you can make room for a cleaning service in the budget, or if you both hate cooking, look into meal delivery services such as Blue Apron. Be open to alternatives as well. When breaking up the chores, you may be imaginative, but just make sure that it feels equal to both of you.

3. Not making your partnership a top priority

Picture this: you've been together for what feels like forever; you're incredibly busy focusing on your career/kids/housework/all the above, and if you get to kiss your other important goodnight before bed, you're lucky. A familiar sound? Although having someone so consistent in your life is a blessing that you know they will be there even when you don't tend to your relationship, it doesn't mean you can take a blessing for granted. And when life gets busy, make sure that neither of you put the other on the back burner.

The Correction: Here's the thing: it may be easy to say "go on date nights more often," or "give them more compliments." While these techniques may benefit some couples fully, other couples might be too exhausted/busy/depressed and end up fighting through date night, or compliments might not be noticed, and when you try, they might leave you feeling uncared for.

So the trick to make sure you both feel that the relationship is a top priority is the good old reliable languages of love. Know the language of love of your partner and prepare meaningful ways to act on their language of love every day. Wake up every morning for your own sake and think about at least three things you are thankful for in your partner. When you appreciate it, prioritizing your relationship won't feel like trying.

4. Issues with money

Money can't buy you love, but it can destroy it ... whether it's conflicted about who's paying for what, frustration about dependence, setting financial targets, or very different spending patterns, money can not only trigger relationship difficulties, but it can lead to breakups. For many individuals, financial status is understandably a common fear, and a disparity in financial values for even strong couples may reflect a deal-breaking disparity in more excellent morals.

The Correction: From the beginning, be truthful about your financial condition and spending habits. Before any significant change, such as moving in together, getting married, or having a child, have a 'money talk' with your significant other. Acknowledge that both of you will have different habits-one might be a spender, and one might be a saver, and both lifestyles are optimistic and negative. Think of wealth, not your wealth, effort, and work against theirs, as the life you create together.

5. Lack of intimacy

When your schedules are crazy, the kids are up all night, or you've just been together for a long time, sex could feel more like an occasional chore than a significant part of the relationship. Plus, emotionally compatible couples may not always be physically compatible. Unfulfilled intimacy, however, can cause relationship problems because physical contact re-leases hormones that bring you closer together and keep the chemistry alive.

The Correction: Focus outside the bedroom on your physical touch-hold hands sometimes, give hugs out of the blue, and kiss more often than routine (such as saying hello or goodbye). Discuss freely what you all want, and make it a priority to have a comfortable space to discuss to-gether. Do not judge your partner and do not be with someone who will judge you. By prioritizing your intimacy, maintain a spark in the rela-tionship, and connect with your partner if you don't feel comfortable with your sex life. It may be challenging to be so frank, but disappointment is not an instant deal breaker. Inability to connect and modify together is.

6. Growing apart

After a celebrity split, we all read the cliché joint statement that says some nonsense like, 'we love and care about each other, yet have just grown apart...' Although relationships don't work out because of "growing apart" has a lot of validity, it can be resolved with the right effort and care. As humans, we are all growing, and you can either grow together or grow apart in your relationship.

The Correction: With the transition, be all right. By definition, a partnership should mean a stable space for growing together, enabling your partner to always develop and be their best selves, without setting standards or limitations. Be mindful of how your overtime shift affects your insecurities, making you feel less valuable if you put more hours into your new company, instead of feeling proud of all their hard work. Always convey every feeling you have, and enjoy watching your partner grow, ensuring that they also share your growth. Let them take part in every career achievement or milestone in life, sharing each new process.

7. Trust

Yes, whether or not you genuinely trust each other will make a relationship or break it. Trust is more than either going to cheat on me or not. You should not only trust the integrity of your partner to have a lasting, successful, satisfying relationship, but trust their thoughts, their character, and that they have your best interest at heart.

The Correction: Since you can only influence your actions, here's what you can do to improve the relationship's trust: make promises you keep, don't lie (even little white lies to save feelings), call when you say you will, don't say things you don't mean, and look at past wounds that impact the way you trust. Do you feel insecure and unlovable, or have you been cheated on? Many times, apart from our history or insecurities, we do not trust our partner for no reason. If that's the case, it's not that your spouse doesn't trust you; it's because you don't trust being in a successful partnership. Be honest about why you feel that way with your partner and what you two can do to overcome those feelings.

But if you just don't trust your partner, they've lied to you before, they don't call when they say they're going to, or they've done stuff behind your back that didn't make you feel comfortable, maybe it's time to reconsider if it's a relationship worth having. Not all inconsistencies can (or should) be corrected.

HOW COUPLES CAN REBUILD MARRIAGE TRUST

Trust is rooted in feeling comfortable with another person in an intimate relationship. The confidence between a husband and wife can be seriously compromised by infidelity, lies, or broken promises. That, however, does not necessarily mean that a partnership can't be redeemed. While rebuilding trust can be difficult when there is a significant breach, it is possible if all partners are committed to the process.

The Bits Pick Up

It takes a lot of time and effort to re-establish the sense of security that a marriage needs to flourish and continue to grow. Recovery from the trauma caused by a split in the trust is where you might get stuck with several couples who want to get back on track.

Research has shown that, to successfully move past a breach of confidence, couples must overcome the following five stumbling points:

1. Knowing about the specifics
2. Releasing the frustration
3. Showing engagement
4. Reconstructing trust
5. Reconstruction of the relationship

To restore the faith in your marriage, whether you were the offending party or the deceived, you will need to renew your loyalty to your marriage and each other.

The Specifics Know

There are still two sides, sometimes in apparently clear-cut instances of betrayal. Besides providing straightforward answers to their partner's questions, the offending partner should be straightforward and truthful with details.

This will offer a broader awareness of the situation to the betrayed side. What, when, and where happened? What emotions or issues may have led to this situation? What were the mitigating circumstances there?

Release the Rage

Also, minor confidence violations can lead to problems with mental, emotional, and physical health. Partners can experience difficulties in sleeping or reduced appetite. About small stuff, they can become easily irritable.

Although pushing all the frustration and feelings down can be tempting, deceived partners must turn in and focus on all the feelings they have. Consider the effect on you and others of the deception of your partner. Reflect on how life, including thinking about all the questions and concerns that are now arising, has been interrupted. Make both of these feelings known to your partner. Because before the incident, even the accused party can share any feelings of disappointment and frustration they may have been harboring.

Show Commitment

Both parties, especially the deceived, may doubt their loyalty to the relationship and wonder if the relationship is still right or even salvageable for them. Empathy actions may heal all parties by expressing pain, frustration, and anger, exhibiting guilt and regret, and providing room for the appreciation and acknowledgment of hurt feelings.

Building on this, specifying what both sides need from the partnership, will allow partners to realize that the relationship continues with reasonable expectations that each individual has agreed to meet in going forward.

To remain committed to making the relationship work, all parties must work to identify what is needed. When expressing this, explain what you see, expect, or want from your partner, avoid using terms that can cause conflict (e.g., always, must, never, should). Alternatively, pick phrases that encourage open dialogue and use non-blaming "I" sentences. For instance, "I need to feel like a priority in your life" over "You never put me first."

Rebuilding Trust

Together, to get your marriage back on track, you must set clear targets and practical deadlines. Recognize that it takes time to restore trust and work on the following.

Decide to forgive or to be forgiven. Make a deliberate effort to love by attempting to let go of the past. Although it may take some time to accomplish this aim entirely, sticking to it is essential.

Be open to change and self-growth. With just promises and declarations of forgiveness, you can't restore broken faith. For the problems to remain latent, the betrayal's underlying factors must be established, investigated, and operated on by both partners.

Be mindful of your innermost emotions, and share your thoughts. It will not fix anything by leaving one side to obsess about the circumstance or action that broke the trust. Instead, freely sharing the specifics and voicing all feelings of anger and hurt is necessary.

Want it to work. There is no room in the process for lip service or more lies. Be frank with and true to your desires.

When both sides have taken the above points to heart, speak about your priorities freely, and check in periodically to ensure you are on target.

For the Offender

It may be difficult or even unpleasant to be reminded of your wrongdoings as the person who damaged the relationship. Note, however, that the above measures are critical to the repair and recovery process. While you're working on them:

Show that by altering your conduct, the errant conduct is gone if you are the one who lied, cheated, or breached the confidence in your marriage. It means no more secrets, deceit, unfaithfulness, or something else of that kind. From now on, be fully straightforward, accessible, and forthcoming.

Be frank and work to understand why bad conduct happened and to state why. Statements like 'I don't know' don't instill confidence or help you get to the root of the problem.

Take responsibility for your acts and decisions; apologize and resist defensiveness for the hurt you caused, which would only perpetuate the dispute or crisis. It's also not constructive to explain your actions based on what your partner is doing or has done in the past.

For Betrayed Ones

Although going forward depends a lot on what your partner can offer, you note that the job you do has a lot to do with your future success. Day by day, as you proceed:

Work on learning why and what went wrong before the betrayal finally took place in the relationship. Although this will not make you forget what happened, it will make you get the answers that you need to move forward.

Provide constructive answers and encouragement to help your partner with clear feedback on things that interest you or make you happy once you commit to giving your partner a second chance.

Know that it is also OK if you do not want to continue the relationship after contemplating the above steps or starting them. Just be honest with yourself and your partner and don't go through the motions just because, as a committed partner, you believe that is what is expected of you.

To the Couple

Although there's independent work to be done, remember to listen to each other. Remind each other that each of you deserves open and truthful responses to your questions about treason.

Rebuilding The Partnership

When couples have dedicated themselves to restoring faith, they have to focus on handling the relationship as though it were a completely new one. Both sides need to ask for what they need and not presume to already hear what they want from their partner.

In this new partnership, do not withhold trust, even though it is with the same person. Withholding trust out of fear or rage will deter you from reconnecting with your partner emotionally. This prevents the relationship stably from going forward.

Instead, work towards restoring the relationship by doing the job needed to create trust and rebuild a bond that helps each other. Come to an understanding with both of you on what a good relationship looks like.

Some examples include setting date nights, working together on a five-year, ten-year, and even 20-year plan, discovering your languages of love, and checking in with your partner about how you feel the relationship is going or whether your goals are being met.

Note that work is needed for all relationships. Also, the closest couples have to work hard on renewing the spark, year after year, when working together to develop in the same direction.

Having professional assistance

Suppose you resolve the problems mentioned above and hang on to the bigger picture. In that case, you will focus on creating a healthier, happier, and more truthful relationship. You will understand that getting through this is only possible if you remain together and commit to working together on it.

To help you both move forward, a therapist will help you process what happened, why, and how. To get a clearer understanding of what caused the trust to be broken, all parties must be open to finding help. But in addition to the care of couples, you might want or need to pursue individual counseling.

Many therapy types can be particularly useful for couples intended to re-establish trust, intimacy, and connection. After going through such a crisis, you can even end up with a more strong marriage through continued work and counseling.

Rebuilding trust after you have been deceived

It can leave you feeling damaged, stunned, and even physically ill to have someone break your trust. In a different context, it could encourage you to reconsider your partnership and your spouse. Here are some excellent starting points if you want to try to restore trust.

Take account of the motive behind the deception or betrayal

You do not care much about the reasons behind it when you've been lied to. But sometimes individuals lie because they don't know what else to do. This does not make their decision right, but in their place, it can help to understand how you would have responded.

Yes, to defend yourself, your partner may have betrayed you, but they may have had a different reason. Have they been trying to safeguard you from bad news? Make the best out of a bad situation with money? A family member helping? Perhaps a miscommunication or confusion resulted from the betrayal of confidence.

It is necessary, whatever happened, to make it clear that what they did was not OK. But understanding the reasons behind their acts will help you determine whether you can start restoring the trust you once shared.

Communicate, collaborate

It may be painful or awkward, but talking to your partner about the situation is one of the main aspects of restoring trust after deception.

Set some time aside to tell them clearly:

- The way you think about the situation
- Why did the betrayal of confidence affect you
- What you need from them to begin to restore trust

Offer them a chance to speak, but heed their sincerity. Are they sorry and appearing to be very regretful? Or are they defensive and hesitant to own up to their betrayal?

During this conversation, you may feel emotional or irritated. These emotions are true. Take a break and come back to the subject later if you are too frustrated to continue talking constructively.

Talking about what happened is just the start. If you can't get through it in just a night or two, it's perfectly fine and natural.

Practice forgiveness

Forgiveness is crucial if you want to restore a relationship after a betrayal. You may not only need to forgive your spouse, but you will need to forgive yourself as well. Blaming yourself for what has happened in any way will keep you trapped in self-doubt. That can hurt the chances of recovering from your relationship.

It may be difficult to forgive your partner and move on, depending on the betrayal. But try to note that your partner isn't saying what they did was OK. Instead, you motivate yourself to come to terms with what happened in the past and leave it behind. You're also allowing your partner to learn from their mistakes and grow.

Prevent dwelling on the past

It's usually best not to put the problem to rest until you've thoroughly addressed the betrayal. This means that in future arguments, you don't want to bring it up.

To ensure that they are not lying to you again, you may also want to go easy on continually checking in on your partner. This, especially at first, isn't always easy. You can find it challenging to let go of the betrayal and find it hard to start trusting your partner, especially if you're worried about another betrayal.

But you're still choosing to trust your partner again as you decide to give the partnership a second chance. You may not be able to trust them fully right away, but you're saying that you're going to give trust a chance to regrow.

If you can't bear to think about what happened or have misgivings about your partner's potential integrity or faithfulness, therapy for couples can help. But these symptoms may also mean that you may not be ready for the relationship to function.

Rebuilding trust after you have hurt others

You've messed up. Perhaps you were lying and hurting your partner or hiding details that you felt would hurt them. No matter your motives, you know that you have caused them pain, and you feel horrible. You can feel like you will do whatever it takes to show them that they can trust you again. First of all, it is essential to know that broken trust might be beyond repair. But if both of you are not going to focus on fixing the relationship, you can take a few helpful steps.

Think about why you did so

You'll first want to check in with yourself to understand why you did it before you embark on the process of reconstructing faith. Is it possible you wanted the relationship to end but didn't know how to do it? Or were there unique needs that your partner wasn't meeting? Or was it just a stupid error? It can be challenging to understand the reasons behind your actions, but it's a vital part of restoring trust.

Sincerely apologize

A sincere apology is an excellent way to start making amends if you lied, cheated, or otherwise undermined your partner's confidence in you. It's essential to admit that you've made an error.

Only note that it's not the time to justify your acts or clarify the situation with your apologies. If any factors have affected your behavior, after apologizing and owning your role in the scenario, you can still share these with your partner.

Be specific

Be specific when you apologize, to demonstrate that you know what you did was wrong. For instance, instead of 'I'm sorry I hurt you,' try 'I apologize for having lied to you about where I was going. I know I was meant to tell you the truth, and I regret having caused you pain. I want you to know that I'm never going to do it again.'

When telling them how you plan to stop making the same mistake again, make sure to follow up. You should ask if you're not sure what they need from you to work on the connection. Only make sure that you're ready and able to listen to their response actively.

Give time to your partner

Your partner may not feel ready yet, even though you're ready to apologize, talk about what happened, and start working through stuff. A betrayal or broken faith may take time to come to terms with.

People process stuff in various ways, too. Maybe your partner wants to chat right away. But they may also require days or weeks to discuss the problem with you before they can. Before they're ready, it's crucial to avoid pushing them to have a conversation. Apologize and let your partner know that when they are, you're able. In the meantime, if you're struggling, consider speaking to a professional who will provide impartial and helpful advice.

Let their need guide you

Before they can address what happened, your partner would need room and time. And also, physical space could be involved in this. This may be hard to face, but respecting your partner's boundaries and needs may go a long way to showing them that they can again count on you.

In the future, your partner may want more accountability and contact from you. After a betrayal of confidence, this is normal. To show your integrity, you can also freely share your phone and computer with your partner.

Now, suppose you have made some progress in improving your relationship and your partner wants to track your behavior and relationships with others. In that case, it may help speak to a counselor for couples.

Commit to clear communication

You may want to answer your partner's questions frankly and commit to being fully available to them in the future in the immediate aftermath of broken faith. You have to make sure that you are consistent with the amount of contact they need to do this.

Let's say, by hiding some details that you didn't think was important, you broke their trust, and you didn't understand why they felt so deceived. This can mean that there is a deeper communication problem in your relationship.

You need to achieve a shared understanding of what good communication looks like if you want to fix your relationship and avoid upsetting your partner again in the future. Sometimes, miscommunications or misunderstandings may cause as much pain as deliberate dishonesty.

What about the specifics of the relationship?

Relationship therapists often warn against revealing explicit information about a sexual experience with anyone else. Your wife might have a lot of questions about what happened if you've cheated. And in an attempt to be straightforward, you might want to address them.

But talking about an encounter's specifics can cause extra pain that is not very effective. Consider telling them to wait until you can see a therapist together if your partner needs specifics.

You should help the therapist navigate the healthiest way to answer these issues. In the meantime, without providing specific information, you can still accurately answer their questions.

How long would it take?

It can be incredibly uncomfortable to be in a relationship of broken faith. Both sides may be anxious to get the whole reconstruction process done as soon as possible. But this takes time, realistically.

Exactly how much time? It depends on several variables, especially the event that broke the confidence. It will take longer to fix long-standing infidelity or deceptive trends. It may be easier to resolve a single lie grounded in a misunderstanding or desire to protect, particularly when the spouse who lied demonstrates genuine regret and a renewed commitment to communication.

For yourself, have faith. Don't let you hurry with your partner. A spouse who regrets hurting you might also be hurting, but if they care about you and want to fix things, they should also know that jumping straight back into the way things were is not helpful.

Is it worthwhile?

It's not an easy job to restore trust. Before you decide to commit to working on your relationship, it is natural to doubt whether it is worth it. If, over a long relationship, your partner makes a mistake or two and owns up to it, working on confidence issues might be the right step.

Working on confidence issues will only improve your relationship as long as there is always love and devotion between the two of you. But if you know you're never going to be able to trust your partner fully again, regardless of what they do, it's usually best to make this clear right away so that you can both start moving forward independently.

If you have uncovered years of infidelity, financial dishonesty, coercion, or other significant confidence violations, it is also worth considering your options.

Other warning flags that may mean that it is time to throw in the towel include:

- Continued deception or tampering
- An insincere pardon
- Conduct which does not fit their words

A rough patch goes through every relationship. In reaching out for support, there's no guilt. Counseling for couples can be a great resource when dealing with confidence issues, particularly those involving infidelity. A therapist may provide an objective view of the relationship and help all parties work through fundamental problems.

It can also bring up painful feelings on both sides to have difficult discussions about betrayal and trust. Finding a reliable counselor will also help you handle the uncomfortable emotions that emerge when they occur. After a breach of confidence, it's possible to restore a relationship. Whether it's worth it depends on your partnership's needs and whether you believe if your partner can be trusted again.

If you plan to try to fix problems, be prepared to take some time to do something. If both sides are committed to the confidence-building process, you will find that, both as a couple and on your own, you both come out stronger than ever.

HOW TO INTERACT WHEN YOU DISAGREE WITH YOUR PARTNER

Now that we have learned how to regain trust in a relationship, let's look at a few ways to connect better when a disagreement arises, and you don't see eye to eye with your partner or spouse.

Care. A lack of respect is one of the key items I see in couples on the brink of marital collapse. You're in trouble when you hit a point where you don't like each other anymore. Unfortunately, we always treat everyday strangers with more respect than people at home. Respect is one of the main factors in a good and happy marriage: respect for those around you and, most importantly, respect for yourself.

Define yourself clearly. Defining yourself means you better understand and know your values, interests, wants, and desires. Marriage is a wonderful place in your life to describe these things, largely because that is the way marriage is planned.

You live with another person who, just like you, has his or her vision of the way things should be. For starters, tables may serve as great places to store piles of mail, magazines, and artwork for children in your family of origin. But the family of origin of your partner feels tables are perfect places to have dinner together, so they ought to be clutter-free.

None of the ways is inherent "right," just different. The way you chose, you're allowed to live life, but so is your partner.

Comprehend the principle of over-functioning and under-functioning. There'll be the one who over-function in any partnership, while the other under-functions. It is a related fact. In answer to the way we do life, over-functioning and under-functioning are positions we hold. None of us is all one way all the time; in some aspects of life, we over-function, and in others, we under-function.

What is important to you and what you value defines this. For instance, if the grades of your child are more important to you than they are to her, you are more likely to do her homework for her, or at least keep up with her about it, so she can under-function, knowing that you are going to pick up the slack.

One thing to keep in mind is that you're under-functioning for yourself if you're over-functioning for others. It's best to start a conversation about the change when you are faced with something you want to change and have a partner who is not on the same page.

Share your opinions. Listen to theirs freely. Together, you are very likely to be able to come up with a solution.

Live according to what you hold dear. Live according to your dignity and beliefs when you are faced with a situation where you and your partner aren't on the same page. Simplify your life if you want to simplify it, and your partner doesn't. Would you like to eat nutritious food, and your partner only wants fast food? Balanced eating.

I'll leave you with this: what you are responsible for is you at the end of the day.

30 LITTLE WAYS TO SHOW HOW MUCH YOU LOVE YOUR PARTNER

1. Tell them.

It's best not to overcomplicate things sometimes. If it's your boyfriend, girlfriend, husband, or wife, choosing the right words and saying them is the best way to express your gratitude. A basic "Thank you" is a good starting point, but you may want to add a little more, such as "Thank you for that." "I am very thankful." "You didn't have to do that, but it shows me that you are a good and loving person." Talk straight from the heart.

2. Send them a letter of appreciation.

A lovely way to thank your loved one is to write a little message to them and leave it somewhere they're going to see it. Perhaps you might drop it in their packed lunch or whatever they are currently reading next to the bookmark. A note helps you to say more than you can while talking to them, and instead of fumbling for the right words at the moment, it gives you time to think about what you want to say.

3. Spend time together with them.

Nothing shouts, "I take you for granted!" more than spending half your free time with your girlfriend away from you. But few things say, "I love you," more than just spending quality time with them. It's awesome that you have your friends and interests, but you need to make sure the two of you have plenty of time to maintain your personal and romantic relationship.

4. Reflect on their passions and hobbies.
Ask yourself what they love most if you want to show others you value them, and then make that a part of what you do for them. Are you an enthusiastic person who enjoys the countryside? Hire some bikes and plan a path that will take you to some nearby spots of beauty. Have they got a favorite sports team? For an upcoming game, purchase tickets and go along with them. Take them to a convention if they enjoy graphic novels. This indicates that you are well aware of them and that you like how enthusiastic they are about these unique things.

5. Become affectionate.
Most people like hugs, so when did you last send one to your partner? Showing them love often expresses respect for them. "I would like to be next to you because you are important to me," it says. Create time for their neck/back/bum embraces, kisses, holding hands, or a soft caress.

6. Take care of their duties.
Relationships often entail sharing responsibilities, so by taking on their duties more often, you can illustrate how thankful you are to have someone in your life. Only do these things yourself if they typically clean the bathroom or set out the dishwasher. This gives them a little bit of free time to enjoy themselves and relax. It also teaches you not to take what they do for granted.

7. Buy flowers for them.
Yes, it's the most convenient way of thanking someone, but it's successful, too. It is a beautiful surprise to send your partner flowers, and

without wanting to be sexist, it possibly has the most significant effect on women. Flowers are beautiful, and they represent the beauty you see in your partner (if you're wondering, that's a nice thing to say, too).

8. Offer them compliments.
People want to hear positive things about them that are talked about, which is universal. It makes us happy, and our self-esteem is improved. So thank your mate, not only for how they look but for how they are and the qualities that you like best. Praise them for the things they've been good at, whether they've been trying to make work-related or lifestyle changes. And if you don't think they're feeling too uncomfortable, tell them these sweet things in front of other people to show how proud you are of them.

9. Let them have a lie in.
For parents of young kids, this one is especially important. If you usually take it in turns to have a lie on the weekend, take one for the team and get up early on both Saturday and Sunday with your kid(s). It is evidence enough that you are willing to give up any precious duvet time that you love them and everything they do for you and your family.

10. Make them breakfast in bed
This one connects with the point before. Why not make use of that time by putting together a delicious breakfast if you let them stay in bed a little while longer while you get up? Dream about what they'd like best, maybe poached eggs and a fresh fruit salad on toast. Or fry some bacon, put it in a nice roll, and put some ketchup on it! Then, in bed, take it to them.

11. Take an interest in their life.
It feels good to have someone ask us what we are like and what is happening in our lives. It's even better when the person recalls things that

we've told them before and asks us about them. Do these things for your partner, and they will know in a larger context that you care for their well-being.

12. Listen attentively to their concerns.

Part of the previous argument would include being an outlet to vent or rant or spill out their worries for them. They will need someone to listen to them when they have stuff they are struggling with or working through. They want to feel respected and to know that you, too, care about their issues. By downplaying the issue, try not to diminish their feelings, but reassure them that you are there to help them through this.

13. Surprise them by getting a night out.

Couples will always fall into habits, and this is by no means a bad thing. But occasionally, it's nice to break out of this by doing something a little more special. Why not treat your partner to a night out every so often? This could include dinner, drinks, a show, a video, a concert, whatever you think they'd like the most. It doesn't have to be a very frequent event, or it might lose its influence, but now and then, show them that you value them by planning a night (or a day) out.

14. Cook (or order takeout) their favorite meal.

Putting your favorite meal on a plate is something to do more often if a night out is something to hold your sleeve up for only a few times a year. Make it yourself if you cook (if you don't, you should still give it a try anyway). Just order takeout, if it's easier. These days, you can get almost every cuisine you might imagine delivered to your door. This shows that you know them well, and because they deserve it, you want them to enjoy themselves.

15. Put yourself in a movie that you think they would enjoy.

Why not pick a movie to watch one night that you know they will enjoy, sticking to the theme of understanding them and allowing them to have fun. Or if you're not sure what they've seen already, give them an option of a few. Again, you make their happiness a priority, which is a strong indication that you value them. Or let them choose what to watch on TV if you don't have time for a movie, even if it means you have to experience something that you don't personally like that much.

16. Put their favorite music on.

If the two of you are just pottering around the house, on a similar note, why not put some music they enjoy on? The same goes for road trips. You should make a travel playlist of songs they can jam to in the car if you have to drive anywhere. It's the little things like these that make a person feel cared for.

17. Give them a massage.

Cheer them up by giving them a message if they have had a bad day or are feeling a little under the weather. Neck and shoulder massages are perfect for relieving stress and can also assist with headaches. If they've been on their feet all day, a foot massage will do wonders. Or go and give them a full body massage with the whole hog as they lie there and relax.

18. Tell them you're missing them.

Do not be afraid to tell your loved one that you miss them if you are apart for more than a day or two. This shows them how much you value having them in your life. It tells them that you are not taking them for granted and that their presence enhances your life.

19. Have faith in them.

There are many aspirations and dreams your partner is bound to have.

It matters to them, so they should be valuable to you. Help them, whether in their work, well-being, or something else, as they strive to accomplish things. Tell them that you believe in them, their talents, and their beliefs, and show them.

20. *Ask them for advice.*

Ask them about it if you are not sure what to do in a specific situation. You are expressing your faith in them by turning to them for advice. You say their opinion means a great deal to you. This demonstrates your respect for them by putting a value on their thoughts, ideas, and opinions.

21. *Reciprocate.*

When your partner does something good for you, take the time to think of how you can return the favor, no matter how small. That doesn't have to be right away, but you create a circle of respect for each other by reciprocating one kind gesture with another. If you're stuck with ideas, you may want to revisit any of the points above.

22. *Send them off sometimes with their mates.*

Often, acknowledging their desire to have a life of their own is the best way to show someone how appreciative you are of them. This implies telling them that it's about time they went out with their mates and let their hair down. If you know your partner prioritizes you and your family above all else, this is incredibly powerful. "Thank you for everything you're doing for me/us, but it's time to put yourself and your friends first for once."

23. *Put your phone away.*

If you're with your partner, ultimately be with them. That implies placing to one side every possible diversion and concentrating on them, what they are saying, and sometimes what they are not saying. Switch off your phone/tablet/ TV and put down something else you may be watching. Be there in the room as you speak to them, not somewhere else in your head. When somebody is not listening properly, people can tell, so do your best to communicate with them as they talk.

24. Make it feel comfortable for them.
Sometimes your partner may doubt themselves, their worth, and even your love for them. Reassure them always that they are the ones for whom you see a future, that you embrace them just the way they are, and that even if they don't always see it, you know how wonderful they are.

25. Trust.
We discussed this at length in this book. Trust is one of the primary pillars of a good partnership. Confidence is also a perfect way for your partner to express your gratitude. It shows you believe in them and their decisions when you trust them and make this clear to them. You know they're trying to do what's right and what's best for you both.

26. Politely and respectfully word your questions.
You'll have to ask your partner to do something occasionally. Maybe you need their help with the chores or somewhere to schedule a trip. Make your demands in a friendly manner if you want them to feel respected and not nagging. It reflects an appreciation for their time and resources and makes them more likely than grudgingly to happily consent.

27. Help them care for themselves.
People don't always find their well-being and health a priority. Life is still busy, and to remain happy and safe, the things we need to do slip by the wayside. An actual demonstration of your love of them is finding ways to enable them to look after themselves. In essence, you say to them, "Look, I need you in tip-top shape, because you're my rock." Do what it takes to

make them make themselves, whether it is the guiding force behind healthy eating plans or putting their mental health higher on the priority list.

28. Focus on yourself and your negative patterns.

Working on your flaws is a perfect way of expressing how happy you are to have your partner in your life. We all have facets of our character that we would like to modify. We have poor habits as well. Some of these things could make your partner a source of irritation. So why not try to fix these problems to show them how much you care about them?

29. Be prepared to apologize when you offend them.

No partnership is flawless. You're going to do stuff that upsets your girl-friend/boyfriend. But that's where respect comes into the equation again. You'll be able to swallow your pride and confess to any wrongdo-ing if you love others. You accept the pain you have caused by saying sorry. The intention not to do it again is also communicated.

30. Cut them some slack.

On the flip side of the previous argument, you have to accept that your partner is not perfect, and from time to time, they will annoy you. They're going to bother you, they're going to make you angry, they're going to make you sad, and several things in between. Accepting anyone as an imperfect human being, but respecting them nonetheless, with all their good points, is a beautiful show of respect.

Chapter 13: HOW TO RECOVER FROM A TOXIC RELATIONSHIP

F
ew things sound as refreshing as leaving a genuinely toxic bond. The relentless criticism, continuous confrontation, and emotional abuse are such a relief to escape. But what if you find out you took the poison with you?

Unfortunately, the toxicity of bad relationships, like a "gift that keeps on giving" (in the worst of ways) long after the relationship is over, most frequently outlasts the relationship itself. You may find that an emotionally manipulative parent's harsh voice has been internalized, and now your self-talk holds the same messages and tone as your parents did. Perhaps you find that the harsh assumptions of your ex-spouse have colored your relationship with your new partner. Or you could have left a partner for gas lighting, only to find that you still question what your senses and instincts tell you.

And decades later, the patterns we witness and the negative messages we hear can be sticky, stuck to our psyches, and continue to influence us. The longest hostages in abusive relationships are also our minds.

But that doesn't mean that we can never be free entirely. I've seen hundreds of individuals manage to liberate their minds from their past relationships. Although the job is never easy or quick, it can be immensely satisfying. In the final step of emancipation, the following concepts can be very beneficial.

Be careful with yourself. Bear in mind that retraining the brain takes time. You are a career in progress. Messages you have sent can be extraordinarily long-lived during childhood. Even if your toxic relationship was in adulthood and relatively brief, it could be challenging to break the habits you learned. When you learn that the harmful association continues to color your thoughts and emotions, grant yourself compassion. The unhealthy voice is only reinforced by being impatient with yourself; instead, give yourself the time and space required to recover.

Note the way you are talking to yourself. Be on the lookout for what your internal speech tells you. Be curious, like a scientist, as you discover your mind's patterns. The ideas you find must be written down. In reality, with pen and paper, getting the thoughts out of your mind is far more productive than just mentally noticing them. To begin learning more useful ways of thinking, you'll be in a much better place.

Adopt a more gentle voice. Start to substitute more positive ones for your harsh, critical feelings. Not sure what I'm going to say? Just imagine how you'd chat with a dear friend or a kid of your own. Practice consciously using this gentle answer when you catch the old way of speaking to yourself. For example, if you're making a dumb mistake, substitute, "You're such an idiot!" "with," They all make mistakes. What will you learn for next time from this one?

Lead with compassion. To practice self-kindness, don't wait until you catch the harsh internal expression. Instead, when you reprogram your mind, be positive. In the morning, begin training your thoughts before your feet even hit the floor. Write down three ideas that you want to reinforce and leave them on your table at the bedside. When you wake up, before you get out of bed, read and repeat those thoughts to yourself. You might, for instance, practice thoughts like, "See what occurs when you fill your head with emotions that serve you well," "I'm enough to face whatever this day brings."

Find your courage. Do more of the tasks that keep you alive, the things you love and are good at. You might have given up these things during your dysfunctional relationship because deceptive individuals usually don't want to see you succeed. A useful antidote to seeing yourself as vulnerable or incompetent is experiencing your competence.

Embracing who you are. Toxic relationships often lead us to conceal essential parts of ourselves or to reject them. For instance, if you were naturally exuberant, you may have been guided to bury the joyful part of yourself by a frequently critical parent. Find quiet moments to listen to what longs to be shared. Look inside for impulses that could squash you. For more of your experience, start to make room.

Be where you are. Toxic relationships can lead you not only to feel bad about who you are but about even current ones, as though you don't have the right to take up any room at all. But nothing to apologize for is your existence. Since the world has seen fit to welcome your presence, you have a right to be here. Don't want to shrink your body from being where you are, or justify yourself. Stand strong, unapologetically, in the room you occupy. They're yours. Say the words to yourself as you breathe in, "I Am." As you exhale, say to yourself, "Here." Exactly where you belong.

Finally, take heart. Your mind will once again be yours with focus and practice. In the method, each time you grab the old patterns, count it a win. The fact that you note them implies that you are learning, that you are developing, and that you are coming home to yourself.

The Purpose of Our Emotions

In how we think and act, emotions can play a significant role. The feelings we experience every day will cause us to take action and affect our decisions, both large and small, about our lives. It is essential to understand the three critical components of emotion to truly understand feelings.

An emotion has three parts:

1. A subjective aspect (how the emotion is experienced)
2. A physiological element (how the body reacts to the feeling)
3. An expressive part (how you act in response to your feelings)

In the function and intent of your emotional responses, these distinct elements may play a role.

Emotions, such as a burst of irritation at a co-worker, may be short-lived or long-lasting, such as sustaining sorrow over a relationship's loss. But why do we experience emotions, exactly? What position are they serving?

Emotions can encourage us to take measures

You will experience a lot of anxiety when faced with a nerve-wracking exam about whether you will do well and how the test will affect your final score. You might be more likely to study because of these emotional answers. You had the drive to take action and do something constructive to increase your chances of having a good grade because you encountered a specific emotion.

To experience positive feelings and decrease the risk of experiencing negative emotions, we also prefer to take these actions. For instance, you could search for social activities or hobbies that offer you a sense of pleasure, contentment, and excitement. On the other hand, circumstances that might lead to boredom, frustration, or anxiety, you would avoid.

Emotions assist us in living, succeeding and escaping danger
The naturalist Charles Darwin claimed that emotions adapt to survival and reproduction in both humans and animals. We are likely to confront the root of our frustration when we are upset. We are more likely to escape the danger when we feel fear. We could look for a mate and reproduce when we feel love. In our lives, emotions play an adaptive role by inspiring us to act quickly and take actions that increase our chances of survival and achievement.

Emotions will assist us in making decisions
From what we decide to have for breakfast to what candidates we want to vote for in political elections, our feelings have a big impact on our decisions. Researchers have also found that individuals with certain brain injury levels that impair their capacity to perceive emotions also have a diminished ability to make good choices.
Even in conditions where we think our choices are driven solely by logic and rationality, feelings play a crucial role. In decision making, Emotional Intelligence, or our ability to recognize and control emotions, feelings have been shown to play an important role.

Emotions help other individuals to recognize us
It is essential to provide clues when we communicate with other individuals to understand how we feel. Via body language, such as different facial expressions associated with the specific emotions we feel, these signals can include emotional expression. It could mean specifically stating how we feel in other situations. We send them valuable details when we tell friends or family members that we feel happy, sad, excited, or afraid, which they can then use to take action.

Emotions Help Us Understand Others
Much as our feelings provide others with useful information, we are

provided a wealth of social information by those around us' emotional expressions. Social communication is an integral part of our everyday lives and relationships, and it is necessary to understand and respond to others' emotions.

It enables us to respond appropriately to our friends, family, and loved ones and develop more profound, more meaningful relationships. It also helps us connect efficiently in several social contexts, from interacting with an unhappy client to handling a hot-headed employee.

One of the first scholars to study emotions scientifically was Charles Darwin. Emotional displays may also play an essential role in protection and survival, he suggested. It would clearly show that the creature was angry and defensive if you met a hissing or spitting animal, causing you to back off and escape the potential threat. Understanding others' emotional displays gives us a good insight into how we would need to respond in a specific situation.

Our emotions serve a wide range of purposes, as you have discovered. Fleeting, constant, intense, complex, and even life-changing emotions can be. They can inspire us to behave in specific ways and give us the support and resources we need to engage in our social environments in a meaningful way.

Chapter 14: ESTABLISHING AND SUSTAINING RELATIONSHIPS QUALITY

Boundaries

In the physical world, boundaries are things that separate one thing from another, like walls separating the outside from the inside of a house. While they have no physical structure, by separating individuals' private parts from the public parts, personal boundaries work quite like walls. Similarly, the relationships with others are defined by boundaries that determine the required degree of closeness to and relationship. For example, one such boundary may distinguish whether or not someone is a 'mate' (friends are 'within' the boundary, while non-friends (strangers, acquaintances, etc.) are outside it). How a person will respond to you, what they will be willing to share with you, and what they expect from you in exchange will be largely driven by where you stand about the boundaries of each other. For instance, you may share personal life details with friends, but your decision to share the same information with the supermarket checkout clerk (a non-friend) will cause people to look at you funny. It's essential to respect the limits of people and your limits, so you don't do or say the wrong thing and ruin a significant relationship. The boundaries of each individual are partly deduced from their culture. Because of this, sharing a shared culture with someone you associate with makes it easier for you to understand what that person is going to be comfortable with and what they are going to be uncomfortable with. Another part of a person's boundaries will be personal, and you'll need to get to know them to know what they are. When you remain within appropriate boundaries (cultural, personal, etc.) for the people you relate to, you will have the greatest success in establishing and sustaining relationships.

Comprehension and respect for cultural differences are especially crucial when communicating with people you don't know very well. For example, respecting existing social tabus is a good idea and never finding yourself 'above the rules' about those with whom you are in relations. For example, telling off-color or 'dirty' jokes may be off-putting in a mixed company. Worse, you might think making an off-color joke is just an attempt at humor, while someone in your audience might see it as sexual assault. Do not presume that it is just because you think a specific action is okay that the person or people to whom you relate agree!

Also, it is necessary to know your boundaries. For example, learning how to feel comfortable avoiding alcohol even though it's socially acceptable to have a drink is part of being a well-recovered alcoholic. Recovering alcoholics who do not learn to accept their alcohol limits and boundaries tend not to remain in treatment for a very long time.

Communication

Boundaries tell you how not to behave, but they're not helping you to be consistent about how to act. Maintenance of relationships gets a lot simpler when you understand how to convey in simple and unambiguous terms what you want from others. If you want to become close to someone emotionally, you'll need to share your feelings and thoughts with that person. When you remain completely emotionally guarded, you ruin the chances of closeness and affection and just debate ideas.

The boundaries control the form of contact that is suitable for any specific partnership between the partners that exist (or should exist). For example, sharing your feelings with your partner is acceptable but not necessarily with your boss. On the other hand, your employer might be more interested in your creative thoughts than your spouse.

If a specific form of conversation is underway, bear in mind that if one partner suddenly wants to turn to some kind of conversation, it can be disorienting. This is exactly what happens in marriages when one partner wants to talk about feelings, and the other partner reacts by providing 'solutions;' by attempting to solve the problem rather than acknowledging the pain, the 'feeling' partner does not feel noticed in such situations and leaves the conversation disappointed. Before you talk or respond to your supervisor or your significant other, it is particularly important to take this into account, as you are likely to rely the most on these people.

Commitment

Being committed to a relationship simply means taking the relationship seriously: showing reciprocity towards the relationship, respecting its limits, and making every effort to connect and listen clearly and well. You build up a kind of trust with your relationship partners by doing those things over time. They come to trust you and care for you and expect you to help them if they experience difficulties. This goodwill is what motivates others to assist you when you need help. The relationships of high quality that will support you through times of need and that inspire your resilience will appear to be the ones you have dedicated yourself to. To the point that you can't commit to a relationship (romantic or otherwise) when you can need it, you won't be able to count on that relationship.

Establishing and sustaining quality relationships

Creating new relationships and nurturing old ones requires time and effort, but a difficult thing to do is not required and can also be a lot of fun. First, you have to determine that relationships will be a priority over other important life-filling things, including your job. Next, you need to find out how to break your limited time and resources. Some people are going to want to concentrate on building new relationships (romances, friendships, etc.) while others are going to want to focus on strengthening established relationships with family members, partners, and important, more significant friends.

Having found out the relationships you want to concentrate on, the next challenge is to build ways to maintain the relationship you have selected. If you're trying to build a new relationship, you'll want to see proper dating partners' meetings. If you're looking for new friends, you'll need to put yourself in new social circumstances that will give you opportunities to meet like-minded individuals. Volunteer programs in the neighborhood, civic groups, clubs and hobby groups, religious groups, gyms and fitness classes, and local sporting activities can be excellent places to meet people. Bear in mind that in most situations, you will have to take the lead by involving yourself in arranging and coordinating events and by extending social deals to people you like. Wait for no longer for anyone else to make their first move. Instead, reach out to others in a constructive way. While most people welcome the opportunity to make new friends, they're also busy and won't necessarily be looking for you (or others) alone. Although getting open to others entails some degree of risk, not having a social network has far greater negative consequences. If relationships are new or old, it's more or less the same method of strengthening them so that they increase consistency and vitality. To express your desire for continued or revived intimacy, you will need to build opportunities. One way of showing concern is to take the lead in arranging get-togethers and events while another is open contact about your positive feelings about the relationship. Your taking the time to do fun and meaningful things that help the people you want to be closer to will also cause reciprocity on their part, which will improve the relation-ship.

Making an effort to preserve current partnerships means going the extra mile even while doing so. We're constantly adjusting the relations we make in our lives. Children are born and grow up, people's expectations and desires change, and families are moving across the world, searching for new opportunities. As a result of this move, a lot of good relationships end because they become difficult to maintain. Such tragic ends do not occur when both parties in the relationship regularly stay in touch. For instance, if you are moving away from family around the country, make it a point to call your family once a week. A little upkeep can go a long way.

TIPS FOR GOOD PARTNERSHIP

Creation of a healthy relationship

All romantic relationships go through ups and downs, and they all re-quire effort, dedication, and willingness with your partner to adapt and adjust. But if your relationship is just beginning or you've been together for years, you should take action to create a healthier relationship. Even if you have endured several broken relationships in the past or have struggled before to rekindle the flames of passion in your current rela-tionship, you will learn to remain connected, find satisfaction and enjoy lasting happiness.

What constitutes a stable relationship?

Every relationship is special, and there are several different reasons why people come together. Part of what determines a good relationship is having a shared vision about exactly what you want to be and where you want the relationship to go. And that's something you'll only know if you speak to your partner sincerely and honestly. There are also some attributes that most stable partnerships have in common, however. Knowing these fundamental concepts will help sustain positive, satisfying, and exciting relationships, whatever goals you work for or challenges you to face together.

You hold a strong emotional bond with each other. You make us feel happy and emotionally pleased with each other. There is a distinction between loving one another and feeling loved. It makes you feel welcomed and appreciated by your partner when you feel special like someone does understand you. Some couples are trapped in peaceful coexistence but without the partners being emotionally very connected to each other. Although the union may seem secure on the surface, a lack of mutual interaction and emotional connection just adds tension between two individuals.

You don't care about (respectful) disagreement. Some couples calmly talk things out while others can lift their voices and disagree passionately. However, the trick of a good connection is not to be afraid of confrontation. You must feel comfortable saying things that concern you without fear of retribution, and you must be able to settle disputes without embarrassment, disrespect, or insistence on being right.

You hold alive partnerships and desires outside. Despite the claims of romantic novels or films, nobody can fulfill all your needs. In reality, it can place undue pressure on a partnership to expect too much from your partner. It is necessary to retain your own identity outside of the relationship to stimulate and enrich your romantic relationship, sustain relationships with family and friends, and retain your hobbies and interests.

You communicate freely, frankly. Good communication is an integral part of every connection. It will increase trust and reinforce the bond between you when both parties know what they want from the relationship and feel comfortable sharing their needs, fears, and desires.

To fall in love, vs. to remain in love

Typically falling in love seems to only happen to most people. It is remaining in love — or maintaining the experience of "falling in love"—that demands dedication and effort. It's well worth the effort, though, with its rewards. A safe, stable romantic relationship will serve as an enduring source of support and satisfaction in your life, improving all aspects of your wellbeing through good and bad times. You can create a lasting relationship that lasts — even for a lifetime — by taking steps now to maintain or rekindle your falling in love experience.

Many couples only concentrate on their relationships when there are real, imminent obstacles to resolve. When the issues are resolved, they frequently turn their focus back to their jobs, children, or other interests. Romantic relationships, however, involve constant focus and dedication to thriving love. This will take your commitment and effort as long as the wellbeing of a romantic relationship remains important to you. Finding and resolving a minor issue in your relationship will also help keep it from getting bigger down the road. The following tips will help you maintain the love connection and sustain your romantic relationship

Tip1: Invest in face-to-face quality time

Looking at and listening to one another, you fall in love. If you carry on looking and listening in the same attentive ways, you will continue the long-term falling in love experience. You still have fond memories of the first time you met your loved one. Everything seemed fresh and exciting, and you probably spent hours just talking or coming up with fun new things to do. However, as time goes on, the pressures of work, family, other responsibilities, and the need for the time we all have for ourselves will make it more difficult to find time together.

Many couples notice that they are steadily replacing the face-to-face touch of their early dating days with rushed texts, emails, and instant messages. Although digital communication is perfect for certain reasons, it does not affect the brain and nervous system as much as face-to-face communication in a positive way. It's nice to give your partner a text or voice message saying, "I love you," but if you barely look at them or have the time to sit down together, they'll always feel you don't understand or respect them. And as a pair, you'll get more distant or separated. The emotional signals that both of you need to feel loved can only be expressed in person so no matter how busy life becomes, it is important to spend time together.

Commit to spend a certain amount of quality time together regularly. No matter how busy you are, take a couple of minutes per day to put your mobile devices down, stop worrying about other things, and just concentrate on and communicate with your partner!

Find something you enjoy doing together, whether it's a joint sport, dance class, day-to-day walk, or relaxing over a morning cup of coffee. Gather something new to do. It can be a fun way to connect and keep things exciting, doing new things together. It can be as easy as trying out a new restaurant or going on a day trip to a place you were never before. To focus on having fun together. In the early stages of a partnership, couples are often more humorous and playful. But often, this playful mindset may be lost as life problems tend to get in the way or old resentments begin to build up. In reality, keeping a sense of humor will help you get through difficult times, minimize stress, and work through problems more easily. Think of fun ways to surprise your partner, such as taking flowers home or booking a table in their favorite restaurant in an unconventional way. Playing with pets or little kids will help you reconnect with your fun side too.

Tip 2: Stay linked through communication
Good communication is a key aspect of a successful partnership. You feel comfortable and secure when you have a healthy emotional bond with your partner. When people stop interacting well, they stop connecting well, and periods of transition or stress will bring the disconnect out. It may sound complicated, but you can generally work through any problems you face as long as you talk.

Say what you need to your partner and don't make them guess. Chatting about what you need isn't always convenient. For one, many of us, in a relationship, do not spend enough time thinking about what is important to us. And even though you know what you need, it can make you feel insecure, humiliated, or even ashamed of talking about it. Yet look at it from your partner's perspective. It's a joy to give support and empathy to those you love, not a burden.

If you've known each other for a while, you might imagine your partner has a pretty good idea of what you're thinking and what you need. Your partner isn't a mind-reader, though. Although your partner may have some idea, voicing your needs explicitly is much easier to prevent any misunderstanding.

Your partner may feel something, but maybe that isn't what you need. What's more, people are evolving, and for example, what you needed and wanted five years ago can be very different now. So instead of allowing frustration, confusion, or rage to develop when your partner gets it wrong all the time, get used to telling them exactly what you need. Take note of the nonverbal clues from your partner (More on this in Chapter 20). Too much of our experience is expressed by what we don't say. Nonverbal signs, which include eye contact, voice tone, stance, and movements like leaning forward, crossing your arms, or touching someone's hand, convey much more than words. If you can pick up the nonverbal signs or "body language" from your partner, you'll be able to tell them how they really feel and respond accordingly.

A person has to understand their own, and the nonverbal signs of their partner, for a relationship to function well. Responses to your partner can vary from yours. For example, one person may find a romantic mode of communication after a stressful day — whereas another may just want to go for a walk or sit and talk together.

Also, making sure that what you say suits your body language is crucial. If you're saying, "I'm fine," but you're clenching your teeth and looking away, then your body indicates that you're anything but "good."

You feel cherished and satisfied when you receive positive emotional signs from your partner, and when you give positive emotional signals, your partner feels the same. When you stop taking an interest in your own or your partner's feelings, the bond between you will be weakened, and your ability to communicate will suffer, particularly during stressful times.

Become a good listener. Although much focus is placed on talking in our culture, if you can learn to listen in a way that makes another person feel respected and understood, you can create a deeper, stronger bond between yourself.

There is a major difference between listening and hearing in this manner. When you listen — when you're involved with what's being said — you're going to hear the subtle intonations in your partner's voice showing you how they feel and the feelings they're trying to communicate.

Being a good listener is not about agreeing with your partner or changing your mind. But it can help you find common viewpoints that will help you overcome disputes.

Tip 3: Keep alive the physical intimacy

Communication is a central aspect of human life. Studies on infants have shown that frequent, affectionate interaction is essential for brain growth. And the advantages don't end in infancy. Affected touch increases the levels of oxytocin in the body, a hormone affecting bonding and connection.

Although sex is always a pillar of a committed relationship, the only form of physical intimacy should not be this. Equally significant is the regular, affectionate touch — holding hands, embracing, kissing. Of course, being sensitive to what your partner likes is crucial. Unwanted contact or unwanted overtures will stress and withdraw the other person – just what you don't want. Like so many other facets of a good partnership, this can be down to how much you interact with your partner about your desires and intentions.

Even if you have to think about pressing workloads or young kids, you can help keep physical intimacy alive by carving out a couple of daily occasions, whether it's in the form of a date night or just an hour at the end of the day where you can relax and chat or hold your hands.

Tip 4: Learn how to give and take in your relationship

If you're going to get what you want in a relationship 100 percent of the time, you're setting up for disappointment. Compromise creates stable relationships. However, ensuring that there is a fair exchange that requires effort on the part of every party.

Recognize what counts for your partner. Knowing what matters to your partner will go a long way towards building goodwill and a consensus environment. On the flip side, it's also critical that your partner understands your desires and that you explicitly state them. Spending endlessly on others at the detriment of your own needs can only create frustration and anger.

Don't set your target to "win." It will be impossible to find a compromise if you approach your partner with the mentality that things have to be your way, or else. This attitude often stems from not getting your needs met while being younger, or it may be years of cumulative frustration in the relationship hitting a boiling point. Having strong opinions about something is OK, but your partner also needs to be heard. Be respectful of the other person and their point of view.

Learn how to settle the conflict with dignity. Conflict is inevitable in any relationship, but both parties need to feel they've been understood to maintain a relationship healthy. The goal is not to win but to preserve and improve the partnership.

Assure that you fight equally. Keep your mind on the problem and respect the other person. Don't launch debates over things that are unchangeable.

Don't threaten anyone explicitly but use comments about "I" to express how you feel. For example, try "I feel bad when you do that," instead of saying, "You make me feel bad."

Do not bring ancient claims into the mix. Instead of looking at past disputes or grudges, and taking the blame, concentrate on what you can do to fix the issue in the here and now.

Take a break as tempers flare. Take a few minutes to ease the tension and calm down before saying anything or doing something that you would regret. Mind that you disagree with the one you love.

Knowing when to let go. Suppose a settlement cannot be made, consent to disagree. It takes two people to go on with an argument. If there is a disagreement, you can opt to disengage and move forward.

Tip 5: Stand ready for ups and downs

It's important to remember that any relationship has ups and downs. You're not going to be on the same page. Often, one person can deal with a problem that stresses them, including the death of a close family member. Other incidents, such as job loss or serious health conditions, may impact both partners and make it difficult to interrelate. You may have various ideas about handling finances or raising kids. Different people deal differently with stress, and misunderstandings may easily turn to irritation and resentment.

Don't take your relationship issues out. The pressures on life will make us tense for short. If you're feeling a lot of tension, it might seem easier to end up with your partner and feel even better to snap at them. Initially, fighting like this may feel like a relief, but it poisons your relationship slowly. Find better ways to handle the tension, anger, and annoyance more healthily.

Trying to force a solution can lead to even more issues. Everyone is working in their way through challenges and issues. Please note you are a team. Continuing together to step forward will get you through the tough spots.

Look back at the relationship's early stages. Share the moments that brought the two of you together, analyze the point at which you started to break apart, and discuss how you can work together to rekindle the feeling of falling in love.

Be open to alterations. Change is inevitable in life, and if you go with it or fight it, it will happen. Flexibility is essential to adapt to the transition that often takes place in every relationship, and it helps you to develop together in both the good and the bad times.

Chapter 15:

UNDERSTANDING THE
IMPORTANCE OF SELF-CARE

These days self-care is a common subject, but it's often poorly explained. Maybe you keep seeing it listed in self-help books or magazine articles, and yet you don't have a good sense of how to apply it to your life. You will find it wishy-washy or ambiguous. Alternatively, you might not be persuaded you should be doing routine self-care. Maybe you think that your money is saved better to work and to look after others.

So, what is self-care, and why does it matter so? As it turns out, there are many different self-care habits, and not all of them suit everyone. This chapter will take you through the reasons in your routine why you need at least some form of self-care, and help you understand the practical changes you need to make.

What Is Self-Care? The Self-Care Concept

Self-care is a broad word that includes just about everything that you do for yourself to be healthy. To put it simply, it's about being as kind to yourself as you will be to anyone. It is partly about understanding when the resources run low, and stepping back to replenish them instead of making them all drain away.

In the meantime, it also includes incorporating self-compassion into your life in a manner that helps avoid even a burnout. It is important to note, however, that not all that feels good is self-care. We can all be tempted to take advantage of unhealthy coping mechanisms such as drugs, alcohol, over-eating, and risk-taking. These self-destructive activities help us regulate emotional challenges, but the relief is temporary. The difference between unhealthy mechanisms of coping and self-care is that the latter is uncontroversially good to you. When properly practiced, self-care has long-term benefits for the mind, body, or both.

Self-care advantages

With a definition of self-care on the table, we can turn now and look at what happens to us when we apply it to our lives. Why is self-care essential, then? As indicated above, the benefits of self-care are many. The most evident relates to the levels of mood and electricity. The study, though, as it turns out, also shows broader benefits.

Top 6 Self-care benefits:

Improved rendering. When you learn to say "no" to things that exaggerate you and begin to make time for things that matter more, you slow down life in a wonderful way. This brings the goals to a sharper focus and lets you concentrate on what you're doing.

Improved disease resistance. There is evidence that most practices of self-care trigger the Parasympathetic Nervous System (PNS). This means that the body enters a calming, rejuvenating state, helping it improve its immune system.

Improved physical fitness. Similar to the previous argument, fewer colds, flu cases, and upset stomachs also come with improved self-care. Surely less tension and a stronger immune system will make you feel more physically healthy and strong inside and outside.

Improved Self-esteem. You send a constructive message to your subconscious when you consistently carve out time that is simply about being nice to yourself and fulfilling your own needs. Specifically, you have intrinsic worth and handle yourself like you matter. This can go a long way towards suppressing your critical inner voice and negative self-talk.

Practicing self-care allows you to think about what you want to do. The task of finding out what makes you feel inspired and motivated will help you understand yourself much better. This can also often spark a career change or a reprioritization of previously neglected hobbies.

Contribute more. You may think you're egoistic when you're good to yourself. Self-care also gives you the support you need to be compassionate towards others. Giving compassion is a bit like filling a bucket; if you don't have enough of your own, you cannot fill anyone else's!

TYPES OF SELF-CARE

One of the principal reasons people make to neglect self-care activities is that they simply don't have time. The great news is that there are many different self-care activities, and none of them are overly daunting or require preparation. The trick is to find any you like and which suits your life and values. When you begin to incorporate emotional self-care into your life, you're likely to become intensely protective and wonder how you've ever been without it!

Here are the five major self-care categories, along with examples of how they can benefit you. We're also going to look at specific self-care examples within categories that should help you think about things you're going to enjoy, especially.

1. Sensory

Sensory self-care helps to help relax the mind. When you are tuning in the specifics of the stimuli all around you, living in the present moment is simpler. And when you're in the moment, you can more easily let go of past-related resentments or potential anxieties.

Consider all the senses as you think about the practice of sensory self-care: touch, smell, sound, and sight. Some people are more sensitive to one sense than others, so ask yourself what that meaning might be for you.

The following sensory self-care examples include at least one sense but sometimes more.

Sensory Suggestions for self-care

- Cuddling under a warm blanket.
- Driving out into the fields and reflecting on the air scent.
- Watching candle fires or a flare.
- During a hot bath or shower, feel the warmth on your face.
- The emphasis on your breathing patterns.
- Lying down with your eyes closed and listening to the album.
- Sitting at sunny afternoon temperatures.
- Have a square of the most delicious chocolate available.
- Walk barefoot across the grass.
- Massage using essential oils.
- Carry a pet in the arms.

2. Emotional

One of the best self-care tips for your mental well-being is to make sure you're completely involved with your emotions. In reality, this helps with tension when you face them head-on.

You may feel tempted to force down feelings like depression or rage but feeling them, acknowledging them, and moving on is safe.

Know the emotions in themselves are not "good" or "evil." You are not to blame for the emotions you feel; you are to blame only for how you react to them.

Consider one or more of the following on this subject if you wish to practice better emotional self-care.

Ideas about mental self-care:

- Carry a regular publication and be completely frank about your thoughts.
- See a psychiatrist, even though this is only for 8-10 general personal growth sessions.
- Write a list of "things you know" to broaden your vocabulary.
- Make time to be with a friend or member of your family who knows you.
- Let's cry when you have to.
- Invite yourself to laugh with old memories or funny images.
- Sing along with a song that reflects the current feelings best.

3. Spiritual

If you are not religious, you might be tempted to skim-read or miss this segment entirely. Spiritual self-care, though, isn't just about believing in a god. It refers just as much to the atheists and agnostics as to religious people. Spiritual self-care is about coming into harmony with your beliefs and what matters to you. Self-care tips for depression also emphasize that it is crucial to your healing to develop a sense of purpose. Below are some flexible examples that can help.

Ideas about personal self-care:

- Continue the daily practice of meditation or mindfulness.
- Attend every service, religious or humanistic.
- Read some poems.
- Walk-in nature, and think of the beauty around you.

213

- Make a regular list of 5-10 items, which will make you feel thankful.
- Be imaginative, be it by painting, music, writing, or something else.
- Make a list of 5-10 items that will make you feel good, then ask yourself how these items can be better integrated into your life.
- Say statements that underpin your sense of self and intent.
- Go on a trip with the sole intention of taking pictures of things that inspire you.

4. Physical

Indeed the value of self-care applies to strictly physical aspects of your wellbeing. Physical exercise is important not only for the well-being of the body but also to help you let off steam. You may think there's nothing fun or self-compassionate about going to the gym, but that's just too limited a physical self-care way to think about. Instead, extend the concept by thinking about the lists below.

Ideas for Physical Self-Care:

- Dance to the songs you love
- Yoga, again. Even if you have never tried it, the poses are perfect for beginners.
- Attend a workshop and learn a new sport.
- Go running with your puppy!
- Cycle down the countryside.
- Go only for a stroll.

Often note that physical self-care is about the stuff you don't do as much as the stuff you're doing! Thus:

- Nap when the need arises. Just 20 minutes will make you feel comfortable mentally and physically.
- Reply "no" to invites when you're just too lazy to have fun with them.

- Do not force yourself to perform your workout routine when you are tired or are unwell.

- Engage in 7-9 hours of nightly sleep, barring extraordinary circumstances.

5. Social

Lastly, social self-care is another category that is important to all of us. Depending on whether you are an introvert or an extrovert, it may look different. However, for a wide number of people, it is important to interact with other people for happiness. It's making you realize you're not alone. Moreover, it can also give us a feeling of being truly "seen" by others. Particularly this can help us battle loneliness and isolation.

Social self-care isn't just about doing things for others' benefit, but about wanting to do things for others that make you feel good.

Social Suggestions for self-care:

- Arrange a lunch or dinner date with a wonderful friend.

- Send an email to someone who lives a long way away but loves you.

- Attain anyone you like but haven't seen them in a while.

- Consider joining a group of individuals who share your interests.

- Avoid socializing with the ones who discredit or kill you.

- Strike up an engaging conversation with others.

- Join a support group for those dealing with the same problems as you do.

- Sign up for the class to learn more at the same time and meet new people.

TIPS ON SELF-CARE

1. Create a list of things that you are feeling restorative.

It might be taking a walk outside, petting your dog, meditating, baking, painting, arranging your wardrobe, listening to a podcast, or something else you enjoy calming tension. "Save it on your tablet or anywhere you can easily access it," said Lauren Donelson, a Seattle writer and yoga instructor who is training to be a therapist. "Ideally, you'd make this list on a day that you're feeling pretty good, so that you don't have to worry about self-care things that you feel burned out — which happens to everybody."

2. Identify that for which you are thankful.
A lot is happening in the world, particularly right now, to be frustrated, angry, and scared about. But in these darker times, it is much more important to find things — large and small — that we're grateful for. "We should turn our focus on what is positive in our lives or question our propensity to be drawn into negative thinking," said Tamara Levitt, head of mindfulness at the Peaceful meditation app. "Gratitude is a practice like everything else, and neuroscience teaches us that if we do our best to maintain love, we will find something to be thankful for, even in times of loss and sorrow."

Write down three items every day for which you are grateful in a newspaper, save them on your phone in the Notes app, or read them out loud with a loved one. "It could be the health care staff or the service sector, the weather or a great piece of toast," "Your attempt to discover goodness in this chaos is a good exercise for your brain and mood."

3. Set Job limits.
With many people working from home, living spaces now act as office spaces and blur the distinction between work and play. "It can be tempting to answer emails as soon as you wake up in the morning, or when you eat dinner, respond to messages from your boss," Donelson said. Consider sticking to the same start and end times for your workday to build more structure.

"If you don't usually enter the office before 9 a.m., don't sign up for work before 9 a.m.," "And when you'd normally leave the workplace, stop working." Place your laptop and any other work supplies in a cabinet, tub, or drawer while you're not on the clock until you need them again. Out of sight, out of the heart.

4. Make a "done" list.
Taking a look at a long list of unfinished projects on your to-do list would just make you feel bad about yourself. Instead, I recommend making a "full" list of all of the things that you've already completed. "Consider all of the things that you have accomplished, big and small, from grocery shopping to folding laundry to getting children through a school day," Donelson said. "Beat yourself on the back to produce something at all at a time."

5. Put limitations on your absorption of news.
"Yeah, keeping up with the news and the latest trends is important, but not at the expense of your wellbeing, "When the news becomes a source of fear, anxiety, and futility, it's time to step back." Block unique time slots to limit your consumption where you encourage yourself to read or watch the news and try to stop looking for updates otherwise. "Respect the boundaries which you set and if you find that even a small dose of news feels too much, be aware of how you feel, and step away."

6. Open a book.
Put your mobile down and pick up a book. Take the book you intended to read and try to get 30 minutes of reading in a day. It just doesn't have to be 30 minutes straight. You might also break it up, three times a day doing something like 10 minutes reading.

7. Let yourself grieve the major and the minor losses.

People are currently grieving all sorts of losses: the loss of their loved ones, their careers, their health, their plans, their daily habits, just to name a few. What might feel like declining wellbeing with the crushing burden of your health care job or three children at home. Take a breath and let yourself feel without judgment whatever you feel. When you're done, I suggest taking a pen and paper and writing down all the supporting forces in your life.

They may be "real, technical, economical, family-friendly." "The top-tier helpful colleagues, mentoring, the outstanding boss, the caring wedding vendors, the things you do, your strengths, or your ability to withstand tough times before and now."

8. Pause every day to check in on yourself.

Taking the time daily to check in with yourself will bring focus and understanding to a dizzying moment, otherwise. I suggest these three questions to ask yourself: "What's captivating your thoughts right now?" "What feelings or physical sensations do you feel or experience?" and "What would you like to achieve today?"

9. Try breathing exercises.

One of my favorite soothing practices is called "box breathing." The technique outlined below is popular among Navy SEALs, and takes only five minutes:

- Step 1: 4 seconds to inhale.
- Step 2: 4 seconds to hold air in your lungs.
- Step 3: Exhale for 4 seconds and clear all the air in your lungs.
- Step 4: Stay your lungs empty for 4 seconds.
- Step 5: Repeat 5 minutes.

10. Creating a bedtime routine to foster healthy sleeping habits.

Having a good night's sleep will set an optimistic tone for your day and help you manage your anxiety and stress better. Create a nighttime routine to encourage this that helps your body wind down and puts you in sleep mode. "Try to have a hot bath or shower because hot water will help lower the core body temperature required to start and sustain a good night's sleep," The sleepy time tea and a decent book – and no scrolling Instagram! – And you're going to be out in no time.

11. Keep a journal.

If you feel weighed down by rushing thoughts, consider beginning a journaling practice. Setting aside some time to focus on yourself will help you relax your busy mind and explain and process what you are feeling. If it's something you're dealing with, try to take 10 minutes a day to focus on how you feel, write down any worries or doubts, and agree if feeling these things is normal.

Not sure where to get started? Some journaling exercises can be found online or in books that contain prompts and questions designed to sharpen your introspection skills. Daily self-reflection helps you remain linked to yourself, which means that you can retain your inner balance and power when external elements in your life start to change.

12. Be extra gentle.

These days, are they not shooting on all the cylinders? Take the slack on yourself. Many people find it hard to feel less inspired than normal when they really should practice self-compassion. Instead of beating yourself up for not being 'leveling-up' right now, consider validating yourself with good self-talking like, "This is hard." "My body reacts to an immediate threat." "I am not alone"'

Consider what you would say during this time to a dear friend or relative who is struggling.

Then say these things to yourself.

40 MORE THOUGHTS ON SELF-CARE

1. Practice replacing the words with the 'should.'

2. Take another path to work or the stores.

3. Catch an episode from your favorite television show. Write down than five reasons why you like it.

4. Build a modern, safe, day-to-day routine, and incorporate it into your life.

5. Ignore spammy emails.

6. Reflect on past successes and milestones.

7. Take 15 minutes to drink the heat.

8. Please visit the nearest library.

9. Do a job in your home that you have put off.

10. Watch videos and speeches which are motivating.

11. Speak to a loved one about their thoughts or habits about self-care.

12. Let's joke!

13. Write a summary of a business you have recently enjoyed (such as a restaurant or product you've bought).

14. Create your room.

15. Work on a puzzle you like, a Sudoku puzzle, crossword, or jigsaw, for example.

16. Start a journal.

17. Write out a new statement.

18. Make sure you currently drink at least eight glasses of water.

19. Dance like nobody watches.

20. Learn how to do a massage to yourself.

21. Write a message to the older self.

22. Write a letter to the old self.

23. Do a Digital Detox for 6 hours.

24. Go to your theater.

25. Do something to benefit charity.

26. Clean your car, handbag, and jacket pockets, if necessary.

27. Find a local counselor or therapist.

28. Do something fun that you used to do as a child.

29. Cook a meal you never had before.

30. Do local history research.

31. Set up regular phone notifications to remind you that you're great!

32. Clean your desk or place of employment.

33. Watch a documentary.

34. Take a day of mental health when you feel especially depressed and call in sick to work.

35. Change your bedsheets and have a night early.

36. Read your favorite book over again.

37. Consider forming a community group in your local area.

38. Read motivational quotes.

39. Create a self-care box filled with items like candles, essential oils, affirmation cards, ideas about self-care, a book, etc.

40. Smile in the mirror!

Chapter 16: THE BENEFITS OF MEDITATION

For thousands of years, meditation has been practiced. Originally meditation was intended to help deepen awareness of the sacred and spiritual powers of creation. Meditation is widely used nowadays for relaxation and reduction of stress. Meditation is used as a form of complementary therapy for the mind-body. Meditation will yield a deep state of relaxation and a relaxed mind.

You concentrate your attention during meditation, removing the stream of jumbled thoughts that can clutter your mind and trigger stress. This process will contribute to better physical and emotional health.

Advantages of meditation

Meditation will give you a sense of relaxation, peace, and stability, which will help both your mental well-being and physical health. And those benefits don't end when your session of meditation is finished. Meditation can help to get you through the day more calmly and can help you control the effects of certain medical conditions.

Emotional health and meditation

When you meditate, you can clear off the abundance of knowledge that builds up every day and contributes to your stress. Meditation can have the emotional benefits of including:

- Gaining new perspectives on difficult conditions
- Competencies building to handle the tension
- Improving self-confidence

- Focusing on the present
- Reducing negative feelings
- Building up imagination and innovation
- Heightened awareness and endurance

Meditation and illness

Meditation can also be helpful if you have a medical problem, in particular one that can be exacerbated by stress. Although a growing variety of clinical evidence supports meditation's health benefits, some researchers feel it is not yet possible to conclude the potential benefits of meditation. With that in mind, some research indicates meditation can help people control disease symptoms such as:

- Anxiety
- Asthma
- Cancer
- Chronic pain
- Depression
- Heart disease
- High blood pressure
- Irritable bowel syndrome
- Problems with sleep
- Headache pain

If you have any of these disorders or other health issues, be sure to speak to your health care professional about the pros and cons of using meditation. In certain cases, meditation can exacerbate the symptoms associated with some conditions of mental and physical health. Meditation is not a substitute for conventional medicine. But it can be a helpful supplement to the other medication.

Meditation Forms

Meditation is a paragliding term with several forms for a peaceful state of being. There are many kinds of meditation and relaxation techniques which have components of meditation. All hold the same aim of having inner peace.

Might include ways to meditate:

Meditation recommended. Often called guided imagery or imagination, you create mental images of locations or situations you find soothing with this type of meditation. You are trying to use as many senses as you can, including smells, sights, sounds, and textures. A guide or instructor may guide you through that method.

Meditation mantra. In this form of meditation, you quietly repeat a soothing expression, feeling, or phrase to avoid distracting thoughts.

Mindfulness meditation. This kind of meditation is focused on being vigilant or getting an increased understanding and appreciation of living at this moment. In meditation on mindfulness, you stretch your conscious consciousness. You reflect on what you feel during meditation, like your breath flowing. You should observe your thoughts and feelings but without judgment, let them pass.

Qi gong. In general, this method incorporates meditation, relaxation, physical activity, and respiratory exercises to preserve and maintain equilibrium. Qi gong (CHEE-gung) is a part of Chinese traditional medicine.

Tai chi. This is a gentle style of Chinese martial arts. In tai chi (TIE-CHEE), as you practice deep breathing, you execute a self-paced sequence of postures or moves in a steady, graceful manner.

Transcendental Meditation. Transcendental meditation is a simple technique which is normal. In Transcendental Meditation, in a particular way, you quietly repeat a personally defined rhythm, like a script, sound, or expression. This form of meditation can allow your body to settle into a state of deep relaxation, and your mind to attain a state of inner peace without the need for concentration or effort.

Yoga. As discussed in the previous chapters, to foster a more relaxed body and a peaceful mind, you perform a series of postures and synchronized breathing exercises. You're encouraged to concentrate less on your busy day and more on the moment as you step through poses that need balance and concentration.

MEDITATION ELEMENTS

Various forms of meditation can include various features to help you meditate. This will differ depending on whose instructions you are following or who is teaching a lesson. In meditation, some of the most common features include:

Focused attention. Generally, one of the essential aspects of meditation is to concentrate your mind.

Focusing your focus is what helps release your mind from the multitude of distractions that trigger tension and worry. You may concentrate your attention on things like a particular object, an image, a mantra, or even a breath.

Relaxed breathing. This technique involves fast, even-paced respiration using the muscle of the diaphragm to expand the lungs. The intention is to slow down your breathing, take in more oxygen, and reduce the use of the shoulder, neck, and upper chest muscles when breathing so that you breathe more effectively.

A quiet setting. If you're a novice, it could be easier to practice meditation if you're in a quiet spot with few distractions, including no television, radios, or cell phones. You may be able to do it anywhere as you become more experienced in meditation, particularly in high-stress situations where you benefit most from meditation, such as a traffic jam, a stressful work meeting, or a long line at the grocery store.

Convenient position. If you are seated, lying down, walking, or in other positions or activities, you should practice meditation. Try to be relaxed enough to get the most out of your meditation. Seek to maintain a healthy posture during meditation.

Transparent heart. Without judgment, let the thoughts flow through your mind.

Practicing meditation daily

Don't let the idea of the "right" way of meditating add to your tension. You may attend special centers of meditation or community classes taught by qualified teachers if you want to. But you can easily practice meditation on your own, too.

And you can do the meditation as formal or casual as you want, but ensure it does match your lifestyle and circumstance. Some people integrate meditation into their everyday routines. They can begin and end each day, for example, with an hour of meditation. But what you need for meditation is a few minutes of quality time.

Here are several ways you can practice your meditation, whenever you want to:

Deep breath. For beginners, this technique is fine, since breathing is a natural feature. Focus your whole concentration on breathing. Concentrate on feeling and listening as you breathe in and exhale through your nostrils. To breathe slowly and deeply. Kindly return your concentration to your breathing when your mind wanderers.

Body scan. Shift attention to various parts of the body when using the technique. Be mindful of the different sensations in your body, whether this is pain, discomfort, warmth, or relaxation. Combine body scanning with breathing exercises and visualize various areas of your body breathing heat or relaxation.

A mantra to repeat. You may make your motto, religious or secular, as it may be. Examples of religious mantras include the Christian practice of Jesus Prayer, the holy name of God in Judaism, or the Hindu om chant, Buddhism, and other Eastern religions.

Walking and meditating. The combination of a walk and meditation is an easy and safe way to relax. You can use this technique anywhere you walk, whether in a peaceful forest, on a town sidewalk, or in the market. When using this process, slow down your walking speed so you can concentrate on every step of your legs or feet. Don't concentrate on a specific destination. Concentrate on your legs and feet, repeating words of action in your mind such as 'lifting,' 'moving' and 'placing' as you raise each foot, move your leg forward, and put your foot on the ground.

Pledge to prayer. Prayer is the best-known form of meditation and the most commonly performed. In most rituals of faith, spoken and written prayers find themselves. You may pray with words of your own, or read prayers written by others. Check your local bookstore's Self-Help section, for example. Speak about possible resources with your rabbi, priest, minister, or any other spiritual leader.

Read and reflect. Many people report enjoying reading poetry or sacred texts and taking a few moments to focus quietly on their significance. You can also listen to sacred music, the words spoken, or any music that you find relaxing or inspiring. You might want to write your thoughts in a journal or talk to a friend or spiritual leader about them.

Focus on caring and gratitude. In this form of meditation, you concentrate your focus on a holy image or being, weaving in your thoughts, feelings of devotion, compassion, and gratitude. You may also close your eyes, using your imagination, or look at image representations.

12 SCIENTIFIC BENEFITS OF MEDITATION

Meditation's popularity is growing, with more people discovering its benefits.

As mentioned earlier, meditation is a repetitive process of training the mind to concentrate your thoughts and redirect them. You can use it to raise awareness about yourself and the environment. Many people see it as a way of lowering stress and improving focus.

People can use the activity to develop other beneficial behaviors and emotions, such as good mood and attitude, self-discipline, healthier patterns of sleep, and even improved tolerance to pains.

Let's look at 12 benefits of meditation for the body.

1. Cuts back on the tension

One of the most common reasons people practice meditation is to reduce stress. One research of more than 3,500 adults found that it lives up to its reputation for reducing stress. Normally, increased levels of stress hormone cortisol are triggered by mental and physical stress. This causes many of the stress's harmful effects, like the release of inflammation-promoting chemicals called cytokines.

These effects can interfere with sleep, trigger depression and anxiety, increase blood pressure, and lead to tiredness and blurry thought. In an eight-week study, a form of meditation called "meditation of mindfulness" decreased the response to inflammation caused by stress.

Another study of nearly 1,300 adults has shown that meditation can reduce stress. This impact was especially greatest in those with the highest stress levels. Research has shown that meditation can also enhance stress-related symptoms, including irritable bowel syndrome, post-traumatic stress disorder, and fibromyalgia.

Many meditation types can help lower the tension. Meditation can also alleviate symptoms of people suffering from stress-induced medical conditions.

2. Control Anxiety

Moderate tension translates into less anxiety. For example, an eight-week meditation study of mindfulness helped attendees minimize their anxiety. It also decreased anxiety disorder symptoms such as phobias, social anxiety, negative thinking, obsessive-compulsive behaviors, and panic attacks.

Another research was followed up three years after 18 volunteers had completed an eight-week mediation program. Most participants had maintained daily therapy and held lower levels of long-term anxiety. A larger study among 2,466 participants also found that several different mediation techniques would lower levels of anxiety. Yoga has been shown, for example, to help people relieve anxiety. This is possibly due to benefits from both the practice of meditation and physical activity. Meditation in high-pressure work environments can also help reduce job-related anxiety. One research showed a mediation program in a group of nurses has decreased anxiety.

Habitual therapy tends to relieve anxiety and mental health-related problems such as social anxiety, phobias, and obsessive-compulsive behaviors.

3. Promotes emotional wellbeing

Some types of meditation can also lead to a better self-image and a better perspective on life. Two meditation carefulness research showed depression decreased in more than 4,600 adults. One research accompanied 18 participants as they had spent three years practicing meditation. The study found that there were long-term decreases in depression among participants.

Inflammatory chemicals called cytokines, released in response to stress, may affect mood, leading to depression. An analysis of several studies indicates that by decreasing these inflammatory chemicals, meditation can alleviate depression.

Another controlled research compared electrical activity between the brains of people who practiced meditation for consciousness and those of those who did not.

Those who meditated showed significant improvements in behavior in positive thought and motivation related areas.

Certain types of meditation can boost depression and establish a more optimistic life outlook. Research indicates that cultivating an ongoing meditation practice will help you to retain certain benefits in the long run.

4. Improves self-confidence

Some meditation types can help you develop a better self-understanding, allowing you to evolve to your best self. For example, a meditation on self-inquiry is specifically intended to help you gain a deeper understanding of yourself and how you relate to those around you. Other types help you to recognize feelings that may be negative or losing yourself. The theory is that, as you become more aware of your thinking habits, you will guide them towards more positive trends.

A study of 21 women battling breast cancer showed that their self-esteem increased more than it did in those who attended social support sessions when they participated in a Tai Chi program. In another report, 40 senior men and women taking a meditation awareness program reported reduced feelings of isolation relative to a control group put on the program's waiting list.

More imaginative problem solving can also be developed by practice in meditation. Self-inquiry and similar meditation methods will allow you to "know yourself," which can be a starting point for other positive improvements.

5. Lengthens Attention Span

Focused-attention meditation is like elevating your attention span by weight. This helps to improve the attention's power and stamina. For example, a study investigated the impact of an eight-week meditation course on mindfulness and found it enhanced the ability of participants to reorient and retain their focus.

A related study found that staff with human resources who frequently practiced meditation on mindfulness remained focused on a mission for longer. These staff often recalled their duties in more detail than their colleagues who didn't practice meditation.

One study also concluded that meditation could also reverse brain patterns that lead to mind-walking, worrying, and poor focus. You can also benefit from meditating for a short time. One study found four days of meditation practice that could be necessary to improve attention span. Miscellaneous meditation styles will develop your ability to focus and sustain attention. This can have an impact with as little as four days of meditation.

6. Can reduce memory loss related to age
Improvements in mindfulness and clarity of thought can help keep your mind young.

Kirtan Kriya is a meditation method that combines a mantra or chant with repetitive finger movement to focus thoughts. It enhanced participants' capacity to perform memory tasks in several studies of memory loss related to aging.

A study of 12 studies showed that, in older participants, multiple meditation styles improved focus, memory, and mental pace. In addition to combating normal age-related memory loss, meditation in patients with dementia can partially improve memory. It may also help to reduce stress and improve coping for those caring for dementia family members. The improved concentration that you can gain through daily meditation can enhance memory and clarity of mind. These benefits can help to prevent memory loss and dementia associated with aging.

7. Can Offer kindness
Especially certain forms of meditation can increase positive feelings and behavior towards yourself and others.

Metta, a form of meditation, also known as a meditation on love-kindness, starts to develop kind thoughts and feelings towards yourself. Via practice, people learn to express this compassion and acceptance outwardly, first to relatives, then to acquaintances and eventually enemies. Twenty-two studies of this method of meditation have shown its capacity to increase the compassion of peoples towards themselves and others. One analysis of 100 adults randomly allocated to a program that included a meditation on loving-kindness found such benefits to be dose-

232

dependent. In other words, the more effort people put into a meditation on Metta, the more they had positive feelings.

Another group of studies showed the positive feelings that people build through Metta meditation could decrease Separation Anxiety, decrease marriage conflict, and help control anger. These benefits often tend to accumulate over time through the practice of meditation on love-kindness.

Metta, or meditation on love-kindness, is a method of cultivating positive emotions, first for oneself and then for others. Metta increases positivity for others, empathy, and caring behavior.

8. May help combat addictions

By increasing your self-control and awareness of triggers for addictive behaviors, the mental discipline you can develop through meditation may help you break dependencies.

Research has shown that meditation can help people learn to focus their attention, increase their resilience, control their emotions and desires, and improve their understanding of the causes behind their addictive behaviors.

One research that taught 19 alcoholics how to meditate found that participants who received the training were getting better at controlling their cravings and stress related to cravings. Meditation can also help you manage your food cravings. A review of 14 studies found the meditation on mindfulness helped participants to reduce emotional and binge eating.

Meditation develops mental discipline and willpower and may help you avoid unwanted impulses triggers. This can help you recover, lose weight, and redirect other undesirable habits.

9. *Improves sleep*

At some point, nearly half the population will be struggling with insomnia. One study compared two meditation programs based on mindfulness by randomly assigning participants to one of two groups. One group had been practicing meditation, while the other did not. Participants who meditated fell asleep earlier than those who did not meditate and stayed asleep longer.

Becoming skilled in meditation can help you control or redirect the thoughts of racing or "runaway," which often lead to insomnia. It can also help relax your body, release tension, and put you in a peaceful state where you're more likely to fall asleep.

10. *Helps relieve pain*

Your perception of pain is related to your state of mind, and in stressful conditions, it can be heightened. For example, one study used functional MRI techniques to analyze brain activity when participants encountered a painful stimulus. Some participants had completed four days of meditation carefulness training, and others had not.

Patients who were meditating displayed increased activity in the brain centers known to control pain. Also, they registered less pain sensitivity. In 3,500 participants, a broader study looked at the impact of repetitive meditation. It found that meditation was associated with reduced chronic or sporadic pain complaints.

Additional research in patients with terminal diseases, discovered that meditation can help to mitigate chronic end-of-life pain. Meditators and non-meditators faced the same causes of pain in both of these cases. Still, meditators demonstrated a better capacity to deal with pain and also faced a decreased pain sensation.

Meditation will lessen the brain's perception of pain. This can benefit when used as an alternative to medical care or physical therapy to treat chronic pain.

11. Can reduce blood pressure

Meditation, too, can improve physical health by reducing heart pressure. Over time, high blood pressure makes it harder for the heart to pump blood, which can result in impaired heart function. High blood pressure also leads to atherosclerosis, or artery narrowing, which can cause heart attacks and strokes.

A study of 996 volunteers found that meditating on a "silent mantra" — a repetitive, non-vocalized phrase — reduced average blood pressure by around five points. This was more common among older volunteers and those who had pre-study higher blood pressure. A review concluded that several types of meditation produced similar blood pressure changes. In part, meditation helps to control blood pressure by calming the nerve signals that guide heart function, blood vessel tension, and the "fight-or-flight" response that increases alertness in stressful situations. In individuals who meditate regularly, blood pressure drops not only during meditation but also over time. This can lower the stress on the heart and arteries and help prevent heart disease.

12. Anywhere you can meditate

People practice several different meditation styles, most of which require no specialized equipment or space, with just a few minutes of daily work. If you want to begin meditation, try choosing a meditation form based on what you want to get out of it.

Chapter 17: THE PURPOSE OF RELATIONSHIPS

It seems like most men and women are chasing the dream of finding a perfect partner, falling in love, and living happily ever after. The proof of this? Well, you don't have to look too far to see the vast number of dating agencies, chat rooms, the columns of 'looking' or 'lonely hearts' in papers and magazines, the ever-increasing number of dating TV programs, and the rows and rows of 'How to' books of relationships.

What are the individuals looking for out of a relationship? What should it be for them to figure out? What is it that should create? Without adding the complexities of a relationship, is there not enough going on in their lives? Why can't they be bothered to work at it while they're in a relationship, or spend time and energy in fixing problems, giving up, and moving on to another toxic relationship?

Why?

A relationship's intent may be as simple as providing an atmosphere to raise children in. That doesn't clarify the people who don't want to have kids, but who wants to be in a relationship, though.

Why don't people just live alone or with friends, and be happy with that? It's not that easy, after all — doesn't it save the heart from being broken again and again? Being single means you don't have to feel insecure, compromise, fight about little things. Being single means being free to do whatever you want, at the drop of a hat anytime you want to.

Where does it start, this desire to be in a relationship, and to live happily ever after?

- Is it a fundamental longing for love and security?
- Is it a genetic imperative to build an opportunity to have babies and pass on the reservoir of genes?
- Are we, as human beings and as social creatures, supposed to be part of a pair, and does it come back to being part of a pair to be pro-creative?
- Want to do so, so we can?
- Is being in a relationship what our culture, our society, and our family expect of us?
- Is the relationship's intention to make us feel 'happy' – whatever that's normal, so we don't stick out as being 'single'?
- Is there a relationship that should make us feel complete?

What do individuals think it would do for them to be in a relationship? They'll make them happy, and somehow complete. And the ever-increasing rate of divorce testifies to unfulfilled desires and failure to work things out.

- Others expect a relationship to relieve their deep sense of isolation.
- Others say it is up to their partners to make them happy.
- Others expect their needs (as they perceive them) to be met in a relationship.
- Others believe it is going to make them feel loved and appropriate. Usually, the thought goes something like "if he/she wants to be with me, then I have to be right."
- Some believe "if I'm in a relationship, anything else will be figured out in my life" As if being in a relationship is like a magic wand which has a positive effect on all aspects of your life. It will fix all my problems.
- Others go into a partnership to make it a very different world than one in which they grew up. A new, improved model that works better.
- Many have an idea of how their partner should love them, act, cook,

housekeep, raise children, entertain, and care for them.

- Others plan to maintain the partnership financially. Getting a comfortable big house with all mod drawbacks, the new car, lavish holidays, and exciting social experience.

THE SOURCE OF ASSUMPTIONS ABOUT RELATION-SHIPS

Histories, romance novels, television, families, nursery rhymes, movies, magazines, newspapers, cartoons, a family of your own, songs, ballads, fairy tales, myths, legends, etc. The perceptions of most individuals rely on a young age on what they are related to, the relationship-wise. The relation is made on a level beyond their consciousness. However, this implicit link becomes the strongest possible catalyst for the relationship sense.

Anything like this could go on the link...

Because of whatever situation the child is in, 'she' can relate to a character like Cinderella. And as the story goes, Cinderella enjoyed meeting her prince and lived happily ever after. 'He' might be interacting with Prince Charming. The prince who's so charming, powerful, the hero who's saving and doing it all right.

The presence of that innocent link has far-reaching implications. 'She' will continue, even as an adult, with the implicit hope that an outsider will save her from her condition. This puts pressure on the male to turn everything from 'rags' into 'riches' in her life. 'He,' on the other hand, needs to have a beautiful maiden by his side, be hailed as a hero, be praised for all his successes, and be cared for in-house. Maybe. This is a generalization of enormity. Or it is.

The habits aren't always good, and when recognized, they can come as quite a shock.

Patterns are formed by studying the child's external relationships. The unintentionally occurring role modeling later sets the standards for relationships. History repeats itself several times, no matter how much the person wishes not to repeat what happened to his/her parents. Unfortunately, even more than once.

After the initial lovey-dovey, desire, infatuation, most relationships do something to please point, consisting of blame, assumptions, anger, unfulfilled desires and claims, lack of confidence, communication, and intimacy.

Despite the initial euphoria of being in love, soon she learns he isn't charming her prince. Being in love hasn't solved all her problems with herself; in fact, he hasn't rescued her from all the other problems in her life. On the contrary, in her mind, by not supplying her with what she wanted, he has simply added to them, and she has to nag him just to get the lawn finished.

He, on the other hand, feels let down too. His fair maiden is no match for his imagination. She doesn't respect or compliment him. She even puts him down in bed. He enjoys a hero's adulation. He has never been thanked, let alone appreciated for things he does for her and around the house. All he gets is relentless criticism, her voice playing in his head telling him what a let down he's, he's expected to know what to do and when and why he's not a mind reader.

Too many games are played to believe one's life is under balance. Typically such games are played in the name of love. Typically running patterns are therefore dependency and possessiveness. Lots of people feel strong in attempting to manipulate another. Typically, however, this control or superiority over another is short-lived. And so it returns to square one. For someone else to take over and conquer. Maybe that person will leave too. Often alone.

Why should you place the responsibility on another person for your personal development? Do you want them to be both your counselor and your lover?

To become the kind of person that you want to be with.

Like attracts. If you're very emotionally demanding, you're likely to find a partner who has the same needs as you. And you end up with a scenario where you want your needs to be met, and your partner may not be able to satisfy them because they have the same need and want you to satisfy theirs. If there is really good communication, it can become a situation of no-win. When you think of the kind of person you want to spend the rest of your life with, are you like who guy? If your response is no, then the odds are stacked against you.

You know your strengths and weakness when you are content with yourself, you take responsibility for your attitude and behavior, you act from an adult viewpoint rather than from a child viewpoint, and you discover a life purpose.

Think about the qualities you're looking for and think about how you can build those up inside yourself. So is your companion when you are positive and compassionate. So does your partner when you respect yourself. The Partnership functions when the relationship's intention is not to have another person who could complete you, but to share your fullness with them.

The object of a relationship may be for companionship. Maybe what we are looking for in a relationship is sharing the self that is not possible elsewhere. A profound sense of love and connection. An appreciation of who we are really, warts and all (after acknowledging our warts). Maybe we want to be identified in the way our parents used to know us.

A partnership based on common beliefs and interests can be supportive, imaginative, and motivating. It can bring peace, affection, comfort, laughter, happiness, and a haven. It can provide a very positive way of providing a forum for personal development and contribution to society. A partnership lets you understand and enjoy the differences that make you special. How different an approach from wanting to make your partner like you exactly to the point of washing the dishes, hoovering, walking, etc.

Relationships are precious because they offer a wonderful opportunity for life to build and generate a magnificent experience of who you want to be with your ideas.

A satisfying relationship may provide your children with a supportive atmosphere. When you think about it, that's going to have a big effect. Based on you being a good role model, your kids will then replicate the model for their kids, and so on.

Examples of goals that can last a lifetime and keep the relationship new and enjoyable are: contribute to the health and well-being of those around you; contribute to the financial prosperity of others; contribute to ending hunger on the planet; contribute to ending tension in people's lives; solve the world's problems of violence, abuse or poverty, etc. Nice, optimistic, safe, and meaningful relationships give us the richest experiences we can have. Your caring partner who shares everything with you; the best friend who interacts as few others do with you; the people at work who support you and motivate you to become the best you can be; this is what brings joy to life!

Chapter 18: THE BEST RELATIONSHIP GOALS TO NURTURE INTIMACY

What are the relationship goals for couples? The short answer is: the goals of the partnership are the hopes, aspirations, and accomplishments you and your partner or spouse create for the life you want to develop together.

You have your career goals or your personal life. You can have your own growth goals and self-improvement goals. Just as we have personal or professional ambitions, partners should carefully consider a list of goals for the partnership and how to achieve them.

Over time, individuals and couples adjust, and these changes can lead to disconnection, tension, and unhappiness. If you don't take the time to envision your perfect future as a couple, and how together you can develop and evolve, you will only develop apart.

But when the two of you work together towards a shared vision, while being flexible and agile when life changes occur, you will secure your relationship and enjoy all the benefits of having those objectives.

Make each Other a priority

Let's be frank — most of us talk about the meaning of our marriage or love relationship in a big game, but when the rubber hits the floor, we don't put each other first. Over time, you're beginning to take each other for granted. You get busy and overwhelmed with your things and forget to respond to your partner's needs and desires. You see your coupling as a given, which is just a by-product of your relationship with this other person.

But the pairing is a different entity. There you are. Your partner's in there. And friendship is there. You will have to accept yourself as the centerpiece of your life. How can you get this done? It is a responsibility you have to uphold with all your decisions and acts every single day. It involves regular recalibration, depending on each other's needs and what happens in your life.

Take a moment every day to ask each other and yourself, "Are we putting one another first today? What do we need to do to feed it today?"

Building a Bubble Pair

A couple of bubbles reinforce the goal of making your relationship a priority by speaking in terms of "us" rather than "me." This is hard for most couples because it involves first seeing yourself as part of a team, above your desires and behaviors.

But instead of weakening you through this interdependence, it strengthens you because everyone feels protected and loved. Creating this couple's aim takes a bit of time and commitment, but the payoff is massive as you create a safe sphere around your partnership.

The first step towards achieving this aim is to come together and make a set of agreements that will improve your relationship care and security. One example of this might be "I would never deliberately scare you or abandon you," or "I would treat your vulnerabilities with respect and caution."

Also, a couple of bubble target includes:

- To become knowledgeable regarding the wants, expectations, and fears of one another.
- Fast repair of damage to the partnership.

- Build up a bank of good memories to offset any suffering.

- Being a pillar to each other in tough times.

Provide Daytime Connection

Spending one-on-one time together to reconnect is an important everyday objective of your relationship. If one or both of you work outside the home, carving this time without disruptions or interruptions (from children or something else) is particularly crucial.

Try to do this both in the morning before the beginning of the workday and in the evening before you're dragged away to the tasks and obligations.

The most important aspect of this period of a relationship is for you to be truly present for each other. This means you don't look at your computer, do a job or watch TV. You concentrate solely on one another. This isn't the time to resolve your problems or work through conflict. It's a time to chat, connect, welcome, and just enjoy the company of one another.

Look into the eyes of each other. Keep your hands up. Attentively listen as the other talks. In the morning, before you get up or over a cup of coffee, you could spend some time chatting in bed. You could go for a walk together in the evening or send the kids out to play while you relax and catch up on your day.

The link-time doesn't have to be long hours. Perhaps 15 or 20 minutes is enough to affirm how much you care for one another.

Communicate with Kindness

Goal-setting for couples must include the ways you interact with one another. But have you ever noticed how couples could talk so cruelly and unkindly to each other? They tell one another things they would never dream of asking a casual acquaintance or even someone they don't like.

It's so quick to lash out and say hurtful things when we feel hurt, angry, or frustrated. Sometimes we use passive-aggressive terms and actions to communicate how we feel, using subtle digs, intimidation, or stonewalling. Both direct and implicit words and actions like these are deeply wounding, accumulating enough over time to cause serious problems in a relationship. You lose confidence, mutual respect, and ultimately love. Make it a priority in all your interactions to be kind. Being kind does not mean agreeing with each other or even feeling loved during a difficult moment. It does mean that you consent not to strike, threaten, or purposely injure each other. It means speaking honestly without using passive or aggressive behavior. It means that when you feel like lashing out, you step away or count to ten, knowing you don't want to say or do something you'll regret later. We are all human, and there will, of course, be moments when you fall short of your target of kindness. But make it a priority to immediately apologize, offer immediate forgiveness, and reset your target of kindness as soon as possible.

Acknowledge vulnerability

Partner enters into a relationship with past baggage, insecurities, ashamed or guilty feelings, and tenuous hopes and dreams. We have vulnerabilities that we want to mask from others so that they don't think less about us. As confidence and trust develop with each other, you share with your partner some of your flaws and inner pain. You show your vulnerable underbelly in hopes of finding a position of comfort where you can truly be yourself.

Nothing is more wounding to the couple than disregarding, or worse, rubbing your flaws back into your face to make you feel worse about yourself. The freedom to be comfortably vulnerable to each other will reinforce the bond between you and cultivate a deeper love and intimacy than you thought possible.

When your partner accepts and treats your flaws with dignity, it can heal past wounds and make you feel more confident about who you are. Make it a priority for one another to be transparent, truthful, and genuine. But most importantly, make it a priority always to treat one another's vulnerabilities with tender loving care.

The Fun Together Strategy

Life is already intense and stressed. You spend your days working, caring for kids, running errands, dealing with problems, and thinking about future issues. Your relationship should be a place of peace and respite from the everyday tribulations. Your relationship should genuinely provide an outlet for the fullest possible enjoyment of life. Think back to when you first met your love partner or spouse, and how much fun you had together. You hadn't had to work too hard to have fun at that early stage of your relationship. Everything was fun, and you've been delighted to find fun things to do together.

When your closeness has grown, you may need to work a little harder together to build fun times, but that's still possible. Make it a priority of scheduling and playing time every week. Sit down with your partner to chat about what you both perceive as fun activities. Be open to trying out new things that could be different from your initial fun ideas. Let yourself be dumb and act like children again. Even brief, spontaneous moments of fun will deepen and bring you closer to your relationship.

Grasp the languages of your love

Gary Chapman outlines five ways people show themselves and feel love. Including:

- Giving-gifts
- Calendar time
- Words of affirmation

- Actions of service
- Body touch

Chapman argues that each of us has a primary and secondary love language that is reflected in the way we show love to others. But we're exposing our deepest needs within the relationship by expressing our love language to our partner.

If you're extremely affectionate with your partner, for example, it shows you're looking for physical affection from him or her. Each of you may not have the same love language, and that's why it's so important that you both learn and respect each other's love language. You can do that by studying how your partner expresses love to you and examining what they talk about within the relationship.

Another way of learning about your love languages is by taking a love language quiz and sharing the results. Once you are both conscious of each other's love language, your goal is to offer your partner more of what he or she needs in the relationship.

Hold a Satisfying Sex Life

No matter how great your sex life was at the start of your relationship, it's inevitable from time to time that it will grow boring or even burdensome. If you're fifteen or twenty years into a marriage, it can take real effort and commitment to maintain that romantic spark. But for a healthy relationship, healthy sex life is crucial.

Maintaining a satisfactory sexual bond involves understanding your partner and their sex-related needs, as well as speaking up for their own needs. Women need to feel comfortable and secure with their partner to be willing to try new things and be sexually adventurous. Men need more variety and visual stimulation than females do.

Sex can become a stressor for women if they see it as yet another chore they must perform. Men see sex as a stress reliever and need to experience closeness to this physical connection. Regular communication is the key to bridging those differences in sexual needs.

Speaking about your sex life may at first feel uncomfortable, but communicating your needs and concerns will protect your relationship from potential problems that could further damage your intimacy. Make it a target for a weekly discussion of your sex life. Be frank with each other about what you want, what does not fit well, and what you're fantasizing about. Work to make your relationship feel secure, comfortable, and connected and try to negotiate a compromise in different needs areas.

Promoting One Other Goal

As important as creating a couple of bubbles in your relationship is, you are two individuals who have their own goals and dreams. Having your own goals and dreams as a person does not weaken your bond. Conversely, as each partner has something unique and interesting to add to the partnership, it should strengthen the relationship.

You both should feel that the most important person in your life — your spouse or partner — will help and respect your ambitions and celebrate your accomplishments. Supporting each other's interests is more than merely offering support or verbal encouragement. It could mean sacrificing time, money, or obligations to prove you are fully on board. Make it a priority to explore your individual goals and dreams, and how you can achieve those goals together. Ask each other questions such as, "What can I do to help your targets?

Have a Yearly Review

If you and your partner take the time to set goals for a relationship and work towards achieving them, measuring your efforts' success is significant.

Sit down together at the end of the year to address each of the priorities you've established for your partnership.

- What have you done to realize those goals in the past year?
- So how good were you?
- What does it take you to continue working on?

Use this time to set new goals for the coming year, building on what you've done and what you've learned from each other in the past year.

Spice Up The Date Nights

If you balked at the 'Hold a Satisfying Sex Life' goal, then it's time to put the spice back into your one-on-one time. And if that doesn't suffice, now is the time to make it a priority. It's not just about getting the kids on well. That's not going to be enough to hold your marriage bond strong. And whether you admit it or not, you will both be miserable if you give each other a quick, goodnight peck on the lips, the closest you get to the intimacy.

So schedule a regular date night with that commitment and let nothing but a real emergency mess. And if you're not sure what to do to reconnect and pave the path to greater intimacy, it can't hurt brainstorming ideas and making it fun together. What can you do this week to remember the fun times you had when you first began dating yourself and your spouse? Which date will make you closer than you've been for a while? Your spouse may still be in the dark about what's turning you on, but you're probably not.

The best time to share that information without putting pressure on your spouse is during these private dates — whether you're chatting in your bedroom together with or talking about a drink at a favorite restaurant. The more you can make your partner feel special and worth some trouble at least, the more likely you're both to make inroads and start building a connection — or repairing it.

And with that in place, it's not hard to get a fire going if you're both open to greater intimacy. Then you can do the work to keep it.

Build a Diary for the Couple

Get a journal and write your partner a letter in it, share your thoughts and worries, and express your expectations for your relationship.

Write down what you love about your partner and what you would love to do as a couple.

Write down how much fun you have had and what you think you can still do as you grow older.

Let your spouse read your submission and write your own.

You can even participate in some quizzes about relationships and share your answers in your blog. Journaling as a couple will start as part of the counseling for couples and become a regular part of your DIY couple therapy.

Keeping a journal together and making it a safe place to be honest about what you think and feel can draw both of you closer together and help each other work through personal challenges. There is sound science behind the benefits of journaling for the mental health of an individual. When two are involved — especially two who are committed to each other's well-being — the combined benefits can only help strengthen their relationship.

Set common goals for long term Relationship

Your marriage or engaged relationship will develop and evolve— and you want your love and closeness to stand the test of time. As the years go by, you and your partner can grow and have different needs, and if you have expectations for shared and actual relationships, you've created a shield against obstacles that often tear couples apart.

Setting goals for couples encourages both of you to set the bar high for your relationship instead of allowing your connection to wilt and erode. A life-long pursuit should be to have expectations for your relationship — one that takes you together and enhances your love year after year. Here are some long-term goals for the relationship:

Schedule Travel Together

Was there a spot for your honeymoon that you both wanted to go but couldn't afford? Or is there another, more accessible paradise that suits both of you? Range it out with your partner and spend the daydreaming time together to make sure you both have a great time. Couples world-wide can attest to the advantages of traveling together. And those trips can be planned together to strengthen your bond and increase intimacy.

How short or long you've got for a couple of holidays or annual vacation, it's always better if you're both involved in planning the specifics that will most affect you both:

- Wherever you go, and where you want to see the sites
- Where to rest
- How much travel budget you should spend
- How long should travel be
- Whether you want to fly with others or not

Don't assume you know what your partner wants, even if you already knew what he or she might want to change for the next holiday.

Planning Dates schedule

The science behind planning your goals as a couple reinforces the idea many couples learned on their own: it can be fun to plan together. It is not just about retirement planning, either. Together you can set goals to...

- Your friendship with them
- Parenting / your kids
- Their professions and their interests
- Your fitness and physical and mental health
- Financial stability

It couldn't sound like the most romantic way of being together. But if you actively involve your partner together in preparing for a better future, this can be very romantic indeed. Together preparation is a powerful way of strengthening the relationship as a couple. So place a date on the calendar, make sure you have no interruptions, and spend a couple of hours on your annual review of the relationship.

Schedule weekly Health Marriage meetings

The best piece of advice that you can get is to discuss your connection's health regularly. It's beneficial to schedule "meetings," along with preparation, to monitor the progress and make any appropriate changes to the plan. It's also a good way to get to grips with how you do it, and whether you can all work together as a team.

Set a weekly "planning date" to review the previous week's progress, draw up a to-do list for the next week, and address any relevant issues. Play the Truth Game if there's a sticky topic that keeps coming up, and one of you likes to chat five or ten times more than the other:

- Take turns to ask the other about a deep personal concern.
- Do not automatically respond to your question with your take on it after the other person answers it; instead, let the other person ask his or her question.

- The next issue shouldn't be linked to the previous one.
- Respond as truthfully as you can to this issue.
- Repeat, if the time is up for more.

If you feel the need to answer one of the answers provided by your spouse, ask before you launch into it. He or she might not be up for an extended conversation, much less debate, depending on the time of day and the sort of day you have both had. Even if you can see it from other viewpoints for both of you, sometimes you just don't have the resources. Accept that and live to speak a different day.

Use Stimuli to improve Romance

This may be a sequence of if-then sentences, such as: "If my wife has trouble finding clothes that make her feel comfortable, then I will do something or say something to remind her that she looks amazing to me no matter what she wears." It's not just a matter of expressing your interest in intimacy, because you could just see her as your only sexual partner for all she knows.

Let those random acts be about persuading your partner that she (or he) still makes your stomach flip (or your heart flip) and that she is still the only woman on earth who can do that.

Try one of the causes, then:

- If my spouse sighs or makes some other noise that shows discomfort or dissatisfaction with his presence, then I'll say something like, "Those pants look phenomenal on you."
- If we eat out and I think my spouse may be nervous about ordering what he or she wants, then I'm going to suggest something like, "Let's just order exactly what we want and savor every bite. No peeking at the nutrition detail. You do not have to think about something."

- If I see flowers dying in our house, I'll buy another bouquet while I'm out and put a note of love in it for him/her.

Give Gifts for Fun

These needn't be costly, and — especially if you save money together. It's best to stick to cheap presents, consumable or otherwise, just to show your partner that you're still very keen to keep the romance alive. Here are some suggestions:

- Borrow films from the library you are both interested in.
- Lend music CDs to party together.
- Take a bouquet of colorful flowers or balloons.
- If your partner is involved or has a hobby, pick up something relevant to that.
- Delight your partner by offering a single treatment that he or she loves.

Especially if your partner's love language is gift-giving, this is a powerful way to keep the romance alive. Suppose you keep the tank full of affection, so intimacy is much more possible.

Carrying out routine thoughtful acts

If your partner's love language is service actions, spontaneous or routine thoughtfulness acts will enhance how much you care. It tells your partner that you have paid attention and that you are always motivated to help out and be there for him or her.

Consider the possibilities of:

- Upon seeing a garbage container complete, clean it, and replace the cover.
- If you find that your partner is distracted with something, offer to do

an errand, pick up someone, etc.

- If you've cooked dinner with your partner, try to clean up — or assist with laundry.

- When your wife is tired, give a massage, a cup of tea, a hot bath, and so on.

- If your partner seems to be on edge, ask if you could do something to make the day easier.

Only displaying your readiness to help can go a long way to telling your partner that their health and well-being are vital to you.

Seeking common ground

Both of you have your interests, but taking a class together at least once a year (if not more often) is a perfect way to grow a common interest and discover a new way to have fun. You might learn something that can save a life, too.

Find out the possibilities here:

- Cooking or baking
- Dance (waltz, tango, salsa, etc.)
- Learning a Language
- Self-defense or martial arts
- Learning to play an instrument
- Compounding
- Vehicle repair
- CPR and First Aid

You may take one class a year and then arrange opportunities to practice what you have learned. Or you could take two classes a year — one in late winter or early spring, and the other one in late summer or early fall. Be sure to consult with your partner and make sure you are both sincerely interested in attending before you pay for the class.

Have a Picnic each month

Possibly you've got your favorite spots, or you might try something new. The important thing is to spend time together, to savor the meal and the company of each other.

You could go for a romantic picnic in your backyard, in a park, on the beach, or on the floor of your apartment. If you do this at home and have children, make sure they don't disturb you unless someone dies or the house is on fire.

You can also plan a horse-drawn carriage ride to the park or the beach or lakeshore where you will have your picnic-either on the sand or a ferry. Do what you can for any date to mix it up. If both of you agree to this, organizing your monthly picnic will take turns, and it can be as simple or elaborate as you want.

Go to Cinema Weekly

Take turns choosing a film each month and go out to watch it together. You can either come out for dinner or dessert (or both) or head home after the movie. It doesn't matter if the film wasn't an Academy Award winner itself. What counts is how much fun you have while, and after-ward, you are there.

You can also choose a drive-in movie theater, enjoy your take-out picnic, and switch to the back seat if more action is taking place in the car than on the screen. If you can't manage this every month, try at least every quarter to do that or something similar. Just spend some time together, watching something that reminds you for as long as you can of what you have together and what you want to have together.

Send Love Notes

You may write these on different pieces of paper (or cardstock) or in the journal of the pair, in which you take turns to write. You should pin up the latest love notes on a bulletin board to keep it open, that you can't help but see every day. Pin it lose or position it in an envelope with an image of the recipient of the letter.

When replacing your letter with a new note, flip the envelope to show the words "You have mail! "Or" Thinking about you" or something else that will get the attention of your spouse. Don't be disappointed if it doesn't open up immediately. If your partner knows how the letters work, it's just a matter of time before your new love note is read.

Use them not to sell but to remind your partner of something you love about them — and perhaps something you want to do together.

Keep it positive, supportive, and caring. Let them intend to remember what you have to each other and celebrate the progress you have made — together and individually.

Give your partner a break from the children

If you can both handle it, you can make this a monthly or quarterly thing. Or one of you might grab a moment when the other needs a break and offer to take the children on vacation. Of course, if your partner responds with "No, don't leave me," you may need to reconsider your strategy and find a babysitter while you are performing a much-needed joint TLC procedure.

It is important to spend time together as a family, but that family's credibility depends on the link between you and your spouse. And when things get bad, it's not enough just to do damage control. Creating the relation and maintaining it must be a regular priority.

If we want to make sure we're doing something that our happiness — and that of those closest to us — depends on, we're not trying to squeeze it into; we're making time for it. And that is what we intend for. If other things get in the way, then we do what's needed to restore order and bring peace to the land (i.e., homefront).

So, take the kids out and give them time to chill your spouse — or have the kids chill while you and your spouse tend to each other.

Do what's required and put your relationship ahead of what people want from you, besides your partner. You will both be proud to have done so.

Chapter 19: THOUGHTS AND STYLE OF THOUGHT: THE ART OF PRACTICAL THINKING

Suppose you think of a thought as an energy atom that can be charged positively or negatively and can influence how we feel emotionally. In that case, it may help you understand what is known as brain plasticity in neuroscience and how it operates with our thought energy and, eventually, how thoughts can generally affect our emotions and mood.

"Brain plasticity refers to the remarkable ability of the brain to alter its structure and function following changes within the body or in the external world. The large outer layer of the brain, known as the cortex, can, in particular, enable such changes."

A highly stimulated left frontal cortex indicates a healthier, lighter heart personality and a highly stimulated right frontal cortex indicating a more melancholic mood. It is the thinking energy we produce ourselves that activates our left and right frontal cortexes, respectively. Human beings can create about 30,000-70,000 thoughts a day, so it is no wonder that negative thinking can affect the mind and body. Our thoughts are directly related to our feelings, moods, and behaviors. They can have a powerful effect on us and shape how we can grow and evolve as human beings in any way we like. We are the builders of our inner residence or the person we are, so to be successful in a holistic sense, we need to cultivate ourselves mentally and physically.

Negative thoughts, especially those of a recurrent nature, can have a detrimental impact on our well-being. Dwelling for a long time on something unpleasant will leave us in a constant state of depression and make us sick. Recurring negative thinking about an issue does not resolve it, e.g., it is not a positive way to use our mental resources to bear grudges against those who might have harmed us in the past; it only causes the problem to affect ourselves. Eventually, it can now become more your adopted issue. Catastrophizing (predicting grim or sad results) is another form of pessimistic thought. Predicting things are or will be worse than they are, having a gloomy outlook, general pessimism and self-criticism are just ways of putting down ourselves and others.

If we think of positive thoughts on a scale of positivity at one end of the spectrum, negative thoughts on the other end, and we are sitting right in the center, this is logical thinking. There is nothing wrong with positive thinking; a positive thought is said to uplift or benefit our mood. At the other end of the scale, pessimistic thinking can be in contrast, and it can hold us in a low-mood state of mind instead of advocating optimum gain for everyone making us feel good about ourselves and others. Although it is a healthy thing to remain optimistic, it is not always easy to do. Realistic thoughts about ourselves are what are easier to accomplish and believe.

We should not persuade ourselves that we are experts in an area in which we have not worked hard to excel or pretend we know more than we do by telling ourselves over and over about those topics. What we are capable of doing is being rational. Realistic thinking can be easier to accomplish than positive thinking, and shifting very negative thinking can be more successful than positive thinking, as it is more readily recognized as credible. This is because before we essentially determine whether to believe it or not, we need to evaluate a situation and understand it. We should ask ourselves, for instance, "What are the facts of the matter? How likely is it that an occurrence will occur? What is feasible?" Yes, it takes a little longer to question a negative thought in this manner. Still, the possibility of internalizing the opinion is greater than an over-positive statement that might verge on illogical.

To enhance our standard of thought, we first need to become conscious of our patterns of thinking. Meditation is an established way of healthily channeling our energy and can lead us to a calmer, more peaceful location. We may begin to slow down and consider what is going on in our minds and clear out unnecessary thoughts or imagery by sitting and contemplating our thoughts or concentrating our attention on an object in a space, a place in the distance, or even our breath. Slowing down the thinking processes allows us to emotionally consider and understand what is happening to us and can give us the chance to question any over-negative use of thinking energy that culminates in motivating us to think more positively or more critically. We can begin to reflect more clearly when faced with dilemmas because we can identify more quickly when we worry too much and maybe enter the loop of concern or the circuit of self-pity.

Meditation will lead us to the awareness of the habits we have formed over time and drain good energy from us. It can help us understand what our default position is on certain topics, how we respond to various dilemmas and distinct personalities, or even just aspects of certain people's personalities. Realistic thinking allows a clearer understanding of how to modify these unnecessary ways of thinking and realign the patterns to deliver more useful ones.

If we compare ourselves to machines, our brain is our hardware, our software is our thoughts, or you may want to think of being a maker or artist with a blank canvas to work on. We may then select our applications, fabrics, and colors we want to use. We can choose to be more optimistic, more resilient, more eager to be whatever we want. Getting to know who we are and knowing and countering our vulnerabilities ensures that we are becoming stronger individuals, who are more capable of coping with the little ups and downs of life and even the bigger things.

25 PRACTICES FOR ENHANCING YOUR LIFE'S QUALITY

Fact: If the number one priority is the standard of living, the quality of life rarely increases. But if the number one target is quality of life, the standard of living increases invariably.

How to make the quality of your life better

Regularly, do you find yourself feeling frustrated? Do you feel like a zombie, waking up to the same boring routine every day that seems endless? Over time, has the quality of your life diminished, resulting in a lack of resources, vitality, and potential enthusiasm?

From time to time, we all get irritated. Even for the most astute-minded people, life can be daunting. The difficult times can feel overbearing without knowing where our lives are heading and why they are heading there. Usually, in silent surrender, we want to throw our hands up and utter the words, "I give up."

Life does not have to overwhelm, though, and most definitely, it does not have to frustrate. By improving your actions and your way of thinking, you can enhance your life quality by making a few minor changes to your routines. Remember that you're not alone; we all go through long stretches of anxiety, fear, rage, worry, and frustration.

Overcoming any of our innate tendencies to fall into a state of marginal depression is not difficult. Life doesn't turn out the way we want it to, sometimes. Yet the quality of our lives always has something to do with the simple behaviors we regularly carry out daily. We will enhance the quality of our lives across various spectrums by changing our behaviors. Talent will give you an unfair advantage in life and allow you on autopilot to achieve any goal!

Defining Life Quality

First, let's explain what we mean by "quality of life." You're wrong for those of you who believe your life's quality is equal to your standard of living. Today, your living standard, which is approximately equivalent to your salary, has a marginal impact on your quality of life, but it's not the complete picture.

The total of your fitness, happiness, vitality, leisure, and income is the quality of life, as described here. This formulaic approach tends to paint a clearer picture of the overall consistency of which individuals are exposed. Yet, by the amount of money they have, many individuals determine their quality of life. And even though money is a decent barometer, it's not a complete equation.

And now, capital is making the world go round. People will most definitely change many aspects of their lives with access to money and resources. But tests have also proved that the same people are not so much happier statistically. Only a transient change in satisfaction is equivalent to an increase in wages.

In your history, think about that. Maybe you got the promotion you wished for, or maybe you found a dream job. You were satisfied for a short time. But it's been fleeting. When it comes to monetary gains, happiness does not last forever, and it is not the complete picture. Although money gives you access to "things," there is a reason for the existence of the saying, "The best things in life are free."

The Hedonic Treadmill

In 1971, the word "Hedonic Treadmill," also known as "Hedonic Adaptation," was coined by two behavioral psychologists, Donald T. Campbell and Phillip Brickman. The word refers to people's normal tendencies to return to a fixed point of satisfaction following significant changes in their lives, either positive or negative.

The Hedonic Set Point, then, is a foundation for pleasure that we all have, to which we prefer to return, even after items such as a traumatic experience or a big cash windfall from winning a lottery suggest. In a study released by Campbell and Brickman, they found that both lottery winners and paraplegics both returned to a baseline level of happiness sometime after the case.

We all have a baseline Hedonic Set Point, which is defined by inherited means and experiential experience, they further claim. And, while the baseline level of happiness might be different for everyone, to recognize the root of happiness and increase your life quality, the definition is very important.

Enhancing your life

There are some ways that you can affect the quality of your life with positivity. For individuals, increasing items such as income is far more apparent than increasing their happiness, health, or vitality. Money seems dry and cut. Either you have enough or you don't. It's easy to calculate. But how about the remainder? Health, pleasure, vitality, and enjoyment are also essential elements of the quality of life. How are you going to boost them? Through the promotion of a certain collection of good behaviors and commitment to them.

Good habits Improve your life quality

You must embrace healthy habits if you want to boost the quality of your life. Bad habits must be removed, and good habits must be established. Easier said than done, isn't it?

Good habits help promote satisfaction, vitality, fitness, jobs, and leisure at an increased level. It's just not going to happen overnight. Here are the top practices to further boost the quality of your life.

The Patterns of Happiness

There are 5 top habits that you can institute regularly to improve your overall level of joy and content when it comes to your overall level of happiness.

1. Even when anxious, smile

They have well-documented the impact of smiling on stress. Smiling helps to give the mind a powerful instinct, which then affects the neurochemistry. Studies have shown that individuals who were told to keep a genuine Duchenne smile on their faces had lower heart rates after stressful events.

Put a pencil in your mouth if you can't force yourself to smile, and the natural curvature of your mouth will allow you to indulge in the traditional smile. For 15 to 20 minutes a day, try this. And if you feel sad, you would be shocked by just how much this elevates your mood.

2. Practice daily gratitude

Spend 15 to 30 minutes every single day reading off what you have to be grateful for. Look for something, even though you feel like you have nothing to be grateful for. You may be in a financial pit, but at least you have the intelligence and the ability to walk, speak, and reason in your mind. You will always find something to be grateful for if you can.

When we think about it, we sometimes dwell on stuff that we're dissatisfied with. We don't know just how good we had it until we lose anything that we took for granted, such as an individual, health, independence, work, or something else. But that's what you should alter. Every single day, thank the universe for all that you have every single day. Through the universe, bring it out there. Make a habit of it.

3. Spread love

The act of bonding and sharing love is one sure-fire habit to cultivate that will improve overall happiness. Offer someone a hug or let yourself be hugged by another. Pick up your phone and tell someone you love them, or just listen to what someone's got to say. You'll be shocked by how rewarding it is to take an interest in the life of someone else.

This includes one phone call a day or an in-person meeting. It might be with someone you're already spending time with. Tell them how much you love them. Show love and compassion to them; pour it from your heart. What you bring out into the universe, you get 10-fold back. Make a habit of this, and you're going to have a much happier life.

4. Meditate

This does not have to be an experience of faith. It will improve your overall satisfaction, decrease stress, lower blood pressure, and relieve anxieties by actually practicing the art of meditation. A recent study published in Internal Medicine by JAMA notes just that: a meditation on mindfulness will relieve the psychological pressures associated with depression, anxiety, and pain.

What it takes is 15 minutes of gentle meditation to fulfill this habit. Sit in silence and make yourself present. Don't be involved in the future or the past. Don't worry or dwell on something; just be there at the moment. Sit in silence with your eyes closed and listen to the sounds around you. Feel the air flowing in and out of your lungs, the warmth of the sun on your shoulders, the coolness of the wind flowing through the room, etc. Simply be present. That's all that is important.

5. Regular Learning

Learning is important for our satisfaction regularly, but it also influences other facets of our lives' quality. It helps us to learn, develop, and gain knowledge of the world through experience. Laying the foundations for our personal and professional lives helps us bring life into perspective and eventually fulfill our dreams.

Find a newspaper, magazine, video guide, blog, or something else you enjoy using as a learning resource. Practice every single day, and do this for 15 to 30 minutes. You don't have to commit to massive time blocks. This practice will help you to be a much happier and well-rounded person, as long as you do a little bit every single day, but you do it every single day, over time.

HABITS OF WELLBEING

Compared to annual health habits, such as visiting the doctor or dentist, there are everyday health habits. Every single day, you should develop at least these top 5 health habits.

1. Eating breakfast

You've heard it before: the most important meal of the day is breakfast. And that isn't a lie. Studies have shown that women who have missed breakfast at least once a week are at higher risk for type II diabetes. Studies have also shown that men have lower incidences of heart failure while eating breakfast.

The benefits of eating breakfast every day are much greater and extend to an increase in memory and weight loss, and a reduction in LDL (bad cholesterol). To help it work optimally during the day, your body needs a healthy, nutritious, and nutritional breakfast. Don't steal from it.

2. Ten thousand moves

You may not be able to exercise every single day. But you should most likely make sure you walk a minimum of 10,000 steps. There are extraordinary health benefits of walking 10,000 steps. Too often, though, we do not travel up to as many steps or get even close to it. Studies have shown that waking up to 10,000 steps a day helps with weight loss and reduces the risk of heart disease and diabetes.

If you're not doing a lot of walking at the moment, then this could pose some difficulties for you. There are hacks here, however. For example, if you are currently driving all over the place, you can change your routine by walking a long distance to and from your car. At first, you could find it cumbersome, but you can slowly build up the habit over time. Do what it takes to achieve your target of 10,000 steps a day.

3. 64 ounces of water

All know of water's health benefits. Human adult bodies consist of up to 60 percent water, 73 percent of water consists of the brain and heart, and about 83 percent of water consists of the lungs. But, all too often, we don't get enough water. We prefer to get our water intake from sugar sodas, coffees, and other unhealthy beverages in general.

Drinking at least eight glasses of water, 64 ounces, is the general rule of thumb. But if you want to be more advanced and obey more scientific recommendations, the Institute of Medicine agreed that 3 liters (13 cups) should be for men and that there should be 2.2 liters (9 cups) for women.

4. Minerals & Vitamins

It's impossible to mention the many health benefits of getting the necessary vitamins and minerals every day. To receive the necessary vitamins and minerals that your body needs every day, ensure that you take at least one daily supplement. They are basically for all kinds of optimum functioning of the mind & body.

Sometimes, we don't get the required vitamins and minerals only from the food and drink we eat. This is no great surprise given that most people eat a largely unhealthy range of food & drink. Make this a must-have wellness routine for you and find a perfect once-a-day supplement that you can take to fulfill your everyday requirements.

5. *Brush & floss teeth*

Brushing & flossing may not sound like a wellness routine that must be had, but it is. Every day, there are so many health benefits connected with brushing and flossing. They help stave off gum disease, leading to even more extreme diseases such as delayed conception in women and heart disease and erectile dysfunction in men if left untreated.

Dementia and arthritis are other side effects of gum disease, and patients suffering from gum disease often have issues with memory loss, joint pain, and rheumatoid arthritis.

VITALITY HABITS

The sum of energy you have has a lot to do with your behaviors on a given day. People with bad habits tend to lack motivation and vitality in their lives. Habits influence not just the physical state-of-being, but also the state-of-mind of the mind.

1. *Management of time*

There is an increased amount of energy and vitality in people who control their time efficiently. Managing your time involves regular focus and a pursuit of the urgent over the important. This means delineating your activities so that you follow certain long-term objectives that are all-important and not simply respond to the urgent issues that come up in your day.

Based on their order of priority and urgency, time management can be accomplished by making lists and constructing tasks for the day. It also requires removing bad behaviors like procrastination, television over-watching, internet over-surfing, and so on.

2. Get a minimum of 7 hours of sleep

Your vitality needs to get at least 7 hours of sleep each night. When we sleep, so many significant tasks take place in the mind and body. It's an opportunity for our bodies to relax, unwind, and refresh. When we are consciously out, our unconscious mind and body are busy rebuilding, re-charging, and re-energizing at work.

Sleep deprivation, which impacts mood, energy, fitness, and mental well-being, affects most people. Several research has shown that not only does sleep help to enhance things such as memory, but it also increases the longevity of life, increases consciousness, and promotes creativity.

3. Eat Green Food

We should eat foods that are alkaline to fulfill this need for an alkaline demand from the body. Green foods, organic foods such as root vegetables, fruit, lemons, peppers, etc. are the best kinds of foods.

4. Exercise

Yes, we already said it, and repeat it again. There can be major health advantages to exercising at least 20 minutes per day. Many individuals do not make exercise a routine and suffer from a lack of vitality in exchange. To be called exercise, the body needs to shift, and you need to break a sweat. And, while your overall wellbeing is improved by taking 10,000 steps a day, it's not the same as exercising.

Find and adhere to an easy workout routine. Regardless of what sort of workout you do, just do something. Whether it is light jogging, weights, yoga, or some other lightly-strenuous exercise, it can help develop the habit by just getting started. Don't plan to go overnight from Zero to

Hero. It takes time to develop this habit. Start small and, over time, develop slowly.

5. Inspirational Input

Via everyday inspiration, one of the best ways to add vitality to your life is your motivation. What drives you to drive towards your goals and motivates you? By finding out some sort of knowledge, whatever it may be, give yourself the added boost necessary.

Imaging is one of the easiest ways to do this. Pictures are most likely worth a thousand words, and you will help to inspire and drive you towards your dreams by hanging those pictures somewhere you can see every day. We all get a little irritated from time to time, but if you spend 15 to 20 minutes every day on inspirational feedback, you'll see big results.

HABITS TO PROFITS

You may be wondering why we should talk about money habits in a relationship book. Well, you may already know it, but many pieces of research show that the more couples argue over money or financial problems, the more likely their relationship is to break up over money. Financial problems are one of the main causes of anxiety, whether or not you are in a relationship. When money issues affect both sides of a couple and how they interact with each other, they become a relationship problem.

The reason for that is that these financial problems are much more than just money. When you argue about spending or investing your money, you're arguing about issues going beyond the actual dollars and cents. If you look deeper, money management and spending habits are closely related to your beliefs, core values, and life goals. These are powerfully emotional issues that can make or break a relationship.

Money also tends to magnify the levels of power and trust in your relationship. This may cause relationships to split. Developing healthy income and money management habits helps push us towards those goals, whether you want to make a thousand dollars more every month, or a million dollars more. Check out the five most common income habits that you need to adopt regularly.

1. Set & Review Goals

It is important to set and review targets regularly to achieve your revenue goals. This is one of the best behaviors for achieving the monetary objectives that you may have. S.M.A.R.T.E.R.'s target setting requires setting (S)pecific, (M)easurable, (A)ttainable, (R)elevant, (T)ime-bound targets that are (E)valuated, and (R)e-adjusted over time.

Establish a goal-setting framework and ensure that you participate every day in setting goals. Pursue the important objectives to you and develop checklists to help you achieve what you want over time.

2. Save 20% of your salary

It also involves adhering to a strict saving schedule for a long period to get ahead. This money is not just for emergencies; it is cash at the moment of opportunity. It's cash that needs to be used when the right investment opportunity presents itself. To build up your assets for investment opportunities, at least 20 percent of your income should be saved. You should automate your savings. Install a savings account any time you get paid to subtract your personal account's funds automatically. Before you can even get used to having it in your bank account, ensure that the money goes out and make sure you can't access it in your savings account.

3. Track & audit costs

Right off the bat, many people will tell you their profits. They know exactly how much money they make because it seems to be set in general. Although most people can't tell you how much they spent last month on a particular expense group. It doesn't pay near enough attention to the money that goes out, just the money that comes in.

Tracking & auditing costs regularly should be something that should be done. It's important to know every penny that goes out the door, whether using a notepad or a digital spreadsheet. Large ships fall through small leaks. $5 a day of latte habits is equivalent to $1825 a year spent on coffee. Each day, $20 lunches are equivalent to $7300 a year. Track all of the expenditures and audit them.

4. Education

Training is one of the most significant income patterns you can endorse. Without schooling, it becomes extremely difficult to develop over time in profession and income. And, regularly, education must be provided, not something that occurs once or twice a year. Spend at least 30 minutes per day on your professional education.

If, in your intended area, you are not subscribing to a newsletter, magazine, or newspaper, then now is the time to do so. Subscribe to something that will help advance your career, whether you read it online or in print. Even better, if you want to teach yourself about investments, spend just a little time learning every day, and over time, you'll see amazing results.

5. Everyday budgeting

Create a budget and stick to it, and religiously execute it. Over time, this should allow you to save and invest your capital. It's much harder to get ahead and meet your revenue targets if you don't adhere to a schedule. It can motivate you to get ahead by understanding exactly how much money you can or can't spend every day.

Take your monthly budget and break it into a budget for each day. Cut

273

spending where you can and add as much money into your savings as possible. Time passes easily, so make sure you put your money where it counts.

HABITS OF LEISURE

What you do in your spare time has a huge effect on the quality of your life. When you do happen to have time for yourself, there are five behaviors that you should institute that will dramatically change your life.

1. Get organized

"Clean home, clean mind." Spend your spare time arranging your surroundings for a few minutes. Take 5 minutes for your desk to clean up, declutter, or just throw away things. When you get organized, you'll be shocked by how much your quality of life can improve.

But, it's not just washing and decluttering to get organized. Getting organized also has a lot to do with forming behaviors that will help shape your life's path and mold it. Understand where you are going and make sure you have a certain sense of clarity. Concentrate, imagine and get prepared.

2. Contribution

Many individuals take their free time for themselves. However, cultivating the leisure habit of contributing would help make an immense difference to improve your life quality. By contributing, you give your unconscious mind a simple message that there is more than enough for you, both your time and your money, to go around.

And, even if you don't have any spare cash to donate, donate your time. There are those out there who are in dire straits and need support somehow, and one of the greatest gifts you can give is to give your time. Every day, spend some time searching for ways you can give back.

3. Socializing & networking

Improve your life's consistency through socializing and networking. Seventy-nine percent of rich people spend 5 hours or more networking; it has been said, while the poor spend 16 percent of their time doing so. But, networking doesn't just have to be for business alone. Take an interest in the lives of other people, and you'll be shocked by how often it comes back to you.

4. Do one thing you fear

Do one thing that every single day you're scared of. By cultivating this habit, take your leisure time to the next level. What are you scared of doing? Why are you scared of doing it? Very often, because of how scared we are of something, we can not get ahead. For us, fear and anxiety tend to be overwhelming. Overcome your fears and push yourself to do the one thing that you hesitate to do.

5. Do one thing you've been putting off

Do one thing you put off every single day. This is a big way of overcoming procrastination and developing the recreational habit of moving your life forward. Build a list of all the items that were put off by you. Then, commit to spending just 15 minutes on one of those things every day. And if it's not possible to complete it, make sure you spend 15 minutes doing it.

Chapter 20:

UNDERSTANDING BODY LANGUAGE AND FACIAL EXPRESSIONS

The look on a person's face can also help decide if we trust or believe what the person is saying. One study found that a subtle eyebrow raise and a soft smile were involved in the most trustworthy facial expressions. The researchers indicated that this term conveys both friendliness and trust.

The universal forms of body language also involve facial expressions. The expressions used to communicate fear, rage, sorrow, and happiness are identical throughout the world. Researcher Paul Ekman has found evidence for various facial expressions' universality, including excitement, rage, fear, surprise, and sadness, linked to unique emotions. Research also suggests that we make assumptions based on their faces and gestures regarding the intelligence of people.

One study found that it was more likely that people who had smaller faces and more pronounced noses were viewed as intelligent. People with happy, cheerful faces were often considered to be smarter than those with angry faces.

The Eyes
The eyes are often referred to as the "windows to the soul" because they can reveal a lot about what a person feels or thinks. Taking note of eye

movements is a normal and essential part of the communication process when you engage in conversation with another person.

If people make direct eye contact or avert their attention, how often they blink, or whether their pupils are dilated are some common things you can find. Pay attention to the following eye gestures when determining body language.

The gaze of the Eye. When an individual looks into your eyes directly while having a conversation, it demonstrates that they are interested in paying attention. Prolonged eye contact, however, can feel menacing. Breaking eye contact and sometimes looking away, on the other hand, might mean that the individual is distracted, embarrassed, or trying to hide his or her true feelings.

Blinks. Blinking is normal, but you should also pay attention to whether too much or too little of a person is blinking. When they are feeling upset or nervous, people sometimes blink more quickly. Infrequent blinking can mean that a person is attempting to regulate his or her eye movements deliberately. For instance, a poker player may blink less frequently because he is intentionally trying to appear unexcited about the hand he was handed.

Scale of Pupil. A very subtle nonverbal communication signal can be pupil size. Although light levels influence pupil dilation in the atmosphere, emotions often may also cause minor changes in the pupil's size. For instance, when they are attracted to another person, you might have heard the word "bedroom eyes" to describe the look someone gives. For instance, highly dilated eyes may mean that a person is interested or even aroused.

The Mouth

In reading body language, mouth expressions and gestures may also be important. Chewing on the bottom lip, for instance, may suggest that the person experiences feelings of concern, anxiety, or insecurity. If the person is yawning or coughing, covering the mouth may be an effort to be polite, but it may also be an attempt to cover up a frown of disapproval. Smiling is probably one of the main signs of body language, but smiles can also be perceived in several respects. A smile can be sincere or can portray fake optimism, sarcasm, or even cynicism.

Pay attention to the following mouth and lip signals when analyzing body language:

- *Pursed lips.* A sign of distaste, disdain, or mistrust may be tightening the mouth.
- *Lips biting.* When they are worried, anxious, or depressed, people often bite their lips.
- *Mouth covering.* When people want to mask an emotional reaction, they may cover their mouths to avoid revealing smiles or smirks.
- *Lips turned up or down.* Slight mouth changes can be subtle indications of what a person thinks, too. When the mouth is slightly turned up, it might suggest that the person feels happy or hopeful. On the other hand, a slightly down-turned lip may be an indication of sorrow, rejection, or even an outright grimace.

Gestures

We could write a whole book about this subject! Some of the clearest and visible signs of body language can be gestures. Waving, pointing, and using fingers to signify numerical quantities are very common movements that are simple to understand.

However, certain signs could be cultural, so giving in another country a

278

thumbs-up or a peace sign may have a different significance than it does in the United States. Only a couple of famous gestures and their possible meanings are the following examples. In certain situations or solidarity in others, a clenched fist can indicate anger. As signals of support and rejection, thumbs up and thumbs down are also used.

The "okay" gesture can be used to signify "okay" or "all right" by touching the thumb and index finger together in a circle while spreading the other three fingers. However, in some parts of Europe, the same symbol is used to show that you are nothing. The symbol is simply a lewd gesture in some South American countries.

In some countries, the V sign, created by raising the index and middle finger and separating them to create a V-shape, implies peace or victory. The emblem takes on an aggressive significance in the United Kingdom and Australia when the hand's back is facing outward.

The Legs and Arms

In conveying nonverbal knowledge, the arms and legs may also be useful. It may mean defensiveness to cross the arms. Crossing legs away from another individual may display dislike or discomfort with that person. An attempt to appear larger or more dominant while holding the arms close to the body can be an effort to diminish oneself or withdraw from view, other subtle gestures such as spreading the arms broadly.

Pay attention to several of the following signals that the arms and legs can convey when evaluating body language. Crossed arms can show that an individual feels defensive, self-protective, or closed-off. Standing with hands placed on the hips may mean that an individual is ready and in control, or may also be a sign of aggressiveness. Clamping the hands be-hind the back can mean that a person feels bored, nervous, or even angry. Tapping fingers or fidgeting rapidly may signify that an individual is bored, irritated, or annoyed. Crossed legs may mean that a person feels closed off or in need of confidentiality.

Posture

As an integral part of body language, how we carry our bodies may also serve. The term posture refers to how we carry our bodies and an individual's overall physical structure. Posture can communicate a wealth of knowledge about how an individual feels and clues about personality characteristics, such as whether an individual is positive, accessible, or submissive.

For instance, sitting up straight can mean that a person is focused and paying attention to what is happening. On the other hand, sitting with the body hunched forward, may mean that the individual is bored or indifferent. Try to note some of the signs a person's posture can send when trying to read body language. The open posture requires holding the body's trunk open and uncovered. Friendliness, transparency, and readiness are suggested in this kind of pose. Closed stance includes covering the trunk of the body by hunching over and holding crossed arms and legs. A sign of aggression, unfriendliness, and anxiety can be this type of pose.

Personal Space

Have you heard someone ever refer to their need for personal space? Have you ever begun to feel awkward when someone just stands a little too close to you?

Proxemics, coined by anthropologist Edward T. Hall, refers to the distance between individuals when they communicate. Just as a great deal of nonverbal knowledge can be conveyed through body gestures and facial expressions, so can the physical space between people.

Hall defined four levels of social distance occurring in various situations.

Intimate Distance: between 6 and 18 inches. This degree of physical distance also suggests a closer relationship between individuals or greater comfort. Intimate interaction, such as kissing, whispering, or touching, typically occurs.

Personal Distance: between 1.5 and 4 feet. At this stage, physical distance typically happens between individuals who are family members or near friends. A measure of the degree of intimacy in their relationship may be the closest people can stand comfortably when communicating.

Social Distance: between 4 and 12 feet. This degree of physical distance with people who are acquaintances is also used. You might feel more comfortable communicating at a greater distance with someone you know reasonably well, such as a co-worker you see many times a week. A distance of 10 to 12 feet may feel more secure in scenarios where you do not know the other person well, such as a postal delivery driver whom you only see once a month.

Public Distance: between 12 and 25 feet. In public speaking contexts, the physical distance at this stage is also used. Good examples of such scenarios include speaking in front of a class full of students or making a presentation at work. It is also important to remember that the degree of personal distance people need to feel relaxed will vary from culture to culture.

The differentiation between individuals from Latin cultures and those from North America is one often-cited example. When communicating, Latin nations seem to feel more comfortable standing next to each other, whereas those from North America need more personal distance.

Body language comprehension will go a long way to helping you connect more with others and to understand what others might be trying to express. While it may be tempting to pick apart signals one by one, about verbal communication, other nonverbal signals, and the situation, it is important to look at these nonverbal signals.

You should also learn more about how to strengthen your nonverbal communication, without even saying a word, to let people know what you feel. More on this in the next chapters.

Chapter 21: EMOTIONAL INTELLIGENCE

The capacity to interpret, regulate, and assess emotions refers to Emotional Intelligence (EI). Some researchers say that it is possible to acquire and reinforce Emotional Intelligence, while others say it is an inborn trait.

It is important to express and regulate emotions, but so is the ability to understand, perceive, and respond to others' emotions. Imagine a world where when a friend is feeling depressed or when a co-worker is upset, you do not understand. Psychologists referred to this ability as Emotional Intelligence, and some experts also say that it may be more important in your overall life performance than IQ.

Emotional Intelligence History

Until around 1990, Emotional Intelligence as a term did not come into our vernacular. Despite being a relatively new term, since then, interest in the notion has grown tremendously.

Early Expansion. Psychologist Edward Thorndike described the concept of 'Social Intelligence' as the ability to get along with other people as early as the 1930s. Psychologist David Wechsler suggested that during the 1940s, various effective components of intelligence could play an important role in how successful individuals are in life.

Later Evolutions. The emergence of the school of thought known as humanistic psychology was seen in the 1950s, and thinkers like Abraham Maslow centered more emphasis on the various ways in which people could create emotional power.

The concept of multiple intelligences was another important conception to arise in the creation of Emotional Intelligence. Howard Gardner put forth this concept in the mid-1970s, presenting the concept that intelligence was more than just a single, general skill.

The Emergence of Emotional Intelligence. The word "Emotional Intelligence" was first used in 1985 by Wayne Payne in a doctoral thesis. In 1987, Keith Beasley used the word "Emotional Quotient" in an article published in Mensa Magazine.

In 1990, in the journal Imagination, Perception, and Personality, psychologists Peter Salovey and John Mayer published their landmark paper, "Emotional Intelligence." They described Emotional Intelligence as "the ability to track the feelings and emotions of one's own and others, to differentiate between them, and to use this data to direct one's thinking and behavior."

In 1995, after the publication of the book "Emotional Intelligence: Why It Can Matter More Than IQ" by Daniel Goleman, the idea of Emotional Intelligence was popularized. The topic of Emotional Intelligence has continued to catch public attention as it has become relevant in fields outside of psychology, including education and industry.

How to test Emotional Intelligence

To assess levels of Emotional Intelligence, a variety of different tests have arisen. Generally, such assessments fall into one of two types: self-report assessments and tests of ability.

The most popular are self-report assessments because they are the simplest to perform and score. On such assessments, by rating their actions, respondents respond to questions or comments. For example, a test taker may describe the statement as disagreeing, slightly disagreeing,

agreeing, or strongly agreeing on a statement such as "I sometimes feel I understand how others feel."

On the other hand, performance assessments include making individuals react to circumstances and then testing their abilities. These assessments also enable individuals to demonstrate their skills, which are then rated by a third party.

Here are two tests that could be included if you are taking an Emotional Intelligence exam provided by a mental health professional.

The MSCEIT (Mayer-Salovey-Caruso Emotional Intelligence Test) is a skill-based test that tests the four branches of Mayer and Salovey's EI model. Test-takers perform activities aimed at evaluating their ability to interpret, recognize, comprehend, and control feelings.

The Emotional and Social Competency Inventory (ESCI) is based on an older instrument known as the Self-Assessment Questionnaire. It includes providing scores of that person's abilities in many different emotional competencies to individuals who know the individual. The test is intended to measure the social and emotional qualities that enable people to be distinguished as strong leaders.

There are also plenty of more informal online resources to investigate your Emotional Intelligence, many of them free.

Components

Researchers say that there are four distinct types of Emotional Intelligence, including emotional awareness, the capacity to use emotions to reason, comprehend emotions, and the ability to control emotions.

1. Emotion perceiving: The first step in recognizing emotions is to interpret them correctly. This might include recognizing nonverbal signs such as body language and facial expressions in certain instances.

2. Emotion reasoning: The next step includes the use of emotions to facilitate thought and cognitive activity. Emotions help prioritize what we pay attention to and respond to; we respond to items that attract our attention emotionally.

3. Emotions understanding: A wide range of interpretations can hold the emotions we experience. The observer must perceive the origin of the person's anger and what it might mean if someone shows angry emotions. If your boss is acting mad, for instance, it could mean that they are unhappy with your job, or it could be because that morning they got a speeding ticket on their way to work or because they were arguing with their wife.

4. Emotion management: The ability to successfully control emotions is a key component of the highest degree of Emotional Intelligence. Regulating emotions, reacting correctly and listening to other people's emotions are important aspects of emotional management.

With the more simple processes at the lower levels and the more sophisticated processes at the higher levels, this model's four divisions are grouped by complexity. For instance, the lowest levels include emotion perception and expression, while higher levels require greater conscious intervention and include emotion regulation.

5 PRIMARY EMOTIONAL INTELLIGENCE COMPONENTS

Emotional Intelligence Effect

In recent years, interest in cognitive and Emotional Intelligence teaching and learning has increased. Social and Emotional Learning (SEL) programs for many schools have become a regular part of the curriculum. In addition to improving health and well-being, these programs' goal is to help students excel academically and avoid bullying. In everyday life, there are several examples of how Emotional Intelligence can play a role.

Thinking Before Responding

Emotionally intelligent people know that emotions can be strong, but transient as well. The emotionally intelligent approach will take some time before reacting when a highly charged emotional event arises, such as becoming upset with a partner or a co-worker. This helps everyone to relax their feelings and think about all the factors surrounding the debate more rationally.

Greater Self-Consciousness

Not only are emotionally intelligent individuals excellent at thinking about how other individuals would feel, but they are also skilled at knowing their own emotions. Self-awareness helps individuals to understand the many different variables that lead to their feelings.

Empathy with Others

Thinking about and empathizing with how other people feel is a big part of Emotional Intelligence. This also includes thinking how, if you were in the same position, you would react. People with high Emotional Intelligence can understand other people's viewpoints, perceptions, and feelings and use this data to explain why individuals act the way they do.

How to Make Use

Emotional Intelligence can be found in daily life in several different ways. Such distinct ways of exercising Emotional Intelligence include:

- Being willing to embrace critique and transparency
- Being willing to pass on despite having made an error
- Being capable of saying no when you need to
- Being willing to share with others your thoughts
- Being capable of addressing issues in ways that work for everyone
- Getting empathy with other people
- Having an excellent listening capacity
- Knowing why the things you do are done for you
- Being not judgmental toward others

For effective interpersonal communication, Emotional Intelligence is important. Some experts claim that in deciding life success, this skill is more important than IQ alone. Fortunately, to improve your own social and Emotional Intelligence, there are things that you can do.

The secret to healthier relationships, increased well-being, and good communication skills can be the understanding of feelings.

Tips for EI Improvement

It is important to be emotionally intelligent, but what steps can you take to develop your own social and emotional skills? Here are a couple of tips.

Listen. The first step is to pay attention if you want to comprehend what other individuals are experiencing. Take time to listen to what people, both verbally and non-verbally, are trying to tell you. Body language can hold a lot of significance. Consider the various factors that may lead to the emotion when you sense that someone is feeling a certain way.

Empathizing. It is important to pick up on emotions, but you need to be able to put yourself in someone else's shoes to truly understand their point of view. Practice empathizing with individuals. Imagine how you would feel in their place. These activities will help you gain an emotional understanding of a specific situation and improve stronger emotional abilities in the long term.

Reflect. The capacity to reason with feelings is a significant feature of Emotional Intelligence. Consider how your thoughts shape your choices and actions. When you think about how other individuals react, determine the role that their feelings play.

Why is this person feeling this way? Are there any hidden variables that could lead to these emotions? How do they differ the emotions from theirs? You can find it easier to understand the role that emotions play in how people think and act when discussing such questions.

EMOTIONALLY INTELLIGENT PEOPLE'S HABITS
Potential Pitfalls
Lower Emotional Intelligence can lead to several potential pitfalls, including work and relationships, that can affect multiple areas of life. People who have fewer emotional abilities tend to have more arguments, lower quality relationships, and poor emotional coping abilities.

Being low in Emotional Intelligence can have several setbacks, but it can also be challenging to have a very high emotional skills level. For instance, research indicates that individuals with high Emotional Intelligence may be less innovative and creative.

It may be difficult for highly emotionally intelligent individuals to provide negative feedback for fear of hurting other individuals' feelings. Research has found that for manipulative and deceptive purposes, high EQ can sometimes be used.

289

8 LOW EMOTIONAL INTELLIGENCE SYMPTOMS

Are you familiar with someone who never seems to be able to control their feelings? Perhaps, at the wrong time, they are continuously doing the wrong things. Or maybe they still judge people, but they have a tough time acknowledging criticism. If someone you know describes this, the chances are high that this individual struggles with low Emotional Intelligence.

Low Emotional Intelligence means the inability to interpret feelings correctly (in both yourself and others) and to use the data to direct your thoughts and actions.

For virtually every aspect of life, Emotional Intelligence (sometimes called "Emotional Quotient" or "EQ") is important. As already mentioned, many experts now agree that EQ may be more important than IQ to decide overall success in life. As such, your interpersonal relationships and your mental and physical well-being can be adversely affected by low EQ or low Emotional Intelligence.

If anyone has a low EQ, there are several ways in which they can show themselves. Eight classic symptoms of people with low Emotional Intelligence are below.

1. They have to always be 'Right.' You also know someone who appears to have arguments with others at all times. In conflicts with these argumentative people, acquaintances, relatives, co-workers, and even total strangers find themselves entangled.

Individuals with low EQ will also argue a death point while refusing to listen to what someone else has to say. They would argue that your facts are incorrect, even though you provide them with evidence that they are accurate. At all costs, they have to win and find it difficult to only "agree to disagree." This is especially true if other individuals are critical of how they do not understand what others feel.

2. They're oblivious to the feelings of other people. Many people with low EQ are unaware of the emotions of others. They may be truly shocked that they are upset at their partner or do not like their co-workers. Not only that, but when people expect them to know how they are feeling, they get irritated.

3. They Act Insensitively. People with low EQ, for the most part, do not know the right thing to say. They might also struggle to grasp the pacing of saying things properly versus improperly. For instance, they may say something offensive at a funeral or make a joke right after a traumatic accident. They behave as if you're overly sensitive if you respond to their out-of-line answer.
Since they have trouble understanding others' emotions, it's no wonder that they cannot perceive the emotional tone and environment and react appropriately.

4. They blame others for their problem. People with low EQ have no insight into how their emotions could trigger issues. The one thing that a person with low Emotional Intelligence is not going to do is take responsibility for their actions.
If something goes wrong, finding someone or something else to blame is their first reaction. They could say that they had no other choice with what they have done and that others don't understand their situation. For instance, it's your fault to leave your phone unlocked if they read through your texts. Somehow, if they miss an assignment, break a lock, don't get the work done, or burn dinner, someone else's mistake will make it.

5. They have poor knowledge in dealing with emotions. An indication of low EQ may be an inability to deal with emotionally-charged circumstances. For those with low Emotional Intelligence, intense emotions, whether their own or others, are hard to comprehend. To avoid dealing with the emotional fallout, these individuals will always walk away from these circumstances. It is also very normal to conceal their true emotions

6. *They have emotional outbursts.* One of the components of Emotional Intelligence is the capacity to control emotions. People with low EQ also fail to grasp their emotions and control them. Without knowing what they feel or why they are so angry, they may lash out reactively. There may also be sudden emotional outbursts that seem overblown and uncontrollable for a person who lacks EQ. In a tirade that can last for minutes, even hours, the slightest things set them off.

7. *They struggle with relationships.* Often, individuals with low EQ have very few close friends. This is because close friendships require reciprocal giving-and-taking, emotional exchange, kindness, and emotional support, usually missing in all features of low-EQ individuals. Alternatively, individuals with low EQ often come off as abrasive and unfeeling.

8. *Conversations are turned towards themselves.* People who are emotionally unintelligent appear to dominate the conversation. They still find a way to move it back to them, even though they ask questions and seem to be listening intently. They usually have to show that whatever you meet, they've had better or worse.

No matter what you say, they did that; they were there. Were you involved in a car accident? They still have... and their dog died. Heading to Mount Kilimanjaro for a climb? Four years ago, they climbed Mount Everest. If you like, they will give you a list of tips!

In many areas of your life, low Emotional Intelligence can cause problems. Learning more about EI can help you connect with your partner and ultimately live a healthier relationship. Fortunately, to increase your

Emotional Intelligence, there are things you can do. Sharpening your talents will strengthen your personal and professional experiences.

Chapter 22: THE SECRETS TO RELATIONSHIP CONTENTMENT

Most of us associate peace with happy relationships: getting along, agreeing, and not disappointing each other. In the extreme, however, it can be exhausting to constantly try to keep things rosy with a spouse or partner, which can strain the bond. Relationship contentment is far more than avoiding wars.

You typically say yes to most of the things your partner asks or needs to keep your relationship free of tension and calm: always go along with their intentions when you would rather do something else, or take on several tasks or tasks to prevent an argument. "You think it is much better than" rocking the relationship boat.

Balance is essential

Granted, denying the individual you love and whom you want to support can be overwhelming. A going-along strategy seems prudent when you're in love, or, at least, you believe it is. You force your desires to the backburner in over-striving for relationship contentment, however. You end up dissatisfied in the extreme, mostly because being trapped in a pattern of the agreement will result in stressful feelings of impotence.

For long stretches, spouses who are endlessly cooperative feel as though they are taken for granted, and their frustration builds, and the relationship suffers. The one mistake that gets replicated over and over in relationships is being unable to deny your partner, and it's the one thing you can improve.

By standing up for what you want, it is possible to make your relationship more equal. You'll feel more like sharing your love and affection by doing so and making your connection stronger.

Three-pointers to communicate your needs

1. Have your yes-patterns tested.

Seek ways of making improvements that are equal and gentle. Say that while your partner can comfortably split the load, you have fallen into the habit of doing a chore, one you hate. It may be that you are still the one who washes or cooks breakfast regularly. Because these tasks pop up frequently, you can feel as if complying is your only choice. Break it if this is a trend you hate. Consider dividing the job instead of going to extremes and making your spouse do the laundry or make breakfast every day. You wash it; your wife folds it and puts it away. Similarly, on less-hectic days, you just plan breakfasts. The improvements are more likely to stick when you say no to being liable for most household duties and propose equal solutions.

2. Know that it isn't a deal-breaker to show disagreement.

Showing unhappiness is not, either. Imagine, on the other hand, you keep your lips zipped, but you're secretly furious. That will intensify tensions that are sure to increase. Note that individuals are not mind-readers. If dread or tension is your knee-jerk response to an appeal, favor, or announcement, speak up. If your partner violates your limits or challenges your tolerance, this is particularly the case. For instance, if your spouse asks if it is okay if the in-laws stay a week longer than you would be able to handle reasonably, try saying, "That's not going to work for me." "We need another strategy." You might also want to follow the expression, "This is what I'm doing, in other cases." Make it clear that you are not asking for permission or approval.

3. When it comes to screen time, just put your foot down.

Our smartphones, TVs, and other computers seem to be too glued by most of us. Say something when your partner's screening patterns conflict with your time together (e.g., dates, meals). For healthy relationships, face-to-face contact is essential. Try to suggest, "Let's just switch our phones off and focus on us." Or, "I don't want to sit here, forget my spaghetti, and have a talk with my spaghetti." You might even suggest a rule to keep smartphones during dinner or when you have company in a container. There is various research with proof to back you up.

In your partnership, accepting the word "no" or its counterpart is something you should do. It helps make way for more positive changes to stand up for yourself: you can start to feel more like complementing and helping each other. You're going to feel linked more.

Partnership is a two-way street when you are in love. As vital as preserving harmony, your needs and justice are just as necessary. Saying no, altering the status quo, goes a long way to creating and sustaining happiness in relationships.

Chapter 23: HOW TO BUILD HEALTHY TIES AND AVOID UNHEALTHY RELATIONSHIPS

While no woman (man) is an island, getting along with others can also be challenging. They all have their ups and downs in friendships and romantic ventures, but you never want to be trapped in a relationship that does more harm than good. That's why, when it comes to your relations with others, it's good to set the right kind of standards. You'll be on your way to establishing healthy relationships and avoiding potentially toxic environments if you follow these rules.

Of who you are, stay real.
It can easily be swept away in a new relationship, whether it's a friend with an infectious personality or a charming partner. And while it's good to respect others for who they are, your special personality should also be welcomed! Know, in the first place: there is a reason they like you, so don't forget your special qualities. Keep in mind your objectives and development, regardless of how much time you spend with someone new.

From day one, be transparent and honest.
Constructing it based on dishonesty would be one of the worst things you might do to undermine a new friendship or relationship. It doesn't necessarily have to be a big old dirty lie that you're hiding. Anything

insignificant might be withheld. For instance, lying and pretending you like spicy food to please your friend at dinner may not seem like a big deal. But later on, when your mouth is constantly on fire, you're going to regret that decision, and they'll be insulted that you didn't feel you should tell them the truth.

Learn empathy for the other person.
Empathy is a fancy way to say, "put yourself in the shoes of someone else." Take a second to think about how your counterpart would feel considering their circumstance and personality. Everyone is on their path, and often it can be difficult to note that anything might have a different effect on another person than it would affect you. Self-centeredness or narcissism is the enemy of empathy, so make efforts to eradicate them from your relationship.

Constant interaction is essential.
Constant contact does not mean you're nonstop texting or calling each other. But it is essential to remain open to contact when there is uncertainty or a misunderstanding. It will only make it harder to simply shut down and avoid a problem. It's best to work things out and start things off with a strategy as they occur to talk about things. Perhaps your friend or partner is someone who needs to take a step back before a conversation, which is fine as long as shortly afterward, you can discuss things civilly.

Be consistent and efficient.
Don't be the one who always flakes out, who nobody likes! Simply turning up and doing what you say, you're going to do part of building a trustworthy relationship. In one area of your life, if you are unreliable, there is a fair possibility that you are unreliable in other respects, too. Establish strong bonds of confidence and belief for any link to a stable backbone.

Where you need them, set boundaries.

Keep in mind that you can apply these "boundaries" to any subject. Set a cap to not let your friend ask for any more before the first amount is paid back if your friend continues borrowing money from you. Set the barrier if your partner wants to spend every waking moment with you, but you need time alone. It's all about reaching an understanding and knowing what's best for you, what's best for them.

There has to be fairness and reciprocity.

Of course, unless all individuals consciously follow them, any previous laws don't work. This doesn't mean that you have to keep a better buddy; just make sure that you both put in the effort and pull your weight. No relationship is flawless, and sometimes it's a lot of work. Only remember that to tango, it takes two!

SIX WAYS TO DEVELOP BETTER RELATIONSHIP

Happiness is an elusive subject that throughout history has been studied and contemplated by many. While there are many ideas and philosophies of what it means to be happy, I wanted to concentrate on the relational aspect of happiness in this book.

It is no accident that online dating and the wedding sector are highly popular firms. Human beings pursue near and intimate relationships and crave them. We feel "whole" when we feel loved and connected. Romantic relationships, however, are not the main or even primary source of relational happiness. Friendships and relationships with family can be just as meaningful.

A psychotherapist may also ask, "Who is your support network?" while someone in therapy is going through a tough time. This is an important question because the better the support network, the easier the recovery. Feeling valued and embraced by a "tribe" is always essential to make us happy. The study, in truth, also reveals the mental and physical benefits of friendship.

On the other end of the continuum, of course, partnerships often have the potential to make us deeply dissatisfied. It can feel bad to be in the wrong relationship or surrounded by people who do not make us feel comfortable or take advantage of us and drain us emotionally. Positive relationships increase our satisfaction, but negative relationships can make us sad. It is essential to know how to build satisfying relationships since relationships are so strong. No one tells us how to be in relationships in our lives. In school, no lessons are teaching us how to have safe and happy relationships. We mostly only handle them on our own and, as we go, learn.

What are the things one can do to develop better relationships with others, considering that we are sometimes uneducated about healthy relationships? Here are a handful of tips.

1. Empathy: The most fruitful relationship dynamics are where there is a clear sense of empathy for each person involved in the relationship. Empathy means that you are deliberately thinking about how another person would feel and behave appropriately and thoughtfully accordingly. Because of the narcissism, selfishness, or superiority of one person, I've seen many relationships end. You need to imagine yourself in their shoes if you want to develop a true sense of closeness and intimacy and with another human. I think the cornerstone and center of any good partnership is empathy.

2. Thoughtfulness and Kindness: I don't mean that you can buy your friends and family lavish gifts (or gifts at all) when I use the term 'generosity.' Generosity is the generosity of feeling. A sign of thoughtfulness and kindness is also only checking in with others regularly to prove you care. It is also a form of thoughtfulness and kindness to express gratitude by words, gift-giving, verbal gratitude, or any thoughtful gesture that shows others you are thinking of them.

3. *Continuity and Follow Through:* Nobody likes someone who keeps bailing, not following through, or making false promises all the time. Before people stop putting up with it, you can only get away with flaky behavior for so long.

4. *Compromise and Fairness:* There should be a sense of reciprocity in all partnerships. This does not imply tit for tat; rather, it implies that both sides should not believe that the relationship is one-sided or unequal. A degree of compromise and fairness is necessary for all strong relationships. People who constantly take from others and expect others without raising a finger to give and bend over backward for them are others who do not have many friends or any real-life friendships.

5. *Only when you need something, don't ask people for things:* When anyone calls you just when they need something from you, isn't it the most irritating thing? Beyond only selfish desires, all good and stable relationships can stem from something. When they feel like you genuinely like them for who they are and not what you can do for them, people are more likely to want to do nice things for you.

6. *Boundaries:* when you're in a relationship with somebody who has little to no empathy, is not emotionally generous, is flaky, does not compromise, or just asks for something from you if they need something from you, set a boundary and distance yourself from the person or terminate the relationship completely. There is no point in getting relationships that make you feel bad, rob you, and leave you resentful.

10 TIPS TO HELP COUPLES CONTINUE TO DEVELOP IN A RELATIONSHIP

We talked extensively about the work that it takes to make a relationship a joyful adventure. Here below, I'm listing a few tips that can keep a relationship growing.

1. You don't need to settle. You can expand your relationship and make it something that improves your life continuously. A good relationship is like something you love. You have to be dedicated to learning, developing, and always looking to change. You need to act when you feel like you settling becomes a chasm of stagnation or worse.

2. Arguing is great. Many studies indicate that there are better marriages for couples who dispute. In a relationship, it takes a while to learn this. Some may see arguments as a weakness, but the reality is that they are essential components of a good partnership. To argue well, i.e., you can speak when the sparks are finished flying, implies that you must value each other and the relationship enough to fight for it.

3. Say that you're sorry and that you own it. If there's a bad argument, just walk away. Then when you're ready to own your share of the fiasco, come back and say you're sorry. In return, expect nothing. A sure sign to your loved one that your friendship is more than skin deep is this sort of unconditional response to adversity.

4. Create time for your relationship to be spoken about. Schedule time where you give each other a chance to speak without prejudice or bitterness about the relationship. And intend to approach your relationship like a third person by "talking about your relationship." Are we communicating properly, are their concerns unresolved, etc.

5. Remind yourself always why in the first place you fell in love. Look at old frames, tell ancient tales, recall the first magnetic embers of love. At this moment, we are not only who we are; we are the product of the past, the present, and the future. For future development, use the victories and lessons of the past as fuel.

6. Share adventures. Our lives can be so crazy that we tend to forget about the little pleasures. Go for walks, together, shopping, coffee, whatever. Even a brief enjoyment will seem like a walk on the beach when life has overwhelmed us.

7. Spend time concentrating completely on your companion. Massage them, listen and don't speak before your fingers cramp up, go with them on an errand that they should do alone, write them a poem or love letter like you did when you fell in love. Only pray for them. Focusing on them would make the bond stronger.

8. Scheduling space for each other. To grow, you need space. A suffocating relationship kills growth. We need liberty in the comfort of a pledge. One that is aware of this space is a good partnership.

9. Keep track of your progress. Set relationship expectations and keep track of them. You need to prepare, set goals, work, and evaluate to develop a relationship like anything else of value.

10. Two people working together is a positive partnership. Two people build something deeper and stronger than themselves, but they are still themselves. A stable relationship is a sort of like a trinity. You must still grow as a person and not lose yourself for a relationship to grow. For mothers, this can be truly challenging. They can get so wrapped up in the office, husband, kids that they can no longer remember who they are. Make sure that's what you support her with.

7 WAYS TO COMMUNICATE WITH YOUR PARTNER

One of the most amazing experiences in life is interacting with a loved one. Loneliness goes away when we interact with someone we love, and we feel full of joy inside. This relation we yearn for, but we always find it elusive.

To help your relationship with your partner, there are quite clear things you should do.

1. Connecting to Yourself

When you are separated from yourself, you cannot communicate with your partner. When you are accessible and flowing inside, communication with another occurs, not when you feel anxious and needy. Do your inner work to bring yourself into a loving place before attempting to communicate with your partner. When you want to express your love, you can communicate with your partner, not when you attempt to receive love.

2. Open to learning

We are in one of two forms at any given moment: the intention of learning about love and reality and the intention to protect against pain with some sort of behavior control. Controlling conduct closes our hearts and divides us from our spouses and ourselves. Our heart opens as we want to be open to learning about loving ourselves and our partner, which helps us bond. With a closed core, we cannot communicate. A connection needs to choose the purpose of learning while with your partner.

3. Be Present

Nothing more disconnects partners than when one talks and the other thinks about other things and does not even hear the partner. This makes you feel invisible to your mate. Be present while you are with your partner. Look at your partner — in the mind of your partner, if you can. Uh, listen. Take note of what your partner thinks and feels. Be reactive. If you are always worried while you are with your partner, do some internal work and find out what you avoid. A lack of presence means that you are separated from both yourself and your partner, so you need to learn to be present with your partner at the moment if you want to communicate.

4. Reflect on what you like in your spouse, not on what you don't like
Then you will also respect your partner's essence as you do your inner work and learn to love and respect who you are in your heart. We just deserve to be seen for who we are — which, when we are transparent, is who we are. As fears are activated, as they do in all relationships, we can turn to different defensive, controlling behaviors that are learned. But these learned habits of defense are not who we are. We are our nature, our spirit, our true self, which is always beautiful and majestic. This is actually what you fell in love with when your partner first fell in love with you. You can build distance and disconnection if you concentrate on your partner's wounded behaviors from fear. You will build the arena for interaction if you reflect on your partner's wonderful core values and always talk to them.

5. Schedule pleasant dates and time together
Relation occurs when partners have time to be together in a fun and comfortable way. Ways include having dinner, having a walk together, sharing interesting things about their day, cooking together, making something together, holding each other and chatting, playing a sport together, watching a comedy show together, etc.

Most people say things like, "We sat in the restaurant and spoke for hours" when they first interacted with each other. This is what generated the bond, and this is what you need to prepare together in your life to sustain the bond.

6. Supporting your partner in what gives him or her pleasure
When we feel encouraged by them in what we love to do, it is much easier to hold our hearts open with our partner. Partners derive pleasure from the other's pleasure in successful relationships.

Supporting your partner's happiness is not the same thing as supporting the addictive behavior of your partner. You need to focus on what you want if your partner's behavior is detrimental to you, such as having an affair or getting drunk. But if your partner is threatening you to spend time with friends or spend time alone or play a sport with someone of their equal capacity, then to value yourself enough not to be threatened, you need to do your internal job. It is part of a healthy partnership and building relationships to encourage each other in what we each love to do.

7. Be there for each other when one is triggered
All of us have our vulnerabilities — that childhood causes, that place us in pain, anxiety, or sadness. Often, through frustration or isolation, a partner defends against the pain. You need to learn how to be there with care and consideration for the other instead of being reactive to your partner's causes and heading into your anger or withdrawal. When old wounds are caused, we all need help and support, and caring partners will learn how to do this for each other. It doesn't mean that you take responsibility for your partner's feelings — this is not at all helpful — but it means that you know how to help your partner cope with the difficult feelings by encouraging him or herself. Compassion for the wounds and

weaknesses of each other goes a long way towards the development of relationships.

For your well-being and the well-being of the partnership, communication with your partner is essential. If you find it difficult for you to make some of these recommendations, then do some inner work to find out what's in the way. If you can't follow these ideas yet, you might want to get some counseling, coaching, or facilitation to cure something that prevents you from communicating with yourself and your partner.

Chapter 24: LOVE FINDING TOOLS: HELP YOU FIND THE PARTNERSHIP YOU WANT

Many of us feel helpless when searching to find a love like it's entirely outside of our control. It's not to say that we need advice on what we should do to find love from well-intended sources, i.e., "put you out there," "smile at strangers," "try this dating website," "have a friend hook you up," "stop dating jerks."

While these are not bad ideas, when it comes to the deeper aim of actually seeking love, they seem to scratch the surface. No matter how many strategies we try, we might still be hitting the same walls that make us think that finding love has more to do with chance than power. However, Dr. Lisa Firestone, psychologist and researcher (we "met" her and her father earlier in this book), make a strong case. She says that there are practical aspects that we should consciously focus on in ourselves that direct us to find love and help us build a strong foundation for long-lasting and fulfilling relationships. For more than 30 years, Dr. Firestone, co-author of Sex and Love in Intimate Relationships, has collaborated with couples and written extensively on romantic relationships. We can learn from her here about the elements that get in our way of finding love and the best advice to conquer internal hurdles and find the love we think we want.

How does our way of seeking love get in the way?

*Holding to Our Defenses. R*etaining those psychological defenses is one of the key ways we get in our way to finding love. These protections come from adaptations we have created, sometimes very early in our lives, to traumatic experiences. Long before we start dating, this phase of being defended starts in our childhoods when hurtful experiences and dynamics lead us to put up walls or view the world through a filter that can adversely affect us as adults. Such changes will cause us to become more and more self-protective and closed off.

In our early lives, dynamics that harmed us could have taught us to keep our guard up, not trust too easily, or to expect people to act in relationships in a certain way. We may assume that potential partners will be dishonest, unreliable, or uninterested because dishonest, dismissive, or rejecting were our earliest caretakers. We could expect people to be intrusive, disruptive, or want too much from us because we had a controlling, inconsiderate, or emotionally hungry parent. As a result, we create obstacles around ourselves in which we feel self-protective or self-critical (i.e., "you don't require anyone else anyway") or self-critical (i.e., "there is something wrong with you that you have to solve if you want anybody to love you"). As a consequence, we create barriers around ourselves. As a result, we create obstacles around ourselves. When making romantic connections, our most in-depth defenses, which flow from old experiences, can lead us to act aloof, insecure, or simply not ourselves.

Pursuing Unhealthy Attractions. They often choose less than ideal romantic partners when individuals act on their defenses. It seems counterintuitive, but many of us are motivated unconsciously to replicate negative trends and dynamics from our experience and reproduce them. As a result, we may be drawn to individuals who have characteristics comparable to people in our history. For instance, we may be drawn to someone who is not emotionally accessible or particularly lit up around someone who takes charge and aggressively pursues us.

It is essential to consider that these initial attractions are not always in our best interest and will not always lead to long-term, loving relationships. For example, if being quiet and withdrawn is a defense that we used in our original family to meet our requirements, we may only feel a "spark" with someone who is outgoing and controls the situation. However, if we aim to find lasting love, this dynamic could prove limiting in the long run. While our partner regulates more and more of the life we share, we may retreat more and more into our shell. Ultimately, we may wind up feeling lost in the relationship or resentful.

Surrendering to our fear of intimacy. Dr. Robert Firestone has presented a case as to why most people fear closeness to varying degrees. "Most people say they want love and positive recognition, but relatively few people, because it threatens their defenses, can tolerate real love and respect from another person." They appear to retreat, get over it, and often respond with true aggression. We may experience this fear by having real anxiety about getting too close (i.e., losing ourselves or our freedom, breaking our heart, refusing, leaving, or letting down). Or we may experience this fear on a more subconscious level, suddenly becoming more irritable or drawn to punish or drive the other person away. The more an individual begins to mean to us, these doubts start to intensify, partially explaining our ambivalence towards and resistance to finding love.

Hearing Our Inner Critic. The vocabulary of our security mechanism and our fear of intimacy are what all Drs. Robert and Lisa Firestone have also referred to as the "important inner voice." People protect their defenses and their fears by preserving an old, pessimistic view of themselves, in which they ultimately see themselves as unlovable or unable to find a romantic relationship." As Dr. Lisa Firestone said, "We all have important inner voices that tell us we're too fat, too hideous, too old, too different. We participate in acts that drive people away when we listen to these voices."

310

Our minds tend to be clouded with negative, undermining thoughts towards ourselves, but critical and suspicious thoughts towards others from the minute we start dating or even thinking about dating. These "voices" reflect a way that is often rooted in our past to see ourselves. It shows up in the self-soothing advice, "Tonight, don't go out." "You're too timid." "You're only going to feel humiliated and let down." With critiques like "You're so pathetic, it bombards us. No one even notices you here." It rears its ugly head as it warns, "You're never going to find anybody you like."

The objective of this "voice" is to hold us back, make us stick to our defenses, and give in to fear. People just let you down. It prevents us from having the self-assurance to go after what we want, even when it sounds self-protective.

Being Picky. Our defenses can make us feel more selective, not in a positive, self-possessed way, but in a more cynical and restrictive way that can lead us to hone on and magnify the flaws in the individuals we meet. Not only are our critical inner voices aimed at us, but at people to whom we may potentially feel an attraction. These voices start from the get-go for some people. "She seems too loud." "He sounds like he might be in need." "She's going to get too serious." "He's probably boring." For some people, the moment they start feeling closer to someone, these thoughts creep in. "We should slow things down, maybe." "She's not that great." "He's kind of high-maintenance." The nitpicky ways we start to become partners or potential partners can prevent us from being open and getting to know someone. Furthermore, sometimes the very characteristics that put us off are what we think we supposedly want or things that would make us happy, such as if a partner "likes us too much" or is "too affectionate." It is essential to consider where our pickiness comes from and what we may rule out by listening to our inner critical voice.

Avoiding competition. Seeking love also means having to be vulnerable and putting ourselves out there. When we know that we will have to join a certain level of competition, this can feel too frightening. This is not to suggest that we have to treat dating like athletes or make any enemies along the way, but we have to acknowledge that both ourselves and others may have to face competitive feelings. Our fear of competition can leave us to avoid putting ourselves out there, as Dr. Firestone said. Maybe we're scared of looking like a fool or not being selected. We might also have worries about winning the match, fearing that we're going to hurt another person's feelings. Going after what we want may feel daunting, but considering the competitive feelings that emerge will help us avoid turning against ourselves by putting ourselves down, or even turning against others by being negative or critical, rather than simply pursuing what we want. We may miss something that would make us happy if we avoid competing because of our frustration with these feelings (i.e., staying at home from a social event, not presenting oneself with confidence, or holding back from talking to anyone new).

Staying in Our Place of Comfort. Many of us create ideas of who we are and what we are capable of, and during our lives, we find ways to keep ourselves in those boxes. We build walls that are built to keep us feeling safe. We may not like that we're not going out often or feeling uncomfortable when we meet someone, but we don't question those things because we want to stay in our comfort zone. This may mean, for some individuals, finding solitude. Even though they can be cruel and unfriendly, many people feel relaxed being self-critical and listening to their critical inner voices; they're familiar. For others, it may mean forcing themselves to work hard and "be responsible." Learning what it is and how it works can help us begin to break out a little and challenge the protected pose that keeps others out, whatever this bubble may be for each of us.

The pursuit of a Soulmate. The propensity to prefer imagination over reality is another factor that can serve as a barrier to finding love. Many of us still believe in the idea of a soulmate when it comes to dating and relationships, one person who can complement and complete us in every way. Although it is a worthwhile endeavor to search for someone we feel a true bond and desire with (and who eventually feels like our soulmate), often we build unrealistic expectations and take a more passive role in our romantic destiny since we keep a fantasy of what it would look like to find love. Maybe, we're waiting to be hit by a sparkly beautiful lightning bolt, or we're writing off anyone the minute they don't suit a clear, unique expectation. Basically, in ways that can shut out possibilities, we limit our quest. "I reject the idea that we have only one person in the world, and we are doomed to a lonely life of romantic suffering until we find that person," said Dr. Firestone. "There are a lot of individuals with whom we can have a highly satisfying, profoundly fulfilling relationship."

EMPOWERING LOVE FINDING TIPS

Exploring the history of your attachment. In chapters 7 and 8, we covered in great detail the various attachment styles and their impact on relationships. As Dr. Firestone said, "Our attachment style affects everything from our partner selection to how well our relationships develop to, unfortunately, how they end." Our caretakers' early attachment styles continue to form our internal working models for how we expect relationships to act like adults. We might be more likely to feel nervous, anxious, or evasive in our interpersonal relationships during our lives if we have developed an insecure attachment as children. Knowing our early attachment patterns will give us amazing insight into the kinds of relationships and relationship partners that we are attracted to select and build. It can help understand why we're so stuck with that one person who just won't open up and give us what we want or why we lose interest the minute someone starts expecting something from us. This understanding guides us to make better decisions, recognize obstacles, and build more stable attachments.

Know what you look for. "The spark that drives a relationship is initial chemistry, but for all the right reasons, the spark doesn't always ignite," says Dr. Firestone. As we have said before, we are not always drawn to people for the right reasons, and often we find people more appealing because they help us reconstruct old dynamics. We can also look unconsciously for partners that affirm the current negative perceptions we have about ourselves. We may feel drawn to someone who acts superior if we think of ourselves as dumb. If we feel vulnerable, we might be looking for someone to unrealistically build us up. Think of the qualities in a partner you usually look for. What are you looking to find? Then, consider the attributes of partners whom you have ended up dating. Are there some characteristics that you can stop in the future? Get to know the trends behind the individuals you pick, so you can find ways to break the loop and find someone you can interact with.

Identify your Pattern. In addition to really focusing on the attributes we are searching for, we should think about the general habits we fall into that restrict us in seeking love. We might not only search out individuals who seem familiar based on our background, for instance, but once we start dating someone, are there ways we misrepresent them? Do we begin to feel hypercritical suddenly? Are we sure we will be rejected, which makes us feel desperate or clingy? Are we starting to feel suffocated, as if we just need space? Even when our partner hasn't changed, based on our concerns and defenses, we can change the way we see him or her. We may also begin to provoke our partner to behave in some way. For instance, if we see ourselves as unresponsible, we can behave in more flaky or absent-minded ways. When our partner begins to sound parental or instructive, we then feel angry. When our partner calls too many times, we may dislike the fact that they want our attention too much, we may behave distant and inaccessible, causing them to be the one who most of the time reaches out. Suppose we can get to know our complex side, the habits, and behaviors that threaten our objective of intimacy. In that case, before they begin to control our relationships, we can begin to question these inclinations.

Take Opportunities. We depend pretty heavily on instinct when it comes to dating. First impressions hold a lot of weight, and we tend to assess and judge individuals very quickly to decide whether they are "right for us." We also tend to rule out individuals based on our defenses and vital inner voices, which push us to select the same type of individual and fall into the same loop. Dr. Firestone wrote, "You should deliberately decide to be open to the possibility of being with someone different from the individuals you usually prefer, for example, someone who communicates a strong appeal to you." Many happy relationships started with one person who was initially reluctant because they were approached by someone who they didn't think was their kind or someone who liked them too much, or who they even described as "too nice." Widening our quest and taking chances doesn't imply that we have to lower our standards or push ourselves to be in relationships that we don't want entirely. It means having a more adventurous attitude and seeing where stuff goes. Too many people are shocked by the emotions (and futures) they generate for people who initially weren't even on their radar.

Listen to Your friends. It is enormously beneficial to have friends whose viewpoint we can turn to when we can not differentiate our true perspective from our pessimistic inner coach because our fears and defenses can lead us astray. "Trusting your friends is a helpful way to assess whether a strong desire or a lack of interest is based on your true state of mind or elements of your experience," said Dr. Firestone. For example, if things are going well with someone new, but you unexpectedly feel the need to pull away, or if you're very compelled by someone who holds you at a distance, now is a good time to talk to a friend. They appear to be far more analytical about you. It will help you step back from the situation and begin to figure out if the situation is worth pursuing and make sense of your responses and better understand your patterns.

Don't listen to the inner coach. Think of your inner coach as an old scripted dialogue in your past and played out in your real life. The purpose of this voice is to ensure that we maintain a relaxed and familiar view of ourselves and your partner (or prospective partners), however highly negative. When it slips in, it criticizes us or anyone we're dating, the more we can catch on to, making us feel less sure about ourselves, poking, prodding, or attacking outright. Get to know this inner critic so that you can confront him, disregard his statements, and ignore his advice.

Learn steps for conquering your vital inner voice. An adventure filled with peaks and lows is finding love. With uncomfortable encounters, epic disappointments, hysterical mishaps, and entangled roads leading nowhere, the road to get there can be packed. Not being pessimistic or trying to harden ourselves against the world can be challenging, but the only way to find love is to remain vulnerable.

The more we shed our barriers and defy our inner critics, the more we're bound to feel nervous and vulnerable. Breaking free from our past chains will cause us to confront the pain of our past. The closer we find love, the more anxiety, and sorrow we may expect to emerge. We may even feel irrationally angry at a loved one for seeing and treating us differently than we're used to being seen and handled by ourselves or others, as Dr. Firestone said. Remaining vulnerable and responsive will likely prove our greatest challenge, not only to find love but to help it last over time. But it's worthwhile. The obstacles can not fall quickly or without injury, but they open up a new world of possibilities for us.

TWELVE SIMPLE RULES FOR FINDING LOVE

As we approach the end of this chapter about finding the right partner, I will leave you with a series of simple rules that could help you make things a little easier.

1. When you're not searching, the 'You'll find love' strategy might be incorrect.

That's like saying, "When you're least looking for a career, you'll find a job," said Pepper Schwartz, a relationship expert and professor of sociology at the University of Washington. It's possible, but it happens rarely. "People who are waiting for a job are mainly unemployed," she said. It's just an excuse for me to be afraid to go and put the effort in. Yeah, it's going to happen, but no, that's not a smart idea. Schwartz agrees with this saying's underlying sentiment: Don't be desperate. Try to locate somebody, but don't behave as any breathing body does.

2. Go where people enjoy the same stuff that you want.

If you don't like them, you can miss singular activities, but you have to go where you can meet people, Schwartz advised. Enter social groups or meet-ups; be a worker bee; get interested in political parties in a cause you believe in. You're doing anything you enjoy, at least, and at best, you're going to find someone like-minded.

Bite the bullet and pursue online dating, Schwartz said, for a wide pool of possible candidates. Try a different dating website if you're already online.

3. Lookup from the phone.

Bela Gandhi, a TODAY blogger and founder of the Smart Dating Academy in Chicago, noted that good men and good women are everywhere if you look. Sometimes, she's surprised people lament that they don't meet anyone, but then go out and hold their heads down all the time, looking at their equipment.

Be present wherever you are and glance around the room to see who is looking at you. Make eye contact with the cute stranger and smile for three seconds, which is an invitation to him to come over and talk to you, she recommended.

4. Don't hunt for affection; aim for collaboration.

Romance is for dates, and it's nice to have in your marriage on occasion, but it's a relationship that can get you through the tough times. Don't look for someone to sweep you away from your feet. That means a control freak, and you won't like what's going to happen later, she said. Look for someone who likes to give-and-take, who wants and acknowledges your opinion, who cares, too, about what you want.

5. Happy people attract individuals.

Perhaps the main problem with not finding love is that you don't feel good about yourself. Like yourself and like your life, Schwartz recommended that you focus on it. You must be the person you'd like to meet. "If you're not a happy, ambitious, self-confident individual, you cut your chances of being in the right space for the right kind of individual," she said.

To see if you're sad, go to a doctor, get a trainer if you haven't been exercising, and visit a nutritionist to start eating healthy. If you're shy, just know that you may be less shy.

"The theory is that for all, you have to prepare, and you also have to prepare for love," Schwartz said. You should make yourself work. If you are gone, you're not a finished product.

6. Take some time to be alone.

After a break-up or divorce, after a long relationship, it is essential to take time to be alone. "If you have time to recover, spend time alone to find out who you are again, focus on what went wrong, you'll be in a better position to meet the 'right' guy," Feuer said. "So, you're not committing the same failures over and over again."

7. Sometimes, instant sexual desire disappears.

Gandhi said that most good love is a slow burn, which takes a while to grow. She believes attraction is important, but since that instant spark is more about lust and less about the material of real relationships, you don't have to feel it right away. Emotions can alter and deepen over time, Feuer added, so give people a fair shot.

8. Beware of the principle of 'opposites attract.'

At first, opposites are drawn, but they are likely to face significant tension points down the road. Like-minded individuals make long-term relationships simpler and healthier, said Dr. Gail Saltz, a psychiatrist from New York. The more you see eye-to-eye, the less debate and compromise there is to complain about.

9. Become a 'psychotic optimist.'

"That means you believe that you're going to find that love at any cost; love is meant for you, and it's going to come to you so that before you find it, you just have to date like hell," Gandhi said.

You have to accept the dating process because it will make it more fun to adopt a "psychotic optimist" attitude until you're persuaded that true love is out there for you. Before you locate one to be exclusive with, Gandhi suggests dating three to five individuals simultaneously. Dating means "getting to know casually," not sleeping with anyone. Until you're in a dedicated, exclusive relationship, she recommends not having sex.

10. *Understand your own needs.*

"Are you in need of a lot of space? Longing for lots of affection? Will you need to know what's happening all the time? It's OK, whatever your style is, but you need to know it and be able to pass it on to your future partner. If you both know what you need, you can train each other," said Tina B. Tessina, Ph.D. - psychotherapist.

11. *Understand the difference between fooling around and creating a real bond.*

"If you're cautious and have healthy sex, you can mess around with anyone," Tessina noted. "But before you put someone in your life or share money or a living room, note that they're carrying luggage." In the beginning, the person you're dating is on their best behavior, she advised. Later, it gets worse, not better, so before going too far, get to know what's secret.

12. *For someone inaccessible, stop pining.*

"Let yourself realize that it is unhealthy to hang on to someone who is not involved or is not there for you, and move on." Schwartz advised," You have to see it as a large dark black pit that you have to crawl out of, or you're going to be trapped in it."

Chapter 25: 10 POSITIVE SUCCESS AFFIRMATIONS THAT WILL CHANGE YOUR LIFE

Strong affirmations matter. The only way for individuals to fulfill their ambitions and aspirations is to meet their full potential. You must practice saying positive affirmations for success every day to accomplish your goals and have the confidence to keep going forward. It sends a positive message to your subconscious mind every time you use positive affirmations for success. Inviting money, good health, love, success, and improved standing in your life will help with a good collection of optimistic claims for success. There are words of wisdom out there to give us a head start, and all we have to do is make great use of it for our gain.

As we discussed throughout this book, the journey to a healthy and successful relationship starts with yourself. As we approach the end of this book and embark on our journey to a healthier relationship and a fulfilling life, I want to leave you with these ten powerful and positive affirmations that you can use daily to improve and grow your inner self.

So here they are, change your life with these affirmations.

1. My soul is happy, healthy, brilliant.
A healthy body begins with a healthy soul and mind. If either suffers from adverse feelings, the others will be impacted.

2. I believe that I can do anything.
You are capable of doing anything and anything you put your mind to by saying this.

3. Everything that is happening now, for my most significant benefit, is happening.
No deaths, no injuries, and no coincidences, ever. In this fact, they don't exist as you and others can only attract what you and their components are. So, from the bottom of your heart, know that everything happens in complete synchronicity and for a reason.

4. I am the architect of my life; I have designed its base and selected its contents.
Affirmation is something that when you wake up every morning, you can tell yourself. A new day provides a fresh start and affects those around you as well. You can do something that you want on that day because you're the architect of your own life.
If you start your day with thought and feeling of positive reinforcement, it will turn your day into something extraordinary. Each time works!

5. I forgive those who have hurt me in my life and remove myself from them peacefully.
That doesn't mean that you forget everything bad they've done to you, but you're at ease with that. What helps you step on is your strength to forgive, and your response to every encounter is independent of what others think of you.

6. My ability to overcome my struggles is unlimited; my ability to excel is unlimited.

Simple and straightforward, you have no boundaries except those that you put on yourself. What kind of life would you like? What stops you? What challenges do you place upon yourself? This optimistic reinforcement will allow you to overcome all the limits.

7. I am abandoning my old habits today and taking on new, optimistic ones.

Understand that every challenging period is only a brief period of life. When you take in the fresh one, this too will move along with your old habits. With creative energy that surges through you, you are entirely adjusting, leading you to fresh and creative ideas and the mentality that enables that energy to flow.

8. I've achieved perfection.

One of the most essential affirmations is to remind yourself that you can do all the goodness in life daily. Rely on your dreams and your vision. Then bind to that vision the emotion. You give yourself the power to build the life you want by telling yourself this optimistic affirmation and believing that you will achieve greatness.

9. I'm brimming with enthusiasm and filled with happiness.

Joy begins from inside yourself, not from outside yourself. It begins as soon as you rise, as well. So make it a habit, first thing in the morning, to repeat encouraging words to yourself.

10. I accept who I am, and I love myself for who I am.

Self-love is supposed to be the purest form of love and the highest form. You immediately start appreciating and loving yourself when you love yourself. You will begin to see yourself in a different light if you have faith and pride in what you do, and you will be motivated and driven to do bigger and better things with statements of achievement.

Believe in yourself in opening up possibilities. Your subconscious will go to work and start attracting the possibilities that will help you accomplish what you continue to say when you say this or some other constructive affirmation. Try any of these ten uplifting positive reinforcement affirmations that help you re-center on the go if you want to have more motivation for positive statements.

CONCLUSION

Love connects all romantic relationships. They will not exist without passion. In this quote, that says, "Love makes all hard hearts tender," George Hebert illustrates the benefits of love in relationships. This quote describes how love can soften a cold person going into a relationship. An individual is given a sense of reassurance, self-esteem, and affection for himself by having a romantic partner. Love improves both partners' lives in the relationship. When two people are in love, for instance, their feelings are at an ultimate peak. This generates a bond that is not easily broken. Love is what makes a relationship last. With friendship, courtship, and affection, romantic bonds enrich life. Good partnerships can combine and expand upon all of these.

In conclusion, not just one thing helps a good relationship, but several things support it. A good relationship where two or more people are related through something, whether it is blood, marriage, or mutual affection, requires a steady dose of contact, similar goals, respect, and trust – the four pillars for any effective connection.

When it comes to people-to-people relationships, the trick is to optimize those moments of selflessness and concentrate on that other person or group. This particularly applies to those who have family members and spouses-or would-be spouses. But without the other three pillars, these relationships would also fall to the ground – without trust and respect, and commonalities shared and practiced among the people comprising these relationships.

Relationships once again require constant work and focus and persistence-but it should be worth it: good, happy, and healthy relationships are equal to a high quality of life. Research indicates that to live long, happy and healthy lives, people need other people. It is, really, a simple notion. But it works, and it has always been working.

To fall in love is supposed to be magical, but to get close to another person is not at the best of times without there being highs and lows. Intimacy is a medium for every possible emotion, from the joy of learning that someone pretty wonderful is as moved by you as you are by them, to the anguish of self-doubt and possible loss, to the comfort, richness and sometimes stillness of a deeper love. Anxiety affects relationships, but you can secure your relationship and make it one that is solid, close and resilient by being open to its effect and actively reacting to it.